The Angels of Klaipėda

Gordon Mott

Published by Gordon Mott

Copyright Gordon Mott 2021

All rights reserved. This book or any portion thereof may not be reproduced or used in any manner whatsoever without the express written permission of the publisher except for the use of brief quotations in a book review.

Disclaimer

Reference is made to real-world historical events and figures, but this is a work of fiction. The characters portrayed, and their personal stories, are fictitious. No identification with actual persons (living or deceased) is intended or should be inferred. Most businesses, places, events, locales, and incidents are either the products of the author's imagination or used in a fictitious manner.

Typesetting and cover design by Candescent Press.

Book Cover

The book cover is based on a 1992 sketch by Vytautas Antanas Jakštys, entitled "Laivai prie senosios Klaipėdos perkėlos"
("Ships at The Old Klaipėda Dock").

The author is grateful to Mr Jakštys, who generously provided permission for its use.

Dedicated to the people of Lebanon and Lithuania whose recent pasts have been difficult, but whose futures will be so bright.

CONTENTS

Foreword i

One: Capture 1

Two: Loose Ends 29

Three: Waiting and Wondering 49

Four: Budget Clarifications 87

Five: Perspective 105

Six: Strange Liaisons 125

Seven: Surprises 155

Eight: Beginnings 193

Nine: Changes 219

Ten: Developments 247

Eleven: Decisions 275

Twelve: Revelations 305

FOREWORD

In 1997, George falls victim to a hostage-taking gone wrong. He enters a place of secrets. While the world believes he's deceased, he remains locked in a cell. As the months pass, monotony and routine are overwhelming, but there is one redeeming grace. With the aid of his captor's daughter, he learns to survive; he also learns about love and perspective. Lessons he will need when he emerges into a world that has moved on without him.

In 1997, Tanja's husband dies after a hostage-taking goes wrong. Rebuilding her life as a single mother takes time and courage. She perseveres and moves her family to her home town of Klaipeda, Lithuania. It's difficult to move on without him; it's even more difficult when he reappears. Now, she must choose between a former life and the one that she has rebuilt. She's about to learn about being held captive by two worlds and one secret.

The Angels of Klaipėda

CHAPTER 1

Capture

George sat blindfolded on the chair and tried to contemplate the past few hours of his life. His wrists hurt and the handcuffs seemed to be cutting off his circulation. His ankles were in a little better shape; the shackles must have been looser as they weren't really hurting him. The sequence of events seemed most confounding.

It was July 1997. The troubles in Beirut should have been well over. No one got kidnapped here anymore. Maybe, someone had targeted him. He tried to think it through in the darkness and quiet. He was a director of a large shipping company, Trans-ship, based out of London. He was the director responsible for European trading and had built his reputation on cracking open the East European markets. That's why they'd wanted him to go to Beirut. They wanted someone with emerging market experience to meet with local shipping experts. The hope was to develop some trading relationships so Trans-ship could find a toe hold into the Beirut port.

Maybe that was it, maybe one of the traders had entrapped him. However, it didn't seem logical. Most of his new acquaintances had been in the trading business for years; they could target any foreigner for ransom. 'Why him?' It was hard to fathom. By July of 1997, foreigners walked freely on the genteel streets of Beirut. The city certainly gave the illusion of safety. Technically, Americans were still warned not to visit; but rumours abounded that the advisory was about to be lifted.

It had been a very odd ending to an otherwise productive trip. The week had been a spectacular success. The local import and export traders

1

were all very excited about meeting him. After all, Trans-ship was not only a significant shipping and trading company, it was also owned by an American parent company. George, himself, was an American, although he lived in London and had used a British passport when he'd entered Lebanon. He was a dual national as his parents had immigrated to the US in the 1950s. However, it was all the American connections that seemed to excite his new potential business partners. George knew he represented a little ray of American sunshine after years of the clouds of war.

The evening had started innocently enough. He'd invited a couple of the traders out to dinner on his final night in the city. The locals seemed to welcome the invitation and the four apparently knew just the place. It was a few miles from his hotel. George enjoyed the company and was surprised to see them all pouring down the drinks. He avoided any sensitive topics and kept ordering rounds. The lamb was excellent. The traders seemed eager to ingratiate themselves; George likewise was anxious to ingratiate himself as well. The celebrations continued until close to midnight. It was then that things went wrong - very wrong.

After paying the bill, one of his new friends had wanted to stay with him to ensure he got home safely. George declined the gesture; he'd travelled round the world; he could find his own way back to the hotel. At first, he started to walk. It was a beautiful evening and he wanted to sober up a little before returning to the hotel. Several cabs honked at him as he walked along the road, but he declined their offers. However, now George began to worry about where exactly he was; he thought he knew the direction, but now he wasn't quite sure; besides, he was in Beirut, not a place to take chances. George soon wished he would have taken that chance and kept walking.

He had warily accepted one of the offers of a cab ride. He'd taken a long look at the driver. He was an older man with a kindly, if weathered face, he was clean and so was the cab. The driver seemed to understand George; the journey started well enough, but things had quickly deteriorated. As they stopped at a traffic light, two men jumped in the back and 'sandwiched' George between them.

If it hadn't been so terrifying, it might have been comical. One man was very fat and older; he wore a dirty old suit and seemed to constantly perspire. The other man was very thin and younger with a t-shirt and jeans and seemed to be shaking with nerves. Both had pulled out pistols when they climbed into the back seat; George remembered thinking it was something they really should have worked out in advance - one man with a pistol would have sufficed. George had braced himself, certain he was about to be robbed. He'd fallen into a trap. The trap part was true, but the robbery wasn't going to happen – the reality was about to be so much worse.

Through a thick Lebanese accent, the fat man had told him not to move. If he co-operated, it would all be okay. He barked an order in Arabic to his partner, who wrapped the blindfold on George. George then sat there in the backseat. He sat in the backseat and pondered what was about to transpire as the fat man continued his demands to both his partner and the driver.

And now, here he sat in this chair, handcuffed and shackled, and wondering. In retrospect, the two didn't seem to be particularly religious-looking – this didn't seem like a terrorist thing. If he could just stay calm, he could try to think clearly; they were likely looking for a ransom. However, he'd been sitting in this chair for some time now and it bothered him that they didn't seem interested in questioning him. 'How were they going to demand a ransom if they didn't know anything about him?' 'Maybe they would work it out from the contents in his wallet or briefcase, but it just seemed odd.'

Hours seemed to pass; George wondered if it was morning. He'd nodded off a few times, but the pain from his wrists was disturbing and the hard chair was not conducive to sleep. After the most recent dozing, George woke and felt incredibly thirsty. He had fallen asleep with his mouth open. He wondered if maybe the two had thought better of it and had abandoned him here. Now, George's mind shifted from a thorough analysis of the last few hours to contemplating scenarios for a 'no show' by his new hosts.

George's scenario contemplation was interrupted by the sound of a door opening. He could hear people enter the room, but no one said anything. George braced; maybe they were about to strike him or beat him. Nothing happened. Nothing happened for several minutes. They must have known he was awake; George was moving around and sitting straight. George wondered when the silence would be broken. Finally, it all became too much, George decided to break it himself.

"Water, please."

"Ahmed!..." George couldn't understand the words that followed, but began to think that he had either been taken hostage by one of the dumbest hostage-takers in Beirut or Ahmed was not a real name; he hoped for the former.

George could hear someone scurry off and, a minute later, a glass of water was put to his lips. George wondered about the water; he'd been told not to drink tap water, but, at this point, he just needed it and he was in no position to question its origin.

"What are you going to do with me?" George asked.

"You'll be ok; you'll be home in no time." George recognized the voice; it was the fat man. George thought, by process of elimination, that Ahmed must be the thin one.

"Are you asking a ransom for me?"

"Something like that."

George thought that an odd response.

"We bring you food. My friend will feed it to you; you understand?"

"Yes, thank you."

George was then fed some food from a plastic fork; he could tell the fork was plastic. The food was rice mixed with some vegetables. He decided to begin a quest. As he was blindfolded, he would make note of everything he could decipher with his other senses. He'd already seen all three of them – well, it wasn't clear if the driver was part of the racket or not. He knew the name Ahmed. He could tell the food was clearly purchased from a vendor. When he was liberated, he'd have enough details to help track them down; if the authorities could be bothered to track them down.

After the first several bites, George began to get curious. The fat man didn't seem upset when he'd asked questions; George decided to keep asking them.

"How long do you think I'll be staying?"

"I hope we have you out by evening. Now, I ask you to stop questions. My friend stay with you; I go work it."

It seemed odd that they'd left him there all night and now he had a jailer. George heard the footsteps as the man walked off. George now got to thinking; it wasn't a bad thing to have a jailer; he was clearly the subordinate – the fat man was the boss; there might be an opportunity to gain some information. George waited a few minutes before he spoke.

"Ahmed?"

"Yes."

"Is there any chance of more water?"

"Yes."

As Ahmed shuffled out of the room, George thought to himself. I may not need any more water, but his name is definitely Ahmed.

Tariq was nervous; he'd never done anything like this before. The fat man plunked himself on his favourite chair beside his telephone. Things hadn't been going well for him, but he was hoping to turn this latest development to his advantage. He had grown tired of the roadside robberies. The scam was always the same. They would wait at traffic lights at night and, if there was no one around, and the timing was right; he and his son would try to hop into a cab and rob the occupants. Some pliable drivers collaborated with them; but he was okay if they didn't. However, this was something new, he'd never hijacked a foreigner before and he was about to see if he could deploy a more profitable scam.

He carefully dialled the number.

"Jaber? Peace be upon you, brother."

Tariq's hope was to broker a deal with an old associate who had been long associated with Hezbollah.

"I have something that may be of interest to you - a British man."

"How do you mean?" replied Jaber.

"I have a hostage for you; I can hand him over – for a price."

"I don't know that we do that anymore; I'd have to check. How much are you asking?"

"$10,000"

"Are you holding Bill Clinton?"

"$5000?"

"Tariq – you are way too high. I'll ask them what they are willing to pay."

"Please can you get me an answer before sunset; I can't hold him here indefinitely."

"I will try; I will try."

At first, George couldn't determine why he was so tired. It had been a rough night's sleep, but he needed to be alert; he needed to garner as much information as possible from Ahmed. However, he kept nodding off and dreaming, then waking up with a dry mouth. When he wasn't sleeping and dreaming, he was thinking about all the wrong stuff. He needed to conceive a plan, yet all he could think about was the last several months. It felt like a long slide from top to bottom.

Just the year before, at the end of 1996, George had been promoted and moved the family from Seattle to London to take on his new director role. It all seemed so wonderful at the time; it was him, his wife, Tanja, whom he dearly loved, his little girl, Maria, and Tanja's little brother, Vlad. Maria was just a baby at the time. They'd settled in a beautiful apartment in Canary Wharf and spent part of Christmas with an old friend from York. Steve and his family had come down to celebrate with them; it all seemed so perfect – great job, wonderful family, close friends.

Tanja – she was heaven. That must be his soul mate. He'd met her while teaching in Lithuania. She was a Russian girl working in a coffee shop. George remembered how they hadn't even shared a common language; he had some basic Lithuanian which he needed to brush up quickly, but true love seemed to conquer all. She'd been 19 when they met; he was 24. Vlad had Down Syndrome and Tanja had initially wanted to stay in Lithuania to support him. However, it all had worked out – well sort of. Against her better judgment, Tanja agreed to leave her mother and Vlad behind and move to Seattle with her new American husband, who had secured a job offer from Trans-ship. She agreed on a trial basis. After Tanja's mother passed away, Vlad came to live with them. Time had drifted and Tanja and Vlad had drifted with him. Now, Vlad attended a decent school in North London; Tanja seemed happy enough; even her

English was finally improving. And little Maria – well, she was just a joy – the love of his life. 1997 had started with such optimism.

1997 – what a curious year. It began with the wonderful news that Tanja was pregnant again. The baby was due in September. Work was going really well; George's influence was growing; his opinion was sought regularly. That's why he'd been chosen for the Beirut excursion. However, something in the universe must have changed with the coming of the spring. His close friend, Steve, had died tragically in a car accident in Yorkshire – and now there was Ahmed and his fat friend.

George suddenly realized that he was daydreaming again, but he just couldn't help it. His head felt heavy; he would just close his eyes for a few minutes.

"Is he asleep?" asked Tariq.

"I think so," replied Ahmed.

"How long has he been sleeping?"

"Hard to tell; he was asleep, then seemed to nod his head and mumble, then sleep again. I think this current sleep is about 10 minutes."

"Good; I bought today's newspaper; let's get a photograph of him."

"Why would we do that?" asked Ahmed.

"They may want some proof and the newspaper will have today's date on it. Then, you need to develop the film. Ok?"

"Yes, father."

Tariq walked closer to George and gently shook his shoulder. There was no response.

"Ok; he's asleep; now, take the photo. I'll hold his head back."

At that moment, Tariq realized that his photo shoot plan was flawed. If he held his hostage's head, his arms would be in the photo. He tried to let gravity do the work. He held George's head back and pushed it gently so it would stay in position. It would hold for a few seconds then flop down again.

"We must have given him too much; he can't keep his head up. I know; I know; let's get him on his back. Help me."

Father and son tried to push the chair backwards, so the chair's back would rest on the floor. It was more difficult than Tariq imagined; they almost lost grip of George at one point, which would have sent his head colliding with the floor. However, finally, the two got the chair into the proper position. George continued to sit in his chair fast asleep, but now it lay on the ground with George's face pointing skyward.

Tariq arranged George's head into a suitable position, then took pains with the Al-Ahd newspaper to lay it on his chest – and ensure the date was prominent. Then, as if preparing a sculpture for its first public appearance, he removed the blindfold. George didn't look asleep; he looked dead.

"Take the photo."

"Ok, ok, but he doesn't look alive."

"It's ok, do it."

Tanja was nervous. George always called each evening and he hadn't. It was now morning and still no call. She decided to wait till 10, then call his assistant.

"Anna?"

"Hi Tanja, nice to hear from you." Tanja thought that Anna always had such a calming voice. She had a Polish accent and an endearing habit of emphasizing the wrong syllables.

"Thanks Anna. Hey, I call with problem. George not call yesterday."

"That's curious; he was meant to be on an 8 am call this morning and missed it. I've been emailing him, but haven't had a response. I don't think it's anything to worry about. Communications can be trying in places like that; let me call his hotel for you. Ok?"

"Thanks Anna; I wait your call."

Anna was now beginning to worry and wondering how she could explain it to Tanja. The hotel had confirmed it - George's key card hadn't been used since the previous morning. Normally, hotels wouldn't disclose that type of information, but it seemed such principles didn't hold in Beirut. They were accustomed to balancing security with the privacy of visiting executives.

No, she wouldn't call Tanja first. She'd talk to Corporate Security first. Anna moved swiftly down the long office hallway; she was making her way to the office of Aaron Flanders, Director of Security, when she spotted him in one of the conference rooms surrounded by other directors. Anna wouldn't typically have interrupted, but she knocked on the door and entered. The assembled were surprised; they were all huddled around a speakerphone; the meeting was well underway.

"Aaron – can I see you please?"

Aaron was a tall Englishman with dark hair and brown eyes. He always seemed so affable, but this morning he looked annoyed. He stood up and followed Anna into the hallway.

Aaron's disposition changed quickly when Anna explained the story of the missing director.

"I'll get on it. Leave it with me."

"What should I tell his wife?"

"Just keep her calm. Tell her it's probably a communication problem; I'll call her in an hour when I find him."

Anna complied, but Tanja hadn't seemed placated. She asked what the hotel had said. Anna thought for a minute and decided to lie, "hotels won't disclose personal information, but don't worry, Aaron will figure it out; again, it's likely just a communications issue."

"What do you mean?" demanded Tariq.

"I'm telling you; I couldn't get a hold of anyone. You'll have to wait," replied Jaber.

"It's hard to wait; I'll have to drug him again. I don't want to keep him overnight."

"Hey, I'm doing my best. I think it will be tomorrow. By the way, I'll need details; who is he; does he have any value to us? I need photographs as well."

"Ok; ok, will you call me if anything changes?"

"I will; I will."

Tariq put down the phone. This was becoming more complicated, what if they didn't want him? He'd have to let him go. Tariq looked down at George's British passport; the emblem on the cover seemed so official. He opened it and looked at George's photograph. No, he couldn't kill him, that would be too much. He'd have to let him go, but he might know too much. He'd seen their faces. Robbing was one thing; taking a foreigner as a hostage was quite another. The Internal Security Forces were not going to let that go. For the first time during this whole escapade, Tariq finally understood that he was over his head. He was a bit player in a crime game; his attempts to elevate himself to international hostage-taker could go very, very badly.

"Dad?" Ahmed stood in the doorway with a very large photograph. Tariq looked toward him. "What do you think?"

"You were right; he looks dead; we can try again; I need to question him. In the meantime, take a photo of his information page in the passport; it might come in handy."

George kept drifting in and out of consciousness, but it was his bladder that was now the problem. It wasn't a bad problem to have. The pain was keeping him awake. They must have used some sort of sedative, but it seemed to be wearing off now. He pulled his head up.

"Ahmed? You there?" George called out.

There was no response.

George decided to try again, but this time he would shout it "Ahmed!!"

George could hear someone scurry toward the door.

"Ahmed, I need the toilet."

"Ok, I bring you a bucket."

"Ahmed, is there any chance of using a toilet? You can keep me blindfolded, but I need to move."

Ahmed looked up the staircase toward his father, who now stood at the landing.

"One minute."

Ahmed climbed the staircase; his father grabbed him and closed the door to the basement.

"How does he know your name? What did you tell him?"

"Nothing, I don't know how he knows. What do I do about the toilet?"

Tariq thought for a minute and then thought again; he needed to think more quickly.

"No, we can't bring him up here. We'll bring him a bucket, but I'll remove the shackles and he can walk around inside the room. That will do the trick. I need him lucid anyway; I need to interrogate him. From now on, I will refer to you as Mohammed. Just go with it; there's a reason why I chose that name; hopefully, he'll think we're terrorists; just go with it."

Tanja was shocked, more than shocked.

"Aaron, what you mean you can't find him?"

"Well, we just know that he hasn't used his key card recently and he missed a call. He should be in the air now; he might just have been incommunicado; he might appear on your doorstep in a couple of hours. We'll keep working on it with the local authorities in Beirut. I've seen this situation before; his mobile phone had a roaming issue or a battery issue and the internet didn't work in the hotel; it could be as simple as that. Again, don't panic; it's too early to panic."

Tanja put down the phone and looked at her watch. It was time to panic, but what could she even do? She didn't know anyone in Lebanon; she didn't even know anyone in Britain who could help with the exception of Mr Aaron Flanders, Director of Security.

And then a rather odd idea came to Tanja. It was a very peculiar idea, but what choice did she have? She found her husband's address book in a desk drawer beneath the phone. She knew one person with influence in this world and she was going to try him. It was a long shot, but she could make one call.

Darius was a friend of George's; he was also a Member of the Lithuanian Parliament. Even better, he was a cabinet minister. There had been a newspaper article about him a few years back. He had served in the Soviet Army in Afghanistan, but secretly helped the Mujahedeen. His involvement had to have been significant. When the Soviet authorities got wind of his activities, the Afghans smuggled him out to Pakistan. From there, he somehow worked with US and UK military authorities and ended up living in England for a while; Tanja wasn't sure if he could help, but she needed someone at least who could advise her. It was almost 1 pm; it would be 3 pm there. She dialled the number.

"Listening," said the familiar voice in Lithuanian. It was Tanja's second language, but the one that she used at home with George. She replied in that second language.

"Dario? It's me. It's Tanja, George's wife."

"Hello to you, Tanja – is there any chance I could call you back? Just finishing a meeting."

"Actually, it's urgent. Can you talk now? George is, well, he's missing."

"Give me a second, I'll step outside," Tanja could hear Darius' muffled voice as he seemed to be apologizing to some people in the meeting room.

"Ok, Tanja," Darius continued. "Sorry, did you say George is missing? Where did he go missing?"

"Beirut."

"What was he doing there?"

"Long story. Business trip. Darius – do you know anyone who could help? Corporate Security at the company is working on it, but I don't know if they have any contacts."

"How long has he been missing?"

"No one's heard from him since yesterday morning."

"OK; it might be too early to panic. I tell you what; I have one friend in MI5; that's British Military Intelligence. I can call him for you. However, I don't want you to mention it to anyone; ok? He's a friend from a previous life. I don't think he can help, but he might have some local contacts in the security forces. Leave it with me. Ok? And don't worry, he'll turn up."

"Bless you, Darius, you'll call me back?"

"Yes, yes."

Darius hated the distraction and felt it would likely turn out to be just that. He hated to leave the meeting. They were finally making progress on advancing Lithuania's application to join the European Union and every meeting was now important. On the other hand, it was already getting late on a Friday afternoon. The staff were looking tired and his friend came first.

Darius opened the conference room door and made his pronouncement. "I'm sorry everyone; I have an emergency; can you complete without me? I'll get the details from the minutes. I'm sorry about this."

Everyone smiled in return. What else could they do? He was the boss and, even though they needed his direction, they would have to complete without him.

It had been a while since Darius had spoken to Zurab, who now worked for MI5. Their relationship had been a long one. Darius smiled as he thought about him and their time in the Soviet army.

Zurab was a Georgian. When Darius was first conscripted, he was one of the first 'comrades' whom he met in Afghanistan. Zurab was a drug dealer, which was fine with Darius. Most of his fellow soldiers were either stoned on Zurab's heroin or filled with vodka. Darius used to laugh and tease Zurab – "you are bringing something sorely missing from this Soviet Army – private enterprise."

One day, Darius asked Zurab how he was going to spend all the money. Zurab replied, "Oh Darius, I don't have any money. I'm donating all my services in support of Afghan forces to bring about the defeat of the Soviet Union."

At the time, the reply wasn't actually as shocking as it may have sounded. Zurab was suspicious that Darius was a kindred spirit. Soon after, Zurab brought him into the trade, which provided many opportunities to work with the local Afghans. The two even shared an Afghan handler, who was responsible for providing them with the drugs and collecting the money, less a commission, which they could keep for themselves. Their local handler, Sayed, was a gregarious fellow; a real patriot as well. He was a 'fixer.' When rumours surfaced that the Soviet authorities were catching on to the drug trading within the ranks, Sayed raised the alarm and arranged to walk with Darius and Zurab to Peshawar in Pakistan. From there, they met up with an American military attaché who arranged for air force transport so they could be 'debriefed' in Oxfordshire. The information which Zurab provided was of such good use to the American and British military intelligence officials that they asked Zurab to stay on with them in a position with MI5.

Darius walked past the rows of MPs' offices as he made his way to his own office. He wouldn't make this call on a mobile phone; only a landline and only a secured landline. He sat at his desk and looked at Zurab's mobile number in his address book.

"Privyet, Zurab."

"Privyet, Darius, but let's speak in English, not that other one."

"Zurab, I'm calling for a favour. Are you at work? Can you call me on a secured line?"

"Absolutely, give me the number."

Darius replied with his landline number and hung up the phone. It rang a few seconds later.

"Zurab, I have an old friend missing in Beirut, called George Smith; he's only been missing a day, but he's a close friend and his wife is very upset. Is there any chance you might have some contacts in the security forces in Lebanon?"

"Sure Darius, I can give you a hand. For you, anything. You know, I'll also get in touch with our old friend, Sayed. I doubt it's an Islamic thing, but just in case, he might be able to get the word out to spare him."

"How would Sayed be able to help with a problem in Lebanon?" Darius then paused a minute. "Actually, forget it. I don't want to know."

Zurab just laughed, "Well, it's not really a secret. The Islamic underground is pretty connected these days. I talk to him occasionally; I'll try to get through to him today for you."

The conversation went on for several minutes. Darius relayed his friend's details and offered to email across a photo that he'd taken of George at a mutual friend's funeral in York in May. Zurab provided Darius with a webmail address. It was a strange webmail address, seemingly belonging to a Pat Lawrence. Zurab also noted a specific directive. Don't include anything else, just the photo. The two then spent a few pleasant moments reminiscing about their time in Afghanistan. They relived the long march to Pakistan, spoke about the stoned comrades and laughed at how their lives had changed. Darius smiled when he put down the phone. 'At least, I got to spend time with an old friend – so it was a productive day.'

The toilet arrangements weren't convenient, but at least George could relieve the pain in his bladder. It was also nice to have the shackles off. The fat man even let him walk around the room, but insisted on keeping the blindfold in place and holding the handcuffs behind his back.

Now, the fat man was peppering him with questions. Where did he work? What position did he have there? Where did he live? George was truthful on questions related to his work; for questions about his personal life, he lied. Finally, the tidal wave of questions was too much for George.

"Can I ask you something?" I've now been here a full day – or close to it. Is there a reason why you're asking all these questions now?"

"We never got to know each other and now it looks like you'll be here one more day. So, I thought we should talk," replied Tariq.

"You know something; it appears to me that you're trying to negotiate a ransom. I don't want to be disrespectful; I'm not in a position to be disrespectful, but I might be able to help you if you tell me about your plan. It's in my vested interest to get out of here, so I'm pretty sure that our goals are aligned – you want money and I want out. Is that correct?"

"You are very clever. That is quite correct."

"So, I can give you the name of the person at Trans-ship you could discuss this with. I'm not sure if he's ever dealt with a hostage situation before, but you could try."

"Oh yes, please do. I'll write it down."

Tariq wrote down the name and phone number for Aaron Flanders; even though he had no intention of ever talking to the man.

Sayed acted swiftly; he always did. Zurab asked few favours, but when he did, Sayed felt he needed to jump. After all, he owed him an enormous debt. Zurab and Darius had been his henchmen and had taken a considerable risk when they'd collaborated with him and now, he would always be there to return a favour. He didn't care that things had changed so much. He'd worked with the Americans and British to defeat the Soviets; now, the Americans and British were the enemy. However, Sayed didn't care so much about today's politics; when it came to two loyal friends, they would always be brothers and that kinship was more important than the tenor of these particular times.

Zurab and Sayed shared a protocol; if others around Sayed discovered it, they'd be horrified; it would be treasonous to communicate with an MI5 man, but Sayed wasn't bothered; he was a senior man now and had paid his dues during the war. After receiving a cryptic email from someone called Billy Smithe, he went onto a website and logged into a portal. The website sold office chairs in Luton, but his password would take him to a different portal; separate from the chair customers.

Sayed stared at the photos that Zurab had sent. The young man looked very glum in one. The other was a passport photo, which Zurab had sent along from one of his databases. Zurab had provided quite a bit of information, including the man's profession and a few details of his personal history. Sayed looked at the date of birth 'poor soul, just had his 28th birthday'.

Sayed thought for a minute while staring at the information in front of him. He looked up and determined that it just wasn't possible. Hezbollah was out of that game; it was likely all a coincidence. However, Sayed believed in fate. God had sent him to Lebanon only a year ago. Bin Laden's bunch had arranged it. Sayed had visited a training camp there. The whole affair was an attempt to mend bridges over disagreements between the two organizations. Sayed thought that the meetings and activities had gone rather well. He had enjoyed the camaraderie and met a few new friends.

Yes, it was too much of a coincidence. God, as well as Zurab, must want his help. Why else would there be the connection between the two – Zurab and Lebanon? In any event, it was worth intervening just to help out his old Georgian friend. Sayed printed the message and photos and then deleted them from the website.

Sayed sent an email requesting contact from the Lebanese. It was to commence a series of painful communications between himself and his Hezbollah interlocutor. Both sides would not allow direct communication, except for the original email to request contact. That email was to contain a code phrase 'the weather in Instanbul has been very pleasant'. The word Istanbul was to be intentionally misspelt.

From there, Sayed visited a web mail account and provided a rough outline of the request to "help ensure a friend was not harmed," but provided no names. He then saved the email in his draft folder; he would not send it. That would mean the message would not pass through the internet. Fifteen minutes later, he logged back into the account, his draft had been deleted, but another draft had been added to say that the organization was amenable to the request. Sayed deleted that draft and composed a new draft with information on the missing man, but with no mention of the original request. He logged out and waited another fifteen minutes. His correspondent had deleted that draft and wrote a new one saying that they'd be in touch. Sayed deleted the draft and uploaded the photos of George. When Sayed logged in again, the photos had been deleted and the remaining draft simply read "message received." Sayed deleted it.

It was another long night in the chair. George was hoping that this would be the last. Ahmed and the fat man seemed like two buffoons. Today, he would be blunter; he would offer to plain out help them get their money so he could get out of here. He only hoped they would accept the offer.

George's neck really hurt; it wasn't natural to sleep in that position. He now really needed to use the bucket again, but this time he needed to use it for both urination and defecation. He wondered if he should shout out. He'd live with the pain a little longer; he still needed to think. He needed to think about how to get the fat man to listen to him. He wanted to go home. He wondered what Tanja was doing; she must know he's missing now. He should have been home last night. He wondered who she might have called; maybe she called corporate security, but what would they do? They might have already been looking for him; he'd already missed a meeting. No, they wouldn't think he'd gone missing for skipping a single meeting. George began to think that there was very likely no one looking for him. To make matters worse, it was Saturday; he wasn't expected anywhere except home. If Tanja didn't know to phone Security, no one in authority would even know he was missing.

The pain was becoming unbearable; he needed the bucket.

"Ahmed!"

There was no response. George would try louder.

"Ahmed!!"

He waited a minute before letting out a screech.

"Ahmed!!!!"

George heard scurrying. His senses were better today. He listened very carefully as he heard the scurrying. It was coming from above him; he then heard the clear sound of someone scrambling down stairs. He must be in a basement. Before Ahmed got to the door, George also had another realization. They hadn't gagged him, but seemed to hurry when he screeched out; maybe they were worried someone else could hear them. He would remember that detail, which could come in handy.

George believed he must have woken Ahmed out of a deep sleep. He seemed groggy and out of breath when he answered 'yes.'

"I'm sorry, Ahmed, to wake you. I really need the bucket again. Is there any chance you could help me?"

There was a long pause. George was beginning to surmise what a minor player that Ahmed was. He clearly didn't want to do anything without the permission of the fat man. He probably needed to consider whether he should help George or wake the fat man.

"Ahmed? Would that be ok?"

"Ok, give me a minute."

George listened carefully now. Ahmed closed a door and walked several paces before climbing stairs. A minute later he repeated the process in reverse. He must need to retrieve a key for the shackles.

For a fleeting moment, George considered that this might be a chance. He might be able to use his body to overpower Ahmed. Then, he thought the better of it. What would he do if he overpowered him? The noise would just alert the fat man, who would take care of him. It wasn't worth it; George surmised that they likely didn't want to kill him, but if he put them in a position where they had to defend themselves, then they probably would kill him.

The shackles were removed; George was raised from his chair; his body seemed to let out a sigh of relief when rising from that chair as the muscles were allowed to move for the first time in several hours. Ahmed helped him toward the bucket and undid his trousers; they had already confiscated his belt.

While George stood, Ahmed gently pushed the bucket so that it made a noise on the floor below.

"I'm sorry, Ahmed; I need to sit."

Now, there was another long pause. George decided he would have to walk Ahmed through it.

"If you move the bucket in a corner, it won't move around very much. If you help me pull down my trousers, I can do the rest."

Ahmed said nothing, but George could hear the bucket being gently pushed a few feet. He was then led those few feet by Ahmed. George felt as the man fumbled to complete the work of pulling the trousers down. It was hard, but with his handcuffed hands, George could pull down at one side of his underwear. It took a bit of doing at first, the sweat from his skin had acted as a kind of weak glue to cement that underwear in place, but once the right side gave way, he moved his hands to the left side of his body and the underwear was more compliant now as he pulled it down. After a few manoeuvres, he stood bottomless, knowing a bucket was out there. The next few seconds were all about manoeuvring his body into position; he'd used squat toilets before but not blindfolded and handcuffed.

It was a relief. George just squatted there; the squat itself felt nice. It was stretching muscles and it was pleasant to relieve himself.

George listened as he squatted there; he heard someone else moving down those stairs, but this person was trying to be much quieter.

"Mohammed, is everything ok?" said the fat man in English.

There was another long pause. George wondered about the name Mohammed and then realized that the fat man was probably now trying to use an alias for Ahmed, but Ahmed probably had forgotten it. Why else would he address him in English?

"Yes, everything ok," replied Ahmed.

"Did you sleep well?" asked the fat man.

George felt a bit awkward making conversation at that particular moment; he was just finishing his toileting. However, he needed the conversation to keep going.

"Yes, is there any chance of a hand?"

George felt someone put their hands on him and help him from the squat position. It must have been the fat man as his gestures were much more confident. The fat man helped him with his underwear and trousers, then began leading him back to the chair.

"Is there any chance I could stand for a minute? You can shackle me if you like; I just want to stand for a minute."

"That's fine," the fat man held the chain of his handcuffs, apparently thinking this would prevent any bolting for the door.

The fat man said something in Arabic to Ahmed; George could hear the bucket being removed.

George decided that it was time to begin the conversation. He started by asking if the fat man had been in touch with Trans-ship.

"I waiting for a call."

"From Aaron?"

"Who?... oh, yes, maybe Aaron."

It was a strange reply. George was about to impart all the advice he'd put together in his head but was cut off.

"Ok; we put you in the chair now," said the fat man. "Mohammed will bring you breakfast soon."

It was a beautiful Saturday morning in the London apartment. Tanja looked out onto Canary Wharf and the Thames River which sat in the distance. The river seemed to flow and flow as if it had no idea that her husband was missing. She watched it; it was going to be a hot day; it was going to be a hard day. She looked around the apartment; it needed cleaning. It was a beautiful place; a rental that George had arranged. It was a far cry from the life that she'd had before she'd met George. She used to share a bedroom with her mother and her brother slept in the sitting room in a tiny flat in Klaipėda, Lithuania. Now, she lived in luxury, but she couldn't enjoy it today; she was terrified. What happens if he doesn't come back?

Her toddler, Maria, would wake soon and Tanja would have to go about her day as if nothing was wrong. Tanja hadn't told her brother, Vlad, about it. He was 12 years old now. With his Down Syndrome, there was a chance of an overreaction. He always tended to overreact to things in the moment. Tanja would have to keep the worry to herself.

During the previous evening, Darius confirmed that he'd contacted a military intelligence friend who said he might be able to help, then she'd heard nothing more. Aaron had phoned as well; obviously hoping that George would have appeared at home; that would have made his job easier, but it was not to be.

Tanja could hear Maria stirring. She walked toward her bedroom and opened the door. When Maria saw her mother, she stood bolt upright in her crib and grabbed the top railing. The fourteen-month-old Maria held her hands out toward her mother with a big smile. Tanja suddenly felt that it was hard to be sad when one was with Maria. She smiled back at her daughter and spoke in Russian, "little mushroom, we will have to get daddy to renovate that crib into a proper toddler's bed; you're getting too clever for it now. Soon, you'll be able to climb right over that bar." Maria just smiled in agreement.

"What do you mean? I can't keep him here any longer, Jaber. He's been here for two days," demanded Tariq; his telephone voice was now becoming animated.

"Again, I haven't heard back from anyone. They could be anywhere – Gaza, Syria. I can't call them; they don't work that way."

"Ahh, I can't keep him here another night. He keeps asking lots of questions and trying to give me advice on getting money from his company."

"Why don't you take that advice?"

"Jaber, I am a simple man trying to make a living. I would end up in prison. You, you have the skill."

It went quiet on the line for a moment; the compliment seemed to work well. Tariq decided to continue.

"This situation calls for someone who can show leadership and be decisive. That's not me. I'm just desperate; I don't want to put him on the street; his memory is too fresh; I won't kill him; I don't know him and it might be an affront to Allah. If only I had a way out of this situation, I'm not even interested in money anymore. I just want out of it."

Tariq was hoping that Jaber would take the bait. He did.

"Well, let me ask you something?" continued Jaber.

"Sure, any advice from you would be welcome. I need someone like you in my life at the moment. I am lost."

"If you are that desperate, I could take him for you. But, I can't pay you; all my labour goes toward the cause. I will hold him myself; if he has no value to the bosses, then I will deal with the infidel."

Tariq waited; he wanted to give the illusion of contemplating the request in his mind. In his heart, he knew that he was well over his head and it was time to get rid of the Briton in his basement.

"I understand, Jaber, you are wiser than your years. Very wise. I will deliver him to you – no charge."

"Please bring the photographs as well. And come to the usual spot; you know it. Be there at midnight," replied Jaber.

Jaber put down the receiver and smiled to himself. An infidel at no cost; if he proved valuable, he would ingratiate himself with his superiors. If not, he could dispose of him. 'Heads I win, tails I win.'

Tariq put down the receiver and allowed himself a relieved smile. 'Sucker,' he thought, 'I will get this Briton out of my house and I will stick to highway robbery; no more kidnapping – that's it; I've learned my lesson.'

George was a little suspicious about the offer of a late evening snack. The fat man seemed very insistent.

"I'm sorry; I am not a fan of rice pudding," replied George.

"OK, I bring you a drink; what would you like?" replied Tariq.

George had had enough of the game playing.

"Can I ask you something? Forgive the impertinence, but is there any chance you are trying to slip me a drug, like you did yesterday. If you are, I'm hardly in a position to decline it. I'll take it with some water. I'm also guessing that means you might be preparing to move me, which I fully support. Again, I'm not your enemy; I think we're on the same side when it comes to getting me out of here."

"Ok, ok, you are too clever for me, my friend. I get Mohammed to bring water."

"So, just for my own edification, are you moving me tonight?"

"Yes, you figured it out."

"Where am I going?"

"You ask too many questions."

George paused a minute; he was pushing his luck but he decided he'd keep asking anyway.

"I'm curious; how much did you get for me?"

"Not as much as I'd hoped; now please keep quiet."

George heard Ahmed scurry back into the room and Tariq asked George to open his mouth. He could feel the two tablets being placed on his tongue; a glass of water quickly followed.

"I'm going to miss both of you," added George, "especially Mohammed; that's a great name."

Sayed looked at the email that morning; it was from an address he'd never seen before, but contained the phrase 'it has turned sunny in cairo' in the message body. Cairo was spelt with a lowercase 'c'. That was his cue. He opened the webmail account.

The draft simply said, "we have no such product; if we find it, we will ensure your instructions are followed." Sayed deleted it and began a new draft that simply said "thank you." A few hours later, he logged in a final time, just to see if there was any follow-up. There was a draft that read, "It is our pleasure to assist. Please pass along our best wishes to your boss." Sayed's heart missed a beat; did they know he was talking to MI5? Were they aware the instructions came from the UK? He thought and reread the note several times, then it dawned on him. They think the request came from Osama! Sayed allowed himself a moment of relief before deleting the draft and logging out of the account.

For George, this was a new level of pain. His head hurt from whatever sedative the buffoon had given him. The shackles were now far too tight and the handcuffs were so tight, they were ripping into his flesh. It hurt to move either his feet or his hands. To top it off, the chair may have been uncomfortable, but now he just lay on a floor and it was a cold floor without a blanket. In addition to the blindfold, something like a bandana had been placed over his mouth to prevent him from talking.

He lay there and considered trying to make some noise. No, he would wait a while; the drugs would wear off a little more and he'd be more lucid. George contemplated what must be happening. They must have dropped him somewhere else; he'd just have to deal with the agony for a few more hours – or maybe it was minutes. Yes, he could survive that – for sure, he could survive a couple of hours or even a day. This was the beginning of the end; he just had to keep up his stamina. He could do it.

He nodded off; George wasn't sure if he was out for a few minutes or a few hours, but then he had a rude awakening.

George could hear someone pacing, pacing incessantly and mumbling, jabbering away like a madman. The man mumbled in Arabic, but George could work out the occasional "Allah." George would just be quiet and try not to move; even though his bladder was now becoming decidedly painful again. He mustn't move; hopefully, someone else would arrive and he would get out of there.

The pacing continued. The more he paced, the angrier the mumbling seemed to become. George could smell him now; it was a rancid smell of body odour mixed with something else like manure of some sort.

"Pig, dog wake!" shouted the madman in English.

George was hoping the comment was not directed at him, but was pretty sure it was.

The blow was unexpected. The man levelled a kick to George's gut; it wasn't that it was a terribly ferocious blow, it was the spontaneous nature of it that caught George off-guard. George let out a gasp and tensed for the next kick, which was swiftly delivered, right to the bladder. George could no longer contain it; his bladder gave way and he could feel the hot spray of urine against his skin. The madman continued with several more kicks to the stomach. George was hoping that his face would not be next, but was fairly certain it would be. The madman kept shouting at him, but in Arabic, a language George couldn't understand. Then, he seemed to march in the opposite direction and slam a door.

George was alone in the room of horrors.

It was a rough Sunday for Tanja. Even Aaron now agreed that there was likely something wrong. Tanja had to be so careful when taking his calls. She couldn't let Vlad hear her on the phone. She needed to maintain the illusion of normalcy. She'd told Vlad that his brother-in-law had to stay a little longer on his business trip. That seemed to suffice.

She looked out to the Thames; 'where are you?' she asked the filthy muddy river. 'You're out there somewhere.' 'This morning had been tough, but tomorrow would be tougher', she thought. 'I'll have to take Vlad to his summer day camp and pretend everything is normal, but nothing is normal.'

She looked down at her very large tummy. 'What if you never meet your father?' she thought. No, she needed to stop thinking these thoughts. They were taking her to a dark place. She had to stop it. She needed to keep busy; she needed to keep her brother and daughter happy; she needed to keep it together; she needed to avoid teetering on the brink of mental collapse.

Jaber was rather proud of himself. He'd gotten out his frustration on the Briton; now, he was about to have his moment to shine. He walked bravely and proudly to the gate. It was an ornate gate and he rang the buzzer as he had so many times before.

"Yes," said the speaker on the buzzer.

"The clouds are wonderful; I have brought sunshine with me."

The code phrase was accepted and Jaber heard the buzzing sound which was his cue to open the gate door. He strode confidently across the courtyard toward the house. He had his prized manila envelope under his arm.

He knew the routine. As he approached the house, he stood about 10 metres in front of the doorway. That was the protocol. Cameras could view him clearly from that position. He was to go no further until invited.

It only took a half minute for the door to open and a security guard in a crisp business suit to wave him in. Jaber stood in the familiar vestibule. It was impressive. Marble tiles bedecked the floors while beautiful paintings adorned the white walls. Jaber had a favourite and looked toward the painting of Mecca. It had been so beautifully done.

"I'm here for Fares; he's expecting me."

"I know," replied the guard, "follow me."

Jaber made his way through beautiful hallways and toward a big wooden door. The security guard knocked and waited for a reply from within.

"Enter," came a voice from behind it.

The guard opened the door for Jaber, allowed him to enter, then closed it behind him, leaving the two alone.

"Peace be upon you, Fares."

"Come sit down," remarked Fares. Jaber made his way toward the giant oak desk and sat across from Fares, who sat in a very elaborate leather business chair. Fares' desk was piled with papers; the phone rang as Jaber sat. Fares ignored it and let it ring; he was anxious to get to the point.

"I'm sorry, Jaber; today is not the best day. You seemed anxious; what's up?"

"I have a prisoner for you."

Fares looked confused. "What prisoner?"

"A Briton; I have a hostage."

"What do you mean? We've dealt with all of them."

"No, a new one."

"I'm sorry Jaber, can I ask for more context? I'm not getting it; you know we don't take western hostages anymore."

"Well, we could trade him, he might be worth something."

Fares could suddenly feel the sweat trickle down his collar; this very unproductive day was about to go from non-productive to just bad. Did this idiot really take a hostage? He was about to open his mouth to screech at the fool, but then he closed it. He needed to calm down; he needed to calm down quickly.

"So, just to confirm, you are holding a British hostage? Is that correct?"

"Yes."

"Where did he come from?"

"I got him from a guy who hijacks taxis."

"So, there is someone in Beirut who took a British hostage and now knows you possess him? Is that right?"

"That's correct and I didn't even have to pay him; it was a gift."

"And does anyone else know?"

"Well, he works with his son; so just two people."

It was too much; it was really too much. Fares had had it.

"You imbecile; you moron. We're trying to keep peace with the West and you're collecting hostages. You know we don't do that anymore. And why on earth do you think we would ever want a hostage? You're a fool – is he harmed?"

Jaber was shocked, not only by the reply, but by the ferocity of its delivery; he began to shake a little "Well, not really."

"What does that mean? Did they hurt him or not?"

"Maybe, his stomach looked bruised."

"Why were you looking at his stomach?"

Jaber was now the one sweating, sweating profusely. He needed to think of a lie, he needed to think it up quickly. He needed a way out of this.

"Um, I looked him over to see if he was ok."

Fares knew it was a lie and wanted to tell Jaber to his face, but he also needed to regain control of the situation.

"Where is he now?"

"At my safe house."

"Whose guarding him?"

There was another long pause. Fares decided to break it.

"I'm glad you weren't around when we were in that business. You're not good at it. Now, I need to think."

Fares stared into the distance to a place on the wall beyond Jaber; he needed to come up with a plan. The two sat in silence with Jaber looking decidedly sheepish. He was over his head; just like Tariq, Jaber was now well over his head.

"Fares? May I speak?" Fares glared at him and nodded his head.

"I'm sorry to have brought you this problem; my intentions were good. I'll take care of it myself; I'll keep you out of it," said Jaber.

"The only people that are going to be taken care of are those two thieves. I'm officially relinquishing your Briton from you. I'll find someone to take him until we can figure out what to do with him."

Fares continued glaring across the desk. "I need to think; I need to think; is he blindfolded?"

"Yes."

"Ok, while I work this out, I'll ask Amar to go with you. He's the guard who let you in. He's had some experience. You are to never speak of this. If you ever speak of this, it could jeopardize so much of what we have done. You must never mention this to a soul. Do you understand?"

"I do; I'm sorry."

"You should be; I'll need the names and addresses of your thieves; eliminating them from our society will serve a double purpose. What's in that envelope?"

"Photos of the Briton."

"Who took them?"

"The thieves."

"Oh God, we're going to have to move quickly; they'll have negatives. Give me that envelope."

Jaber placed the manila envelope on Fares' desk. He had been so proud of it only a few minutes before; now he was ashamed, deeply ashamed; he'd dishonoured himself and he knew it.

Fares didn't open it. Instead, he leapt out of his chair and ordered Jaber to follow. He opened the large wooden door; Jaber followed like a mule to slaughter.

Fares walked him to the beautiful vestibule with the painting of Mecca while Fares provided instructions to the guard. Jaber had so loved that painting; now it seemed to mock him from its vantage point on the white walls.

CHAPTER 2

Loose Ends

George could hear movement; it was coming from outside. He heard what sounded like at least two cars pulling up outside. He must be somewhere rural; he hadn't heard anything for several hours. The madman must have left him alone, but now, he must be back. George wasn't looking forward to the interaction. His stomach still hurt; he knew his flesh was now well and truly torn around his wrists and his ankles were faring little better. He just wanted the ordeal to be over. During the madman's absence, George had been able to push the gag out of his mouth; he now used his chin, lips and teeth to drag it back on; he didn't want his captor to know he'd been able to slip it off.

It took several minutes before any more activity. Then, he heard the noise that he dreaded, he heard the noise of a door opening. A minute or so passed before he heard something being dragged on the floor. It must be a concrete floor, he thought. It sounded like furniture was being moved into the room. George knew that wouldn't be good; they were going to torture him.

The madman worked in complete silence now. In contrast to the frightening noises of equipment being put in place, he could also smell something that smelled rather nice. The jailer had food with him; maybe he'd give some to him. He had forgotten how hungry he was, but the aroma now reminded him. Or, maybe this was part of the torture, he'd be hungry and he wouldn't feed him. George just tried to lie very still.

George heard the man close the door and then he did something rather odd; he could hear him secure the deadbolt lock. That seemed like a peculiar thing to do; why would he lock himself in with him? George wasn't looking forward to finding out.

After several minutes of furniture moving and various organizational sounds and the sound of the deadbolt, George could feel the man approaching him. It was more than just footsteps; it felt almost like the man was accompanied by a cold breeze, or maybe it was all his imagination; he was exhausted and scared and having his sense of sight denied might be propelling that sense of fear.

George felt the man tug at the gag. God, why did he choose that? He must have seen it was out of place, now he'd be punished. Then, George heard the noise of the gag being cut with something sharp. Oh God, he's got a knife.

Next, the madman gently placed his hands on one of the ankle shackles. At that moment, George thought something odd - the smell. His smell - it was different than earlier; it wasn't unpleasant; in fact, this man smelled clean, like laundry soap. George began to think; his actions were different; this man moved in a far more assured fashion. He thought he'd heard two cars; this must be someone else.

George felt a sense of instant relief as the shackle on his left ankle suddenly released. It was such a relief that George let out a groan; he didn't mean to and wondered if the man would react. He then heard the key in the second shackle and then that one too was released. The man threw the shackles a few feet away; George could hear them clang on the floor. Next, the handcuffs were removed. This wasn't quite as pleasant; it really hurt when they were removed; the raw flesh was irritated by the removal process. What happened next was not expected. The man gently pulled up on the blindfold; then more firmly until it could be removed by slipping it over his head.

It was a strange setting. The room was illuminated by a single lightbulb, which was cloistered in an old fashion cloth fixture, which hung above him. The room only contained two pieces of furniture – a little old wooden table and a single wooden chair. There was a Styrofoam food container on the table and various drinks. There also appeared to be a doctor's bag or first aid kit on the other side of that table. There were some cloths or garments on the chair. A bucket had been placed in another corner of the room. There were no windows, but this wasn't a jail room. It just seemed like someone's basement; it may have been a utility room at some point.

However, the most bizarre thing of all wasn't his ad hoc prison room; it was his jailer. He was a giant; dressed head to toe in black. A burka covered his face. There was a meshed area where the jailer's eyes should have been. George couldn't glimpse even a hint of flesh. He wore gloves. George's mind was wandering. He was terrified, but couldn't help think that his life had become some sort of cartoon. He had now been delivered into the hands of someone who appeared to be the grim reaper, who would feed him and then complete what needed to be done.

George looked at him; he needed to say something.

"Do you speak English?"

The shadowy figure just shook his head and raised his gloved index finger to his mouth to make the silence gesture.

The giant placed his hands under George's armpits and raised him to his feet. George just stood there in a hunched position; the pain was unbearable; he couldn't stand straight. It took him several seconds before he attempted to straighten his back.

It was a relief to feel the circulation in his feet and hands again. George just took a moment to gently move his body around while ensuring his feet remained exactly where they'd been; he didn't want to give the impression he was about to run.

The man pointed to the wooden chair where there appeared to be some clothes. George had forgotten about his earlier beating, but now became very aware. He tried to walk toward the chair, but stumbled; the man grabbed him and led him to the chair.

George wasn't sure how the next few minutes would pan out. The man placed the pile of clothes on the table which seemed to indicate a request for George to change. He started removing his trousers, then sat on the chair to complete the process; he couldn't remember which hostage-taker had taken his dress shirt, shoes and socks. He was going to have trouble with his t-shirt. He tried to get it over his head, but the combination of the pain from his wrists and torso made it difficult. The man interceded at one point and helped him remove it. George now stood. He looked down at his urine-soaked underwear while the man seemed to just stare at him. George was about to remove them when the man made a gesture – he pointed toward the bucket. It was a welcome suggestion. George hobbled toward it and removed the undergarment which clung to his body. He wasn't sure what to do with it, so he left it by the bucket and relieved himself.

While George completed his toileting, he could hear the man move the chair away from the table. When complete, George turned round to face him. George was naked now. Another bucket had been placed in front of the chair with a washcloth hanging from the side of it; a towel was neatly folded beside it on the floor. The man motioned George toward it; it was filled with water. George sat again on the chair and, using the cloth, tried to wash his face and hands, then extended the wash to include his wounded areas and then his chest and armpits. He stood again and moved a little away from the chair and tried to clean the urine around his groin area and, finally, he tried to clean his bottom. He returned the washcloth to the side of the bucket. He then took the towel and tried to dry himself, completing the same ritual in the same order as with the washcloth. After the perfunctory cleanup, he looked back toward the man for guidance. The man pointed him back toward the clothes, which sat on the table; near the Styrofoam container and drinks. The clothes consisted of a pair of underwear and a robe; like the type worn by Islamic men in the middle east. George was still struggling, but was able to don the underwear. At that point, the man did something that seemed slightly surprising.

He motioned George to sit again in the chair. George understood that he was to do it now and not dress in the robe. George obeyed; the man removed the doctor's bag from the table and seemed to study his wrists, then his ankles and then his stomach. Some rubbing alcohol was produced from the bag and cotton balls. George couldn't help it; he screeched when the man started dabbing his right wrist. George thought he would be angry with the outburst, but the jailer seemed unfazed as he continued the cleaning of the various gashes. Once complete, cotton bandages were wrapped around his wrists and ankles. George was then motioned to don his robe.

George put it on and thought how comfortable it felt; he thought he must look rather handsome in it; like Lawrence of Arabia, it was a decent fit. The strange places your mind goes in times like this, he thought. He looked back at the man, who pointed at the Styrofoam container. George sat beside it and opened it.

Dinner was a falafel wrap and chips with a peculiar selection of drinks – there was a Pepsi, 7UP, Mirinda and a bottle of water. It seemed curious, but George was so dehydrated that he finished off the entire selection along with every morsel of food. Because of all the preceding rituals, the chips were now completely cold, but the falafel still maintained a small amount of warmth. It didn't matter. George realized how hungry he had become; he enjoyed it.

Once the meal was complete, he looked up from his chair to his executioner. With his last meal complete, George now believed he was about to take his final journey with his new friend, the grim reaper of Lebanon.

Tariq would have been disappointed at just how easily they were able to gain access to his house. He had spent a small fortune on security. There were quality locks; there was even a little camera that faced the front door, but the intruders didn't use that as an entrance. It was all rather simple, there were four men in total. One was the break and enter specialist. He carefully inspected all the main floor windows, which were located about 10 feet from ground level – they had bars; there were also barred basement windows, just above ground level. There was just one obvious flaw and the man knew how to exploit it. There was a single unbarred small window on the ground floor for the bathroom. It was typical to leave that flaw as it wouldn't be big enough for someone to get through, but the assassins were prepared for that eventuality.

The break and enter specialist signalled toward the window; he was going to need a ladder to get up there. Two men moved like cats, quietly but swiftly to fulfil the request; they brought a ladder from the van. The specialist climbed it and a man handed him a knife and a suction cup affixed to a little handle. It would have surprised the occupants how quietly that man could attach a suction cup to that window and then cut into the glass. Once a circle had been cut, he handed his knife and the piece of glass attached to the suction down to his colleague. The lock was a joke – it was a simple hook and eye lock. The hook was removed and the man opened the window; he needed to be careful, it would close shut by itself and the noise would be unwelcome. After testing to ensure that he could fully open that window, he gently let it rest in the closed position.

The next piece of the scheme would have impressed even the most diehard aficionado of break and enter. That tiny window wouldn't be big enough for a man to get through or even a normal-sized boy. However, there was one man of the four who suffered an affliction. That affliction was not always an advantage in life, but tonight, in this type of work, it would be invaluable.

The specialist climbed down the ladder and the little man with dwarfism climbed up it. He was followed again by the specialist. While the tall man opened the window and held it, the little man pulled his way through it. He made the manoeuvre slowly and held the sill to allow himself to drop quietly into the waiting bathtub. The manoeuvre would have impressed most acrobats. Once standing in the bathtub, tools of the trade were handed up that ladder and presented, through the window, by the big man to the little man. The little man was now armed.

The plan was well-rehearsed and the team had been trained on a number of scenarios. The little man was to complete a site survey. If he could handle the job himself, he would do it. If it looked like he'd need more men, he would search the house for ways to grant them access. The three stood at the bottom of the ladder. They readied their gear either for a quick entry to the house or a quick getaway to the van. Either way, it was to be done quietly.

They stood in silence. Other men would not have even heard the sound, but these men were familiar with it. It was a 'swoosh' sound peculiar to a unique tool called a silencer. The men knew instantly which option their colleague had chosen.

On that summer evening, in a suburb of Beirut, the unusual story of Tariq and Ahmed came to a close. It was a peculiar story of two incidental hijackers who had made the unfortunate decision to diversify their trade. They may have continued to get away with their usual business, but that diversification would not be tolerated.

Fares was at the Communications Centre at 9 am on that Monday morning. It was over a 30-minute drive to Kfour, so he left early. He had worked the phone most of the night; he had wanted to move George the night before, but it was not going to work. He had started to get leads on where he could move him, if he would have to move him, but that's not why he was at the Communications Centre today. He needed to know whom he now had in custody.

He handed the photos to Wissam, who gasped when he saw them.

"He's dead!?" pronounced Wissam.

"No, no, they did a poor job with the photo. He's alive. I just want to find out anything about him; then we can figure out what to do. I'd like to let him go, but he mustn't figure out that we're involved and preferably, I don't want to spook the British with this. It was just a stupid taxi hijacker and a very stupid one of our bunch that got him into all of this. I just want to get him home and not provoke him to talk about it. I was thinking that we could send some men around and pretend it was a raid and 'rescue' him."

Wissam just stared at the photo, "It's not going to be that easy. I know about this one. Bin Laden is looking for him; I've been talking to one of his henchmen. We were told not to harm him. I told them we didn't have him. Before you do anything, I need to get direction from them. There is already too much friction between us. If they find out that we had him and let him go without talking to them, there is going to be more trouble. I'm sorry, Fares. You need to buy me more time."

Back in Afghanistan, Sayed spent most of his Sunday afternoon on a long hike around Kabul. He was out of shape and did not want it to be quite as obvious when he got to the camp in Kandahar. The plan was that they would leave very early in the morning and drive to the training camp. As he walked, he thought to himself that the camps were becoming too religious; the whole country was becoming too religious. But, having Islam govern seemed preferable to the Soviets or the British or the Americans. The camps were necessary; they couldn't allow another occupation; they needed to be prepared.

Sayed pondered his own fight against one of the most recent conquerors. The Russians seemed so stupid and yet they were able to occupy his country. He recalled his own contribution. He had learned decent Russian and already spoke English. His job was to spy and encourage the consumption of a local delicacy by occupying forces. Some of those Russian dunderheads would trade their own weapons for a spoonful of heroin. Dumb lot.

Sayed kept walking; he needed to get some of this fat off him somehow and he needed to move. He was about to spend at least 14 hours in the van. He wanted to spend today moving around.

By the time he returned home, he was exhausted. He had some work to do but decided that it could wait; he'd have a nice meal and rise a half-hour early to tie things up before the fortnight's retreat.

Sayed rose a little after 3:30 the next morning; the van wouldn't leave for an hour. He washed and dressed and then started the computer in his room. It took a long time to boot. He then pressed the button to connect the modem and heard the familiar fax tones.

He looked at his email; he hadn't missed much, except there was one email mentioning 'it has turned sunny in cairo'. That's a pity; it had arrived the previous day. They wouldn't be online now and Sayed wouldn't have internet access again for two weeks.

He logged into the familiar email account and read the draft. "The package has been intercepted by us; it was shipped in the wrong taxi." Sayed deleted the message. "Thank you; will be away after midnight GMT. If unavailable now, please await recontact."

Sayed opened a word session and began typing a draft for Zurab. If the Lebanese didn't reply, he could at least contact Zurab through the website; it wasn't much, but at least it looked like they found him. He completed typing the draft in word format.

It was 4:20, 10 minutes before midnight GMT. Sayed could hear them packing the van. He looked out the window to the dark; then heard someone honk the horn. 'Ahh', he thought, 'the young ones get so excited about these damn camps. They'll have to wait.'

He would check the account one last time before 4:30; he couldn't risk a draft being left behind. He checked again. There was a new draft, but it was only a draft with an attachment; it was George's photo with the newspaper.

'Gees, these guys are poor communicators; it sounded like they'd intercepted him alive.' Sayed saved the photo to his computer and deleted the draft and created a new draft, "Thank you; over and out; please await recontact. I am leaving now." He logged out of the account.

Before leaving, he logged into the website and attached the photo in the web portal; he also completed a comment in the portal for Zurab, "Sorry, my friend, looks like they found him too late. It doesn't sound like a political thing; sounds like he took the wrong taxi."

Normally, Darius would have let the call go to voicemail. His turn to speak at the conference was about to be called. However, the call display looked odd; Zurab had provided a hint in that call display. It appeared to be coming from the UK. Darius decided to step outside the conference hall.

"Hello."

"Dario, it's me."

"Hello to you; I can't really talk; I'm about to speak; I'm at a conference."

There was silence for a moment on the line.

"Dario, it's about that matter we discussed. I have news."

"Is it urgent?"

"I suppose it could be described that way."

Darius did not want to blow this speaking engagement. It was important. It was a celebration of the work completed to date on European Union accession. He then thought about his old friend, George, and about Tanja, both had always shown him such love and respect.

"Ok; give me 30 minutes; I'll get them to bump me till later."

"I'll keep the line free for you, my friend."

Things were much more civil now. After dinner, the jailer in black handcuffed George's right hand to the chair. He did it carefully and ensured that the handcuff was placed directly above the bandage. The man then opened the door and dragged a mattress through it along with some other items. The handcuff was then removed. George was even given blankets and a pillow. After being directed to the mattress, George made up his bed and lay there in his robe. He closed his eyes; he felt a little better now that he'd eaten and had a chance to clean up a little. If he co-operated, it didn't look like this new jailer was actually going to hurt him. It was a significant improvement over his previous captor. George realized how much the stress had exhausted him; although the light in the room remained on, he fell asleep quickly.

The man was still there when he woke along with a new bucket of water and fresh washcloth and towel. There was even more food on the table. Breakfast appeared to be a fancy affair with a selection of pastries and a paper cup of coffee. It was really unclear what was happening; it seemed like a game of bad cop and good cop, but why did they even need that first bad cop?

Shortly before lunch, a different man replaced the man in black. This man was also dressed head to toe in black and refused to speak. The second grim reaper came bearing another meal – lunch was a shawarma plate of lamb, pita bread, couscous, salad; it was also served with a selection of soft drinks.

After lunch, George sat on his mattress staring into space. Grim reaper number 2 seemed to have a plan for that. From the medical bag, he presented George with a copy of a book: Charles Dickens' "David Copperfield." It was a used copy and clearly very worn, but George was pleased with it. It had been one of his favourites from when he was a boy; he sat there and read it while the grim reaper looked on at him. The scene felt surreal, but alas, it was a marked improvement over the first captor and now, George had some way to entertain himself under that lightbulb.

Dinner eventually arrived; it was something akin to a pizza, but different. It was tasty and George was now beginning to relax a little as he made his way through the various soft drinks. He'd enjoyed reading and felt a bit better after all the food. There was only one thing that was bothering him. He felt filthy. Oh, he'd been allowed two buckets of clean water and a wash cloth, but he still could feel and smell the urine against his skin. He desperately wanted a shower, but knew it was unlikely anytime soon.

After dinner, George returned to the book. At one point, there was a knock at the door and grim reaper 2 attended to it. There was a discussion, the man took a bottle of water from whoever was on the other side and then he closed the door and made his way back to the medical bag. After having the book retrieved from that bag, George imagined what might be next; perhaps another book or some sort of game.

George watched carefully as the man removed a plastic pill bottle from the bag and then walked toward him. The jailer extracted two small tablets from the bottle, placed them in the palm of his gloved hand and offered them to George. George dreaded the thought of another knock-out evening followed by a headache, but knew this might be the end of the ordeal – for good or bad. They might take him away and kill him or they might set him free. Either way, he knew he had no choice. He would have to take them.

"Ok, I'm on a secure line. Can you hear me?" asked Darius.

"Yes, my friend; it's good to hear your voice," replied Zurab.

"Yours as well. Thank you again for your help. He's a good friend of the family."

"I understand, Dario. I wish it were better news; I'm afraid your friend is dead."

Both men went quiet; Darius knew that Zurab was giving him a moment to digest the information. Zurab continued.

"It wasn't political; sounds like a taxi ride gone wrong. I have a photo; he was posed with a newspaper; it was on Friday."

"Can I see it?" asked Darius.

"I can't send it by email; are you beside a fax? I can fax it to you but only if you are beside the fax now; you'll then have to destroy it. I'm going to have to hand the case off to someone; you also need to be careful; we can't let anything trail back to our friend. This conversation and the photo must be between us."

Darius contemplated a moment. Did he really need to see it?

"Of course, I think I need to see it; my secretary has a fax machine at her desk. Give me 1 minute; just stay on the line; I'll ask her to take a break."

Darius provided the fax number to Zurab. He went to the next room and asked his secretary to run an urgent errand. He returned to the phone and asked Zurab to send it while he remained on the line.

Darius stared in horror as that photo slowly generated itself from the waiting fax machine.

He then returned to his phone. "Thank you again, I'm sorry to say, you were quite right; it is him."

Darius just sat in his office; he needed to get back to the conference. He didn't know how he was going to make the next call; maybe he should wait; maybe more information would come. No, it was the wrong thing to do; Tanja deserved to hear it from him; he hated to do it by telephone, but what choice did he have? He picked up the phone and dialled the apartment number, it went to voicemail. Darius was unsure what to do next, he decided to try Tanja's mobile number. Part of him was very disappointed when she picked up.

"Hello."

Darius continued in Lithuanian, "Tanja? It's Darius."

"Hi, have you heard anything?"

"Where are you?"

"On the train, have you heard anything?"

"How long till you get home?"

"I just dropped off Vlad at day camp; Maria and I are heading home. Darius – if you know something, can you tell me? I can't wait any longer, no one is telling me anything."

Darius paused a minute before continuing, but it was Tanja who spoke first.

"I'll get off at the next station. Ok?"

It was only a few seconds before Darius heard the familiar 'mind the gap.' He'd been in London many times and was familiar with that announcement. He needed to think; how was he going to explain this? He'd had to deliver bad news on so many occasions, but he'd never had to tell a pregnant woman on a train that her husband was dead while she pushed his child around in a pram on a station platform.

"Darius? I'm off; I'm off the train. Can you hear me?"

"I can. Tanja... I'm afraid It's not good news. My contact at military intelligence has intercepted a photo of George. It looks like he took the wrong taxi." Darius then went quiet.

"What does that mean?" Tanja was pretty sure she knew what it meant but she had to hear the words.

"It hasn't been confirmed by the local authorities as far as I know." Darius decided to change gears; if he was going to deliver this message, it needed to be delivered without ambiguity, "I'm sorry Tanja, it looks like he's dead... I love him; I'm so sorry."

Tanja went quiet for a moment and then her thoughts ran wild and then she felt overwhelmed with sadness and then with anger and then, in one instant, a tidal wave of emotions seemed to come at the same time – Tanja erupted on the platform at Stratford Station in East London. She collapsed and screeched so loudly that the entire busy station seemed to come to a complete standstill. People stared at the crazy woman as she collapsed to her knees and kept screeching in a foreign tongue as she declared, "No, no, why? Why God? Why me? Why him?" Tanja sobbed and sobbed; part of her wanted to throw that mobile phone onto the tracks for delivering this disgusting news. She was repulsed at it and felt a sense of rage toward it.

"Tanja?" said Darius quietly. "Tanja?"

She looked at the phone; she'd felt disgusted toward it, but not toward Darius; he was only providing her the news that no one else was able to give her. It was the truth, even if it were a repugnant truth.

She sobbed and tried to compose herself; she sniffled her reply, "I'm here."

"Can you get home and call me when you get there? I'll be on my mobile. I am so sorry; I love him; I love you too. We're going to get through this."

"I will," she replied.

She disconnected the call and stared at the trains passing her; she watched them come and go. She was past the outburst now; she was just numb and stood on that platform, her face stained with tears as she watched the trains come and go. People passed and looked at her. She didn't care; she was alone now; she was alone to fend for herself. As the next train arrived, she pushed the pram onto it and waited for the doors to close. She was returning home – to her apartment at Canary Wharf.

It was a new day, or maybe it was the same day, but, in any event, it was a new prison for George. He woke groggily; he was accustomed to it now.

He had been drugged several times now and this was his third prison cell. He couldn't seem to recall how many days had passed. Was this Wednesday today or was it Thursday? He couldn't be sure; the drugs and the pain from the beating and the handcuffs and shackles had discombobulated him; the mental stress was producing strange dreams that were also beginning to confuse him. Some of the dreams were so real that he had trouble understanding that they weren't real; his mind was beginning to wander all over. He needed to refocus.

He felt around to see if he was still handcuffed; they were gone. That was something. The first grim reaper had done an admirable job of cleaning up his wounds; wrapping them in cotton bandages. George touched one of his blood-soaked bandages; it needed to be changed, but that was the least of his problems.

He tried to see in the darkness; it was really dark in that room; it was impossible to see anything. Wherever he was, there was no access even to residual light. It must be another basement. He felt around; he was now sleeping on a bed. It was his first real bed; it was comfortable enough, but he didn't want to lie there anymore. George lifted himself just to sit on the bed and stare into the darkness. He felt along the side of the mattress, then started to grope around in the area just in front of him. He took his hands and carefully let them circle in front of him in the hope of touching something. He kept them around the level of the mattress and lower in the hopes of finding something in the darkness.

He had some luck. He could touch a table; likely a nightstand of some sort. He felt around and detected a plastic bottle of liquid. He grasped it and felt its shape. He tried to hold it in front of his eyes; it's likely water, he thought. George twisted the top and smelled the contents, then slowly took a sip, just to test. It was water; George sat on his new bed and drank it. He was thirsty and the water gave him comfort, a rare reprieve of sanity in a world that had become quite insane.

Fares looked over at Wissam and asked the predictable question.

"How much longer?"

"I don't know; they operate the same way that we do. They don't accept communication when they go on location. They want to keep their movements to themselves. However, they're up to something. Our Security Services have heard from the UK; the British think your hostage is dead."

"Really?" asked Fares.

"Yes, and someone's done a good job at it. The British think it was a taxi driver, just bad luck. The incident hasn't even appeared in the media yet. We may not be fond of them, but those Al Qaeda bunch are slick operators. I'm not sure how they convinced them, and the British could still change their minds or they might be telling our people what we want to hear, but at the moment, it looks ok. But we still need direction from them; we need to wait till he reconnects with us."

Fares needed a moment to ponder the last statement. It was good news; they might be allowed just to dispose of the hostage; if there wasn't going to be a reaction, they could just get rid of him.

Wissam continued, "Where's he now?"

"I got a lucky break. I found someone who could help; he used to do it during the war. He still had a family with a facility in the basement." Fares gave a nervous laugh, "They were using it for storage, but they were able to restore it quickly. They don't know who they are holding. I told my contact that they are never to know that we are involved and he's not to do anything until I say so. Apparently, the family is just happy to get the money and serve the cause."

Wissam smiled; it was better to smile than deal with all the stress of that job all the time. "You're quite a fixer, Mr Fares. I will be asking you to co-ordinate my children's weddings."

"If my current luck continues in this job, I will gladly take that job."

It had been hard to get through the day. Tanja was able to get back to the apartment, but then she just sat there in the sitting room. She sat and cried; this made Maria get antsy and difficult, which made Tanja even more upset. It was hard to go about her chores; her mind was spinning. She should phone Milwaukee. She dreaded it; how would she tell his parents? They already hated her; now she would deliver the news that their only child was gone. No, she couldn't deal with it right now. Besides, Darius said that the locals hadn't confirmed it yet. Tanja had grasped onto that sliver of hope since the call. Maybe, just maybe, Darius was wrong, received bad intelligence. It was unlikely; she knew that; he'd served in the Soviet military; she was aware that he'd worked with British and American intelligence as part of his collaboration with the Afghans. He very likely knew much more than the local authorities.

She was finally able to get Maria down for her nap; the only other chore that would have to be undertaken today was collecting her brother from day camp. God, that's another thing, how was she going to tell him? The place really needed cleaning and there were dirty dishes, but Tanja just didn't have the motivation.

She looked at the dirty river out her window. 'So, you've taken him,' she thought to herself. Her mind kept wandering; it wandered to the moment when she first met George. She was only 19 and working part-time at a coffee shop; it seemed like another lifetime. She needed the money from that job; she worked full-time at Vlad's Children's Centre for Down Syndrome kids, but that job paid next to nothing in those days. George used to come in once a week for coffee; it was unusual to have western foreigners in that café. She had tried to learn a few English words to impress the handsome school teacher. It had impressed him; little did she know, he was actively trying to learn as much Lithuanian as possible so he could impress her.

A tragic love story – it was all a tragic love story. It was two destined lovers who couldn't even speak the same language and yet they had fallen in love. She hadn't wanted to go to America, but George had a job offer. They needed to marry to get a visa for her; she loved George, but not America. She was glad when he was promoted again and redeployed from Seattle to London. It was closer to home. And now, she was a Russian girl from Klaipėda, Lithuania staring out a window at a river. There was one baby in her crib; another in her womb and one Down Syndrome 12-year-old who would soon need to be collected from day camp. Not only was she sad; she was over her head.

Tanja was glad when the day was over. She'd made Vlad spaghetti for dinner; it was easy to make, that's why she'd chosen it. She decided not to tell him the news. She would buy the rest of the day to think about how to do it. She needed to deal with her own stress first. She kept looking at her watch and subtracting six hours; she felt odd about not calling his parents. Now, it would have to wait until at least noon tomorrow before she could try again, but this was the right thing, she needed to wait, she needed to think and the fact that she had only heard from Darius helped with that decision; she didn't 'officially' know anything and; if she said anything, she'd be exposing Darius, who shouldn't have been involved. However, even that one ray of hope was about to be extinguished.

She heard the buzzer; there was someone at the answerphone outside the lobby at the main entrance. It may be Aaron, she thought. It wasn't.

"Hello," said the official-sounding voice. "It's Chief Superintendent Brown here from the London Metropolitan Police and a colleague; may we come in?"

Tanja pressed the button to give them access. She looked over at Vlad; he was watching cartoons in the sitting room.

"Who is it?" asked Vlad.

"It's nothing, some policeman investigating something." Then Tanja had a thought; it was the first lucid thought of the day, "I'll talk to them in our bedroom, so we don't interfere with your cartoons."

"That's ok; I'd like to see them."

"No, Vladie, I'm not up to it; I'll just deal with them; you can talk to them another time."

The two policemen looked confused when Tanja greeted them at the door and waved them past the sitting room and into the master bedroom without saying a word; just gesturing that they should follow. She asked them to sit on the bed while she stood. She looked at the older policeman; he had stars on his lapels, like something out of one of Vlad's cartoons. His uniform was meant to deliver a sense of superiority. The other cop was a woman and looked more like regular police.

"Sorry, my brother not know about George," said Tanja.

"I understand completely. I'm Chief Superintendent Brown and this is Sergeant Frank; we're from Special Operations at the London Metropolitan Police. Before we get started, would you be more comfortable sitting on the bed with us?"

"I ok."

The Superintendent continued, "So, I'm afraid we've come with some difficult news."

Tanja looked down; she didn't say anything; she knew what was coming.

"So, we've been working with the Internal Security Forces Directorate in Lebanon as well as the Home Office regarding your husband's disappearance." He paused at that point, then Tanja could see that he also looked down; he was about to deliver it, she wasn't allowed to portray that she already knew.

"Intelligence has gained access to a photograph of your husband. As we understand it, it appears he took a late-night taxi after a business meal with some local colleagues. The Lebanese are still investigating, but the photograph…" The policeman stopped and seemed to pause as if not knowing how to deliver the next few words, "The photograph appears to show that he is no longer with us."

He stopped talking. Tanja thought how odd that the English never liked to use the word 'dead'. Had she not known what he was going to say, she would have had to ask him what it meant. He was clearly staring at her now and waiting for a reaction, but Tanja had spent the whole day reacting. She just looked down and said, "Ok."

The Superintendent continued, "Again, we will continue to work with the local authorities. We have asked them to prioritize an investigation and try to; try to recover any remains. We just have the photograph; our own intelligence currently indicates a robbery that went wrong. I'm sorry, we don't like to deliver this type of news so crassly, but we also want to be transparent and truthful with you."

"I understand," said Tanja, "Can I see it?"

"I have a copy, but please, may I ask you to sit. Please sit beside Sergeant Frank. Tanja complied and she now became aware why the woman policeman was brought along; she was to be the one to comfort the distraught pregnant wife.

Chief Superintendent Brown removed an A4-sized photograph from his briefcase and handed it to her. She looked at her husband's lifeless face; it was a final confirmation of something she already knew, but part of her still rejected. The truth was a difficult thing, but it was also the truth.

"Can I keep it?"

The chief superintendent seemed surprised at the lack of emotion; perhaps it was a cultural thing.

"Of course."

CHAPTER 3

Waiting and Wondering

George just sat there and stared into the darkness; he wasn't sure how long he'd been staring into that darkness. He'd finished the first bottle of water; then found another one. He hesitated before drinking it; he was thirsty, but it would also mean he'd need to use the toilet. It was too dark to determine if there was a bucket in the room. He drank it anyway; he was now so thirsty, he just needed it.

After the second bottle was consumed, he waited. He wondered if maybe there had been a problem with the ransom. Maybe, Trans-ship didn't pay ransoms; it might be a first for that type of request. He knew the US government wouldn't pay one; the UK was unlikely to pay as well. Maybe, they were shaking down Tanja. He had never really shown her where all the financial information was kept; he regretted that now. She'd have trouble finding money quickly. And she didn't need the stress in her condition. He felt a sense of guilt come over him; 'I shouldn't have come and I shouldn't have risked that taxi. I should have taken up the offer of the Lebanese trader; he knew better.' It was an amateur's mistake.

After a while, he could hear a peculiar noise, like a bolt being removed from a steel door. Then, he heard that door open. A ray of light shone down into the corridor. He leapt to his feet. There were bars on his door, he could see light emanating into the hallway from above; there must be a staircase and the door has been opened above.

It wasn't long before someone turned on the lights. Whatever switch was turned, illuminated several lights, flooding the space. It was really too much light. His room had fluorescent lights which were encased in the ceiling; the hallway lights were just bare lightbulbs.

He squinted and watched the man come down the hall. He was dressed the same as his two predecessors, but this man was much shorter. He carried a tray with him; George thought maybe it would be food.

When he arrived at George's cell, he waved George away from the door, pointing him to the bed. George sat on the bed. The man, dressed completely in black, put the tray on the floor and produced some keys. However, he didn't unlock the whole door. George's cell door contained a mini door at the bottom. It was part of the main door, but, when opened, it only liberated about a foot of height and a foot of width – just enough for the man to push forward the tray.

His guard then locked the trap door, turned round and made his way back down the hall and toward the stairs. George couldn't see the staircase or what sounded like a steel door, but he could hear it being shut and then the bolt being reapplied. He was alone again, but now he had food and light.

George took a moment just to review his new accommodations. They actually weren't bad, but they were odd. Beside him was the night table with no drawers, where he'd found his water. Beside that was an empty table – a small dining room table with a single wooden chair. On the other side of the cell, there was another table with bedding, towels and what appeared to be fresh robes and underwear. None of that was particularly odd, but it was the bizarre design of the bathroom that was so peculiar. There was a steel toilet and sink combination; the kind that prisoners in the West might be familiar with and beside that – right in the corner were two taps attached to a long metal hose with a shower head on the top. There was also a drain beneath that shower head. It was odd because there was no door - no way to separate his room from the facilities.

The prison room walls were concrete, save the one side which contained the steel bars. That side was just large enough to ensure that any prisoner would be denied privacy no matter where they stood. George looked around wondering if there was a camera somewhere; there must be one but he couldn't see it.

He stood up again and made his way toward the tray. The food looked decent enough: more pastries, bottled water and coffee. The food was served on proper china plates, the coffee was in a lovely cup and saucer but the utensils were all plastic. He took the tray and put it on his new dining table.

Before eating it, he had one ritual that he was looking forward to completing. He found a towel on his linen table; there was even a small bar of soap, wrapped in paper, which he unwrapped and smelled. He then made his way to the metal sink; he was going to wash his hands before breakfast, just like a real human.

Fares was getting anxious. It had been going on too long. He needed to put a bit of gentle pressure on Wissam. If he couldn't reach his interlocutor, he would have to find someone else within Al Qaeda to negotiate. They couldn't hold the Briton indefinitely. They needed to get their permission for him to disappear, so they could move on with things. The village of Kfour was painfully hot, even for early evening, but Fares needed to make the trip; he would never dream of having this type of conversation over the phone. They'd been warned that the Israelis were getting particularly vigilant at their spying efforts. There were even concerns that they may have information on Kfour itself.

He was hoping Wissam would still be there. With the various time zones and the unpredictability of the secret world in which he dealt, he often worked at odd hours to send and deliver messages.

Fares was surprised to be stopped as he drove to the village. One of the guard's superiors recognized him, but still insisted that his subordinate search the car. Security at the Communications Centre seemed particularly tight. Armed guards were, unusually, in plain view; they normally kept out of view.

When he tried to drive into the underground car park, his car was searched again and he was surprised to be frisked. He'd entered that building dozens of times and this seemed excessive.

He was in luck. Wissam was still there; in fact, most of the staff seemed to be there.

Fares knocked before entering; Wissam smiled and waved him in.

"Why all the security tonight?"

"Likely nothing," replied Wissam. "We're hearing a lot of chatter about an Israeli attack, but we can't authenticate it and it's not clear where they might hit. Don't worry, with men like you in charge, we'll hit them right back."

Fares allowed himself a smile; Wissam was always so charming, but now he needed to get to the point.

"Wissam – can I put some gentle pressure on you? Is there anyone else on their side that we can talk to?"

Wissam thought a minute. "How about I try one more time with my contact? I have a coded message I can send, then I have a protocol. I shouldn't request contact when he's told me to wait for him, but I can try. I'll send it early tomorrow. I'll give him 36 hours, then recall the request and find someone else to talk to. We need to be careful, Fares, Bin Laden may not have informed all his henchmen; we need to be careful."

"Ok," sighed Fares, "I appreciate the efforts. Can I return in, say, three days to check-in?"

"Of course, you are always welcome here. But unfortunately, your welcome will be a bit extended tonight. The road to Beirut isn't safe at the moment; it's just been closed. We may have to defend it if they hit in the area."

It was the last thing Fares wanted to hear, but it wasn't the first time that he'd been ordered to stay put. He would have to spend his night asleep in the backseat in the underground car park of the Communications Centre. It wasn't the end of the world. Except, for Fares, that wasn't quite right.

During that evening, a series of bombs packed with ball bearings were detonated in and around the village of Kfour. It was believed that Israeli special forces had planted them and that the Israeli Air Force had detonated them from the air. The bombs appeared targeted at certain individuals and a couple of strategic buildings. The building which took the greatest impact was the Communications Centre which was completely destroyed.

Tanja stared at the telephone; she had spent most of the morning staring at it. She had delayed calling Milwaukee, but she had promised herself that she would call at noon; that would be 6 am their time. She didn't know what she was going to say. She wished she didn't have to do it; she was the last person who they likely wanted to hear from and her English was still so poor. She needed to be careful about the wording that she would use; she didn't want to offend with a wrong phrase or word; there were so many sensitivities around the issue which she needed to raise.

She looked at the clock; there were still 15 minutes to go. Maria was busy smiling and walking around the place in search of objects to throw onto the floor. Normally, Tanja would have followed her around and discouraged it, but not today, today she could throw anything she wanted. Tanja didn't care. Her wobbly legs sometimes gave way. Tanja had to smile at one point at her determination to keep those legs straight long enough so she could get round the place in search of things to toss.

Tanja's smile soon faded. She started to feel a little angry. She'd never been accepted by her in-laws. She'd only met them twice; the first time was shortly after they'd been married, when the newlyweds flew out from Seattle to see them in Milwaukee. The second time was when the in-laws flew to Seattle for a few days after Maria was born. They seemed so cold. Tanja thought that many Russians objected to their children's choice of spouse, but then they'd let it go. Those two didn't seem capable of it. They seemed determined, in advance, that Tanja was a gold-digging Russian in search of a western passport and a western lifestyle. Tanja didn't want either; she wanted to stay in Lithuania. It was George who wanted to take the job in Seattle; she wanted to stay in Klaipėda, which was a beautiful city, not Seattle which was filled with beggars.

The mother-in-law seemed to warm slightly when Maria entered the picture. They had made a special effort to see their new granddaughter, but they stayed in a hotel, which Tanja felt did not show respect and everything was so formal with them. George tried to explain that that is how English people act and they stayed at a hotel so they didn't get in the way, but Tanja thought he was just covering for their bad behaviour. She was a member of their family, but didn't feel like it.

It was noon. It was time to call. She dialled all the digits; there were so many.

A very weary voice answered on the other end.

"Hello."

"Barb – it is me, Tanja."

There was a pause on the phone. Tanja knew what that was about. She had never called them, only George ever called, why would she call? Barb would know something was wrong.

"Hi dear, everything ok?" Tanja thought the question was asked in an overly polite way, the way only the English speak.

"No, not ok; I'm sorry, Barb... I get news last night... George is dead... they say he killed by taxi driver in Beirut."

It wasn't what Tanja had rehearsed. She knew that she was supposed to be more diplomatic, but she blurted it out and then she began to sob again, and sob louder and kept sobbing. She felt she should stop; the woman had just lost her son, but she couldn't stop, Tanja just sobbed.

Tanja could hear Barb saying something to George's father. Tanja tried to gasp to get some air so she could calm herself.

"That's ok, dear, I put you on the speakerphone. Doug is here now. Could you repeat that?"

Tanja thought that an outlandish request, why couldn't the woman repeat it to her husband? She had just lost her husband, the father of her two children – and one wasn't even born yet. She tried to cut back on the sobs.

"I sorry to you, Doug. George is dead. They give me photo; very very bad."

Tanja thought to herself that her English was better than that, but when she talked to those two, she became the stupid Russian girl from a city no one had ever heard of. Tanja could hear that they'd taken her off the speakerphone; she could hear voices in the background, then she heard Doug's voice.

"Tanja, we're so sorry. Would it be ok if we called you back in a couple of minutes; we just need to digest things. Would that be ok?"

"Ok."

Tanja put down the phone. She had to admit that the English always seemed to be able to control their emotions and when they couldn't, they tried to buy time until they *could* control their emotions. It was worthy of respect, but it also seemed very very cold. Still, at that moment, she was glad of it. She was anxious to put down that receiver; she'd set out with a goal in mind and she'd now achieved it. The gold-digger had delivered the news – their son was gone.

The news about Kfour was difficult for Ibrahim to comprehend. The bombing had been unexpected; the Israelis had gotten lucky. It also showed that there must have been information leaks. How did they know? It was bad news for the movement, but it was particularly difficult news for Ibrahim. One of the dead was his own handler, Fares. All of his directives came from Fares. The orders often involved co-ordinating covert operations – smuggling people to and from the West Bank or Gaza, smuggling drugs to the West, assassinations, hostage-takings; whatever was required. Ibrahim was happy to serve, but Fares' death caused a very specific problem. He had a number of operations currently underway that were being paid for by money that Fares had secured. He needed that funding to continue and he'd need direction on how to proceed with the operations. He was meant to smuggle several people over the coming weeks, he was also supposed to arrange a shipment of heroin to be moved to Italy, he controlled cell members who were holding captives – they were holding 2 Israeli soldiers, a Briton and numerous operatives connected to the South Lebanon Army. He needed direction and confirmation that funding would continue, but wasn't even sure whom to address. It was complicated, very complicated.

It was even further complicated by the fact that the whole operation was now under threat, extreme threat from the Israelis. Ibrahim decided not to ask for direction at that moment, he would wait until the situation became clearer. He didn't want to risk exposing anything to spies within their own ranks. Asking around could lead to real problems. He had enough money to pay for operations over the next several weeks; he had time; he just couldn't leave it too long.

In the end, Ibrahim's worries were for nought. About a week after the bombing, he received a phone call from someone he would never have dared to call himself. If he had, it would have been an admission that he knew the man's position; it was Fares' boss.

"Hello," said Ibrahim.

"Don't say my name; it's me."

"I understand."

"I just wanted to say that everything is all a go; there are no changes. I met with our friend two weeks before the issue, I am aware of everything."

"I see."

"Everything will be funded - no problems, business as usual. However, I know you had some items going west. Is that still going?"

"It is."

"Brilliant. Very fine work. We will talk when things are calmer. God bless!"

Ibrahim checked to ensure the call had been disconnected. It must be desperate times for someone like that to speak on a mobile phone, the destruction of the Communications Centre must have been a blow, but the caller had provided the authorization that he needed. It would be business as usual.

It was hard for George to keep track of the days. They all seemed exactly the same. He must have been here for weeks now. The daily routine was always the same. The day would commence when pitch black would be instantly converted to bright white light as the man threw the switch upstairs. Breakfast would then be served with the tray through the trap door and then the man would swiftly depart. He never stayed for long; his role seemed to focus on the delivery and retrieval of the trays. George was to put his finished tray beside that same trap door along with any dirty laundry. The man would bring clean replacements with the next tray delivery. After breakfast would be exercises. George would stretch and do push-ups and run for a few minutes on the spot, then it was time for a cold shower. There were two taps there, both producing only cold water, but that was ok. It was much preferred to his previous circumstance. Besides, he was accustomed to cold showers; he'd worked in Lithuania after Independence when the Russians had turned off the gas. There was always soap. One that he left in the shower and an unopened one. If he unwrapped the unopened one, then, on his next visit, the man in black would include a new wrapped bar on his next tray. The dressing table also had an unlabelled tube of very poor-quality toothpaste, but no toothbrush; he learned to use his finger to complete his dental hygiene regime.

WAITING AND WONDERING

George wished he could have shampoo and he wanted to shave, but no attempt at communication was ever reciprocated; George decided not to ask.

After the shower, he would towel off and don new underwear and a fresh robe. This was a bit of a highlight for the day. The robe material somehow seemed soft and was more comfortable than the suits that he normally wore. If he ever got out of here, maybe he would buy one.

Most of the rest of the day was spent rereading David Copperfield, which somehow accompanied him when he was delivered to his new cell.

Lunch would arrive with the same procedure as breakfast. It would be followed by more exercises and reading. Then would come dinner. After dinner, George would take another shower, not because he particularly needed it, but because it just broke the monotony and the cold water gave him a shot of adrenaline. About two hours later, lights would suddenly shut off and he would be in darkness again.

He couldn't work out how many hours they would leave him in darkness, but he guessed it was somewhere between 10 to 12 hours. It gave him plenty of time to sleep, to think, to dream. Sometimes, he repeated the words from David Copperfield in his head, sometimes, he would think about Tanja and Maria and Vlad; sometimes he would think about his parents, sometimes he would think about his friends. He thought about Steve who had been killed in a car accident in Yorkshire; he wondered how his girlfriend and son were doing. He thought about Darius, he'd been such a good friend to Steve and to him. He sometimes fantasized; sometimes he had fantasies that he had super powers and could spread open the bars. Sometimes, he fantasized about women; he wished he had one with him, especially Tanja; she was a wonderful lover. She was just a great person; God must have brought her as a present for him; he was so lucky to have her. She had such an aura of kindness; it wasn't something you often found in a western woman; well, at least any woman he'd ever met in the West. He thought about her beautiful blond hair and her beautiful blue eyes; he thought about her slender body and that skin that was so soft. 'I only wish I could get out of here and feel that softness again.'

Tanja found a creative way to tell Vlad. Before school had let out during the preceding June, a Lithuanian woman, Giedrė, used to take him to and from school. Giedrė was Darius' cousin and Vlad loved her to bits. He was very upset when the school year ended and Giedrė had returned to Lithuania. Tanja called Giedrė and begged her to return. Now that George was gone, she needed help with Vlad and the new baby. Tanja offered additional money and flight costs if she would come. To her relief, Giedrė agreed. When breaking the news to Vlad, Tanja was able to mix the Giedrė news in with the George news. To Tanja, it was a weird mix; a pleasant tiny surprise with a tragedy, but to Vlad, they appeared to have equal weight. So, he was able to take it relatively calmly.

The day camp ended in mid-August, so now the days were about entertaining Vlad and Maria until school start. Tanja found it particularly hard work. Aaron had come round at one point and brought a lady from Human Resources; it should have been good news. George had plenty of insurance and the HR lady offered to help with the forms. That was a good thing; the forms were complicated; Aaron then hinted there could be a problem as there wasn't actually a death certificate. Tanja started to cry and Aaron offered to make some phone calls to see if he could get one. Now, she waited, waited on him and waited on her life.

When she woke during those late August mornings, she would think how she couldn't wait for it to be night. She was never a drinker, but she really wanted one, but not now, she was carrying new life inside her; new life that would never meet the man that had provided it.

On the penultimate day of August, Giedrė arrived. The young woman had long dark hair, a dark complexion and very blue eyes; how exotic she looked. It was nice to have another adult around. Tanja spoke Lithuanian to her; it was comforting to converse in a language she understood so perfectly. It was a beautiful language – not like English.

During the previous school year, Giedrė had volunteered at Vlad's school. As a result, she had been offered a part-time job there as a teaching assistant for the new academic year. She hadn't intended to take them up on the offer, but the position was still open and her working holiday visa was still valid, so it was a wonderful opportunity for her. It also meant that, during the daytime, Tanja and Maria would be left alone in the apartment. The first day of school felt so odd. It was as if the world was all returning to normal – except for her; there would never be a return to normal for Tanja. She had no plan; she had nowhere to be; she had had the love of her life taken from her and no one really cared.

To pass the time, George decided he would now speak with the guard; he would speak to him each time he appeared to service the trays. He wished him a cheery 'good morning' and would politely ask about shampoo or the possibility of a shave or a new book. He was never sure if the man in black could understand English. So, George would accompany the words with gestures; he would pretend to lather his head when saying 'shampoo,' imitate a razor dragging across his thick beard for 'shave' or open the palms in front of him to indicate a 'book'. The man never reacted; he acted more like a ghost than a human. George began to wonder about him; the whole arrangement was very peculiar.

The meals were of very high quality; a typical day might include fresh pastries or eggs for breakfast; a pita filled with assorted meats and vegetables for lunch, accompanied by olives and salads. Dinner could be an extraordinary affair with all kinds of wonderful dishes from seafood to beef with rice dishes to accompany. George very much doubted that the ghost was preparing those meals. It wasn't institutional food; it was home cooking. Could his mother or wife be preparing them?

He also tried to understand if the meals provided a hint of where he might be; he accompanied that investigative thought with inspection of the labels on the towel, his underwear and robe. The towels and underwear were made in China and he couldn't make out the tag in the robe; it was in Arabic only. He spent time trying to inspect the pipes and mattress and pillow for hints as well. Was it possible that he wasn't in Lebanon anymore? Is it possible they had moved him to Gaza or Syria or Iran? When they drugged him, he wasn't really sure how long he was unconscious. George wished he knew more about middle east politics; who would want a western hostage and why?

One evening, he heard the steel door open at the landing and the man began his descent down the stairs. George knew the routine; he went and sat on his bed; the man always insisted on it. He looked toward his new tray for hints on what might be on the menu and spotted something unusual on it. There was a little bottle of what appeared to be shampoo!

George clapped his hands together and then put them in front of his face as if praying and, with a giant smile, he used the only Arabic word he knew, "Chokran, praise be to Allah, thank you, thank you."

The man in black giggled from behind the burka. George had never heard him make a sound before. It was a surprise.

Today had been a success; he had dragged a giggle out of the ghost.

It was September 15th when Tanja got the call from Barb. It wasn't a surprise; she'd called a few times since George's death, but this call was not what Tanja expected. It was a shock; Doug was dead; he'd had a heart attack. Tanja couldn't believe it; he was fit; it must have been the news about George that did it, but she was surprised about it; surprised that someone who seemed so cold could be impacted that way. Barb continued; she seemed to be steady; she was delivering the news as if it were just bad news, not the calamity that it was.

"Don't worry dear, we don't expect you at the funeral. You have to stay where you are and deliver us grandbaby number 2."

Tanja was surprised by the remark. She never even thought about going there; now Barb had made it clear that she wouldn't be welcome either or maybe it was a jibe that she'd never arranged any service for George. That was fine either way, she had greater priorities; the baby was due September 24th; exactly nine months after Christmas Eve.

George sat in the dark and waited for the lights. Over time, his internal clock was gaining a rhythm. He was under the impression that the lights were illuminated at the same time each morning, but the evening lights were extinguished on a less precise schedule. George focused on that early morning timeslot. When he knew that the lights would be going on, he would sit on his bed and begin to feel hungry. He was like Pavlov's dog and, from that internal clock, he knew that the lights would go on in the next few minutes and then he'd be served his food. He probably had just another 5 minutes left before illumination that morning. It gave him one more chance to think about Tanja; she'd likely had the baby now. He wondered if it were a boy; he wanted a boy, then they'd have the full set. He remembered the expected delivery date. It was September 24th. He remembered how Tanja used to tease him about the date. "You got quite a Christmas present; next year, you're getting socks." She had a funny sense of humour; he allowed himself a little smile. When he got back, he'd have to make some changes. There would be more time for her and little Maria and the new one. He'd also make more of an effort to see his own parents. He'd only seen them twice in the last many years – it was probably close to ten years.

At that moment, the pitch-black instantly turned to bright light. George was excited; there was little to get excited about in that cell, so the beginning of the morning routine would have to suffice. However, this particular morning was about to get a little more interesting than he could have expected. George was beyond pleased to see it. As the man came into view with his tray, George watched with elation; there appeared to be two books stacked beside his plate on his morning breakfast tray.

As was expected of him, George clasped his hands together and thanked his guard profusely. The man in black nodded at him; it was the first gesture he'd ever made toward him. George was excited; he couldn't wait for today's tray exchange to complete and for the trap door to be locked, so he could get at the books. The man in black seemed to understand the urgency of the moment and appeared to work extra quickly that morning to complete his drop-off.

Once the trap was shut, George scurried to the tray and the two books which sat upon it. He wasn't sure if he resembled a hungry dog running to food or a child on Christmas morning but he wanted to get his hands on those books.

He heard the man begin climbing the stairs as he grabbed the first one and then looked at the second one. It was a disappointment. One was an English edition of the Koran; the second was a copy of the New Testament. George contemplated a minute; he was hoping for something a little different, but who knows, maybe these were the books he needed.

Tanja thought that it had been such curious timing. It started as a normal Friday. It was Friday, September 19th. It had begun in the usual way. Maria woke first and Tanja went to attend to her; Maria was always so happy. Tanja brought her back to the master bedroom to play a little and for a nappy change. She didn't want to disturb Giedrė who slept in the sitting room. After a while, Tanja took the toddler and quietly passed Giedrė's sofa bed through semidarkness as she made her way to the kitchen to begin making breakfast for the family.

And, it continued normally, everyone got up, had breakfast and completed their morning routines. Vlad went to school with Giedrė. Maria began pushing around boxes and looking for things to toss. Then, there was a phone call from Aaron. It shouldn't have been particularly disturbing, but somehow it was. He had managed to convince the British authorities to pressure the Lebanese authorities to issue a death certificate – and now he'd received it. He said that he'd have it translated and then they could meet one more time to go through the insurance paperwork again. Tanja should have been grateful; but to her, it was an additional confirmation that she was alone. She took Maria for a walk in her stroller that morning; it was a beautiful day, but Tanja just kept thinking about the death certificate. She thought more about it in the afternoon. By dinner, she was starting to get contractions.

She didn't say anything about the contractions and she tried not to show anything. She made the evening meal; Giedrė normally did the dishes, but Tanja asked to do them that night. She wanted to keep moving; it helped subdue some of the pain. While Vlad watched television and Giedrė read in the sitting room, she spent the evening with Maria in the master bedroom. Tanja paced back and forth in the room. She was experienced in this now; she had put on a sanitary pad in an attempt to save the carpets from the brunt of the impending flood. She kept pacing and pacing until it was time to put Maria down for the night. Her water broke a little after that.

She waited for Vlad to go to bed before talking to Giedrė. Giedrė would need to take care of both of them on Saturday. Giedrė looked horrified by the news as Tanja simply explained that she'd 'gone into labour and had had contractions for several hours.' Tanja smiled at the woman; she would have felt the same horror just two years ago, but there was no emergency yet. It was going to be a while.

There was more pacing, but about 2:30 am, there was no disputing it. That baby was on his way. She called the pager service for the doctor. The operator took down the details. She then called a taxi, she took her overnight bag and waited for the cab on the forecourt of the building.

It didn't take long for the taxi to arrive and then she began the lonely journey into the night to give birth to a child – Tanja would be alone when that baby came into the world. As she stared out into the night from that taxicab, she reflected on the events of earlier that day. She recalled the call from Aaron; a final reminder that he was gone and now she was about to drag new life into the world – out with the old, in with the new. It was ironic and it made her feel sad.

Tanja paid the driver and walked past the wheelchairs at the emergency door; she checked herself in. It wasn't long before she was in a hospital room. A doctor came and completed an ultrasound; it wasn't her doctor; perhaps her doctor wouldn't make it. Then, she was left alone in her hospital room. This part was much different; in Seattle, when Maria was born, she seemed always surrounded by doctors and nurses; this was much less intense. Finally, a nurse came round to explain that they were waiting for Tanja's doctor.

The nurse left but then Tanja began to worry; 'I hope the other doctor is available right now. My little guy is not interested in being patient.' The pain suddenly became intense; he was trying to get out of there and the contractions went from dull and painful to very very very sharp. Tanja screamed out for help; the nurse ran into the room. She pulled up the guard rails on the bed; they would deliver him right there on the bed.

Tanja knew it was going to be a boy. She had already chosen the name. It would be 'George'; he would forever remind him of her lost husband. It would be nice to have a boy, they were so different than girls; she suddenly realized that her feelings of gloominess about the day were starting to give way. She was about to give birth; she loved being a mother, it was the one thing she was good at; she was going to get through this, she was a tough woman, she'd survived poverty; she'd survived communism, she'd survived cold water and immigration, she'd survived her own mother's death, she'd raised her brother. She was going to be fine; it was all going to be fine.

And it was fine. It took a few more hours before that baby blessed the morning with its arrival. When it finally arrived, Tanja looked toward the doctor. She knew what he was about to say and then he said something else, "It's a girl."

Tanja smiled; it wasn't what she'd expected, but that didn't matter; she would have a house of women; Vlad would serve as the token man. She smiled and put her hands out beckoning the doctor to put her little treasure in her arms.

By evening, the nurses seemed keen to get Tanja out of there, but Tanja wasn't in the mood. She asked to stay overnight. They obliged; perhaps they knew that the little girl in the crib beside her was a bastard child. There was no one to really help her at home; well, Giedrė would help, but Tanja needed a break right now; she needed to focus on her newborn just for one day before giving her life back to Vlad and Maria.

She stared at the paperwork on her meal table. She pulled the table close to her and opened the manila envelope. There was all sorts of information in there but the important document for her to complete was the registration of birth. As the nurse had also left behind a pen, Tanja thought she'd complete that document right now. However, the first question was difficult. It simply said 'Name of Child.'

Tanja stared at her little gem. "You were meant to be a boy. What name would you like?" Maria had been chosen in a similar manner; originally, she'd agreed a different name with George, but then Tanja had looked at Maria and determined that she was a Maria and Maria was a good name because it worked in Russian and English. But, as she looked at her new offspring, another idea came to Tanja's mind. It was a name that didn't work in either language.

"Edita." Tanja loved that name. Some of the Lithuanian girls in her old neighbourhood were called Edita and Tanja loved the melody of it. It was so beautiful. She didn't care that it didn't quite work; it was beautiful, just like the little girl herself. It might work.

She knew it was a big decision and studied her little girl one more time to see if it really fit. Then, an odd thought came to Tanja about the name 'Edita' - why had she thought of that particular name? It was very strange timing; it seemed to be a sign – maybe it was time to go back; there was no reason to stay here. She missed her country; she missed not having fluent conversations; she missed the culture of the place; she was homesick.

Under forename, she wrote 'Edita.' Then, she looked at the box for middle name. A thought came to Tanja; she didn't like that thought, but it made sense. She would never use it; it would just be a word on a birth certificate. It sounded awful, but she'd just chosen a beautiful name that didn't make sense, she could choose a practical name that did make sense even if it were decidedly not beautiful. It would be a gesture, a gesture toward him; it might help bring peace to a difficult situation. It had been a hard summer for her too. She pondered; it made sense; she would make the concession. She wrote the name 'Barbara' in the little box.

George had a new tradition. Every time the man came down the stairs, he would sit on his bed and open the Koran. It might be a way to build some trust. He wasn't sure if the man was a religious person, but the gifts of the two books seemed to indicate something. The man would always nod when greeted now. It was a better relationship; maybe one day, George would hear his voice. However, it wouldn't be today; today he would hear a different voice.

At first, it seemed very confusing. He had been there for months and the routine was breakfast service, lunch service, then dinner service. There were no other timeslots when visitations occurred by the man in black, but this visit was way too early for dinner. George could hear the door open and the familiar steps. He decided he didn't like the sound of it; something was going on and it violated the ritual that had coincided with his survival for these last several weeks.

The man walked down the stairs; George recognized the way he walked now. George sat on the bed and waited. When the man finally came into view, he was carrying a chair. The chair was identical to the wooden chair in his cell; a simple but functional chair that had served him well. The man carefully put the chair down near his cell door; then seemed to pull it back a bit as if he were ensuring it was at a safe distance. George definitely didn't like it; the chair likely meant torture; but why would they torture him now and who was going to do it? He didn't think the ghost would do it; George felt he'd managed to gain a grudging camaraderie with him. It must be someone more senior.

As the man stood there, still holding the back of the chair, George could hear the footsteps coming down the staircase. He was about to meet his torturer. He began to sweat.

The newest grim reaper was cloaked in the same uniform as the three before him - all black; no skin showing; a burka covered the face. The torturer seemed to hesitate before coming closer to the chair that had been placed for his use; George thought that maybe it was his first interrogation. George just sat there as his regular ghost beckoned the new grim reaper forward. He seemed to have to coax him closer to the chair. He even pulled the chair back a little further as if to show that George wouldn't be able to reach him through the bars.

As the new man walked closer to the chair, George sat on the bed and studied him. He was taller than the first one; it was hard to tell with the torturer's loose-fitting robe, but he looked more slender and the walk was somehow slightly effeminate. They couldn't use a woman; George tried to see if he could see the form of any breasts; oh yes, as she walked, the robe clung at one point, it was a woman. A woman was about to torture him or maybe he was wrong, it was difficult to tell.

The ghost beckoned the new reaper to sit. She or he sat on the chair and then just looked at George. The man gently touched his or her shoulder as if to indicate that the communication should commence.

One of George's curiosities was about to be answered.

"Hello," it was a woman's voice who uttered that English word; it had been disguised to be a lower octave, which was fairly obvious to George.

"Hello," replied George.

"You help please."

In case the woman hadn't noticed, George was locked in a cage and at the absolute mercy of the man who stood just behind her. He was absolutely going to help.

"Yes."

"My English, you help?"

"Yes?"

"I want learn it."

It was a surprise that George had not seen coming. This was somebody's daughter; the voice sounded very young. A moment ago, he thought he was about to be beaten. They only wanted an English lesson. For a moment, he smiled to himself, maybe that's why they had taken him, maybe they knew he was a former English teacher.

George thought some more; this was going to be a nice break from the boredom; he could give her some English lessons. He also thought he was very likely to be teaching 'Jihad Julie;' he could teach her a language that would make it easy for her to get on the campus of Sheffield University or in the Mitchell Mall in Milwaukee or, maybe they had higher aspirations for her, maybe she could use her new skill for access to the United Nations or the World Trade Centre.

George continued the conversation. He had a plan and was curious if it might work.

"I will help you. I will be your teacher. My name is George. Now, let us start by finding out how much English you know. How old are you?"

"16."

The reply brought a swift slap on the shoulder from the man. George's plan had worked; he'd actually turned the tables a little and obtained some information from his hostage-takers.

"What is your name?"

There was an uneasy pause, so George continued; he was pushing this too far. "That's ok. I will call you Julie. Do you understand? Is it alright if I call you Julie?"

The girl nodded her head.

"So, if I ask you a question, you must respond with English words. If I ask if that is alright, you should say yes or no. So, is it alright if I call you Julie?"

"Yes."

"Ok, what is your name?"

"My name is Julie."

"Perfect and great pronunciation. Your English is already good. Let's move on."

The lesson seemed to go on for almost 30 minutes. George wanted to make it the best introduction to English that she could ever have received. He spoke slowly and took every opportunity to heap praise on her. New language students always reacted to praise; it was unwise to provide correction until their confidence level was higher.

Once she'd left, George reflected on how this new development opened up all sorts of possibilities; it seemed like she would return, which would help with the boredom, but she might also slip again; it might help to determine a way out of here. It also might help with building a relationship with the man in black; the swat on the shoulder was curious; only a father would do that to a teenage girl.

George was pleased when the chair was left in the hallway; it was a sign that another lesson might occur. When he woke the next morning, he was anxious to see what the day would bring. The usual breakfast and lunch were served and then it happened again. The man came down first, this time followed very closely by Julie. George was looking forward to it.

Julie took the chair this time and carefully positioned it in exactly the same spot. This time, she had a book with her. She placed it on her lap, but it was too far from the bed for George to see the title.

"Hi Julie. What is the name of your book?"

"English."

Julie held up the book, it looked like something akin to English 11. George wondered if that was a grade or a level or something.

George continued. "Can you read me something from your book?"

She opened the book and began reading a passage. George recognized some of the phrases; this was some kind of British Council book; he'd used similar textbooks when he taught in Lithuania. Julie was torturing the text; emphasis was on the wrong syllables; pronunciation was terrible; she was likely not the best student, but George wouldn't let her know that.

After sentence three, George decided to interrupt. "That is great work, Julie. Now, can I read those sentences back to you and ask you some questions?"

George knew this would be a test of trust. He needed to make his next move very carefully. He extended his hand and slowly got to his feet to indicate that he wanted to take the book through the bars. He stopped for a second and looked toward the man to indicate that he wanted permission. The man waved him closer to retrieve it. Julie slotted it through the bars.

George slowly re-read the three sentences then completed the last two in the paragraph. Conveniently, there were comprehension questions printed right at the bottom of the page, but some of the language looked complex, George dumbed it down and only asked easy stuff.

At the end of approximately 30 minutes or what seemed like 30 minutes, George decided to end the lesson; "Good work today, Julie. You're a good student. Will I see you tomorrow?"

"Yes, thank you, George."

It wasn't what she said; it was the way that she said it. The phrase was delivered with some enthusiasm as if the kid rarely received such praise or she'd just understood a concept that she just couldn't get before. George was pleased with himself, 'maybe I should go back into teaching,' he thought.

Weeks passed and George looked forward to that particular daily routine. Father and daughter would arrive; they must be coming just after the school day, George thought. She must be a high school student. There was one day a week when they didn't come; it must be Friday, he thought. They were likely observing the sabbath. The lessons were going surprisingly well. When he'd first met Julie, George didn't know if she were really interested in the subject or whether a parent had goaded her, but as the weeks progressed, she was obviously putting effort into it. She no longer tried to disguise her voice and seemed to relax. George also had to admit that her English was improving and quite quickly; he was surprised at the progress considering that he'd only been helping a few weeks.

He was glad when he heard the door open that afternoon; he had thought up a lesson plan for today. He was keen to do the paragraphs on English cuisine; this might be an opportunity to stray from the topic if she were willing and if the father allowed. He was keen to move the relationship to a more personal level. He needed to establish rapport if he were going to get any more information or help from her.

Once Julie sat in the familiar seat, it was clear something was going on; there was some kind of tension; George thought there may have been an argument between her and her father who stood in his usual place behind her. She said nothing but instead stood up and held a stapled bunch of papers through the cell bars.

George stood up from his bed and walked over to the cell door; he took the papers in his hand and then just stood there. He intentionally didn't walk back to the bed; he now took every opportunity to be physically closer to them. Julie sat down again while George inspected the papers.

It was some sort of test, but it seemed like a simple English test. It was all about verb tenses and it was a fill-in-the-blank type of test; that seemed strange; they were working on much harder concepts in the textbook; this was just fundamentals. Or, maybe that's it; they'd been working on conversational English; maybe the school focused more on mechanics. If that was the case, this would be easy, George knew exactly how to teach it.

Julie started to speak, "My... My friend want I do good. I have test tomorrow about verbs."

George looked at the questions; he had a difficult question but didn't know how to phrase it in a simple way, so he just asked it. "Are these *the* test questions you will answer or are these *sample* questions?"

"Sample."

George was surprised that she knew that word; it hadn't come up before.

George continued, "Ok, please stand up. I'm going to start with a song and dance and then we're going to sing it together and do the actions together." George had done this many times before, he was going to sing the 'I am' song which would entail pointing a finger to himself, then to her for 'you' and then the father for 'he' and then it would continue to the plural pronouns.

She stood a few feet from the bars and George began to sing and point with plenty of gesticulation. "I am George, you are Julie, he is Fred." At the moment, George said 'Fred' and pointed at her father, the girl keeled over with laughter. She keeled over so quickly and with such spontaneity, that her burka nearly flew off. George could see strands of her dark hair; the father tried to grab the dark hood, but he was also laughing. The hilarity of seeing the two black ghosts in convulsions of laughter was also now too funny for George. He started to laugh; he hadn't laughed since that dinner party in July with the Lebanese traders. It felt so good to laugh that George just kept doing it. Whatever tension was in the room, it had been broken.

Once the assembled had regained composure, George was able to complete his song and then George made Julie sing it with him; they then went onto the rules for regular present tense verbs; George had some tricks to remember the exception to the rule. "Fred and Julie and it always need an 's'; everyone else gets no 's'. I walk, you walk, he/she it *walks*, George completed the we, you and they, but reminded her not to worry about them – only worry about Fred." George called it the Fred and Julie rule. He then made her repeat the conjugation, then threw out various pronouns.

"I," said George.

"Walk," said Julie.

"We"

"Walk"

"He"

"Walks"

"You are too clever for this stuff, Julie. Well done. Now stand up and do the song for us. This time, do it by yourself."

Julie completed the pointing song and giggled a little way through it. George then went back to regular verbs and then past tense, which was really simple. When in doubt, just add 'ed'. Remember, everyone walked – even Fred. The irregular verbs were a bit more tricky, but she was getting it. The person who was most surprised that she was getting it seemed to be Julie. She seemed to be thoroughly enjoying herself while learning her new language. George began to wonder if they weren't quite as creative in the local school system.

He completed by getting her to write a few pages of the sample test. She did really well on the simpler stuff – the regular verbs. She had a little more difficulty on the irregular verbs, but that was to be expected. These just needed practice. George thought to himself; it makes more sense to 'runned' than 'ran,' but that's the way it is.

George thought that the lesson was at least 90 minutes that afternoon; maybe longer. When it was finally complete, he was pleased with himself. He'd accomplished one thing; it might have been teaching the devil, but it would be a bilingual devil.

The next day's lesson was back to 30 minutes. George asked about the test; Julie thought she'd done ok.

It was the following day that was such a shock. It wasn't the normal time; lunch had only been an hour ago, but the door seemed to fly open upstairs and Julie seemed to take wing down the stairs. She was coming so quickly that George had no time to get to his bed.

"Look!" she exclaimed. George looked at the papers, but there was something else that attracted George's attention; it wasn't the papers, it was the fact that she was wearing no gloves. He looked at her hands, they were cute little things; dark and somehow elegant with a couple of rings on some of the fingers.

George took the papers; there was an 'A' written in red ink on it with an accompanying comment 'great improvement.' George smiled and then tugged at his ever-growing beard.

"Well done, Julie. You deserve it. You worked hard."

George handed back the papers through the bars. She took them with her left hand and then she did something that George considered quite odd. She extended her right hand to offer a handshake through the bars. George accepted the offer and shook her hand which was now on his side of the bars. It had been months since he'd had any human contact. Her skin was so soft; she'd clearly had little experience with handshakes – maybe she'd never given one; it was a limp shake but that made her hands feel even softer. George felt a pang of guilt for thinking about the softness of that cute little hand; she was a child.

"Thank you," pronounced Julie as she shook his hand through the bars.

That evening, there was something curious left on the tray to accompany the evening meal. It was a pack of Marlboro cigarettes. George didn't smoke, but it seemed like a pleasant gesture. While enjoying the meal, he thought what was he supposed to do with them. Without a way to light them, they were quite useless. After dinner, he decided that he would put the pack on the nightstand; he could look at them; that would be his trophy for helping achieve the A that day.

When he heard the door open about a half-hour later, it dawned on him, it was to be an after-dinner smoke. The father ghost brandished a lighter and carried a little metal ashtray. He waved George toward the cell door, which was a first. George retrieved the Marlboros from the nightstand, removed the cellophane strip and extracted one from the pack. He moved close to the cell door, where father lit the cigarette for him and handed him the ashtray through the bars. With his lighter, Father wandered back toward the stairs and began the ascent from the dungeon.

George puffed on the cigarette. He hadn't smoked in ten years. He breathed the smoke in heavily, then let a little escape from his nose before blowing the residual out through his mouth. Geez, it felt good. He'd forgotten how much he liked it. It had been a good day in the dungeon.

The peace offering of the newborn's middle name had worked. Barb was overjoyed to receive the news of little Edita and her beautiful middle name 'Barbara.' However, as the weeks progressed, Tanja felt the plan had worked too well and now it was beginning to backfire. George's mother now called regularly and would want to talk. Tanja thought that Barb was probably very lonely, but Tanja was busy with two little girls and a brother with Down Syndrome. During the first few calls, Tanja listened a lot. It was a call in early November that caught her off-guard. Barb wanted to come and spend Christmas with her and the children.

Tanja needed to think; she needed to be diplomatic, but she definitely did not need that in her life. She was trying to come up with something and then she realized that she was stopping the woman from meeting her own granddaughter; only weeks after losing her son and husband.

"Of course, children love to see granny. You come; we very happy about it."

"Is there room? I can sleep on a sofa, anywhere."

Tanja was surprised about the request. She was expecting her to stay at a hotel. She would have to deal with her around the clock without having George there to run any defence.

"Don't worry; we find place for you, Barb."

Tanja put down the receiver and thought to herself 'a perfectly awful end to a perfectly dreadful year' and then she began to think about the consequences of the invitation she'd just offered. She would have to ask Giedrė to leave for a break; Giedrė was intending to stay with them. Tanja had tried to make her feel part of the family and now she was about to ask her to leave as the real family would be here. Then, she thought about Vlad. Barb had never met Vlad; she hoped she wouldn't ignore him or complain about his weird behaviour; she probably didn't approve of Down Syndrome kids. Yes, it was all going to be a perfectly miserable end to a perfectly dreadful year.

Tanja's first task was to talk to Giedrė. She had planned what to say in advance. It would be paid leave and Tanja would pay for a return ticket home to Lithuania. Giedrė seemed a little disappointed, but accepted the offer; she didn't have a lot of money and she'd get a chance to see her family for a fortnight. Tanja would book the flight for the first Saturday after Vlad's final Friday at school before the winter break. There, that would free up the sofa bed or should she give her mother-in-law the master bedroom? No, she couldn't nurse a newborn in the sitting room; Barb would have to lump it.

Tanja had one day in mind for those next several weeks – it was December 20th. That was the day that Giedrė would return to Lithuania and Barb would appear for 10 days. Barb would stay till December 30th and Giedrė would return on January 2nd, 1998. Tanja always wanted to have something to look forward to, so she decided the date she was most looking forward to would be December 31st. She was looking forward to seeing the end of 1997. She would be there with her girls and her brother; she would make it a happy day for everyone and she was going to find a way to enjoy it as well. It would be her reward for having to deal with the period between December 20th and December 30th, 1997.

On Thursday, December 18th, after Vlad and Giedrė left for school, Tanja attempted to do a thorough clean top to bottom of the Canary Wharf apartment. It failed. Maria ran round and round while Edita demanded nursing and nappy changes. To make matters worse, she'd started Maria on potty training and it now appeared to be too early. Tanja had to stop twice to clean up accidents and another several times to help her with the little plastic toilet which sat beside the main toilet in the bathroom. By the time that Vlad and Giedrė returned from school, the place really didn't look much better than when she'd started.

Giedrė was kind; she offered to help. She set Vlad in front of the Cartoon Network and watched the girls while Tanja cleaned. Once Edita got fussy, so they switched places and Giedrė cleaned. By 10 pm, the place looked presentable, quite presentable. Tanja would just give it a little going over on Saturday morning. It would be fine.

Saturday morning came and Giedrė left early. Tanja found that her 'going over' plan was doomed to failure. The place was like a zoo with three uncontrollable monkeys. One constantly demanded the use of her body, the other went from room to room tossing things to the floor and wetting herself and Vlad; well, Vlad was Vlad. He watched the television and dropped crumbs everywhere. Tanja wanted to give up and at least get them out of there for some fresh air, but she couldn't. Barb's flight was already supposed to have landed. She was very likely on her way from Gatwick Airport.

Tanja had prepared a nice lunch, but had to guard the dining room table from Vlad who seemed to be constantly hungry – maybe he was undergoing a growth spurt. Yes, it was all going as expected – it was going to be a disaster – and then she heard the buzzer. It was Barb and she was coming up.

Tanja opened the apartment door and, after a few minutes, Barb appeared from the lift; the woman looked exhausted. She was surprised by the greeting that Barb provided. With luggage in hand, Barb seemed to run down the hallway and then, dropped that luggage, and slung her arms around Tanja so forcefully that Tanja stumbled into the apartment and then Barb just hugged her, she hugged her for close to a minute, then she kissed her on the cheek. Tanja began to wonder if this was just a woman that looked like Barb; where was the ogre? Tanja smiled and beckoned her to come in.

"Granny!" shouted Vlad.

Oh, no, thought Tanja; here we go, but Barb handled it diplomatically.

"You must be Vlad, it's nice to meet you." Vlad jumped up, crumbs falling everywhere and grabbed his 'granny' and gave her a big hug.

"Oh my, aren't you a kind boy... and where are my little princesses?"

At that moment, Princess Maria ran through the sitting room, ignoring granny, but tossing a coaster on the floor while shouting 'pee pee pee pee' and darted to the bathroom. Maria didn't bother closing the door and just sat staring at the assembled in the living room as she relieved herself. Tanja wanted to divert Barb's attention from the chaos which was her daily life.

"Come, you meet baby." Tanja put her finger to her lips to indicate that the baby was sleeping and invited Barb into the master bedroom.

In a little crib, lay Edita; Tanja thought she looked just like an angel. She noticed that Barb had a tear in her eye. She heard the woman whisper, "Little Barbara; you are so precious." Then there was a crash from the sitting room and a scream. Maria had managed to push over a floor lamp and it had hit Vlad. The commotion woke Edita who started to cry in solidarity.

Yes, it was all going as expected. It was a miserable end to a dreadful year.

The next day was a little better. Tanja was up early for a feeding with Edita. It was a little before 5 am; Tanja was surprised to hear the soft knock on her bedroom door.

"Come," whispered Tanja.

Barb peaked her head around the door and whispered, "Good morning. May I come in?"

Tanja smiled and waved her forward. Barb came into the room, closed the door, then made her way to sit on the bed right beside Tanja, where George used to sleep.

Tanja looked up for a minute, "You want see Edita having breakfast?"

Barb looked down at the infant suckling away at Tanja, "She's such a treasure; these are such special moments; they only come round once in a lifetime."

Tanja thought it was a peculiar thing for her to say. It wasn't that it was particularly peculiar for anyone to say; her own mother would have said stuff like that. It just didn't seem like Barb.

The two sat in almost darkness; the half-moon outside the window produced the only light; Tanja liked to keep the early morning feeding dark as Edita had a wonderful habit of nodding off after her morning snack. Normally, Tanja would have felt obligated to say something at that moment, but Barb seemed content to sit there in the dark with them and it was too early for small talk.

"Tanja? Vlad and I were talking. Would it be ok if I took Maria and Vlad for an outing today? It might give you a little break as well."

Tanja thought that sounded like a terrible idea. Vlad would drive her crazy with his ongoing commentary, which oscillated between English, Russian and Lithuanian. Maria was absolutely going to wet herself and, if allowed out of the stroller, was very likely to cause wanton destruction as that seemed to correspond with her current stage of development.

"Sure, Barb, but they are," she thought for a minute, "bandits."

Barb smiled. "You're doing such a wonderful job, Tanja. You are such a strong woman. My son was very lucky."

Tanja didn't know where that came from. There was still some wine in the fridge, but Barb polished most of it during the previous evening; she couldn't have been drinking. It must be jet lag, poor woman. She looked so exhausted the preceding day that, after lunch, Tanja offered her the master bedroom to lie down for a couple of hours and now she was up before 5 am. Yes, it was jetlag and time change.

After a late breakfast and early lunch, Barb helped with the dishes and then was true to her word. A little after noon, Barb set out with Maria in a stroller and Vlad trudged along. Tanja had packed changes of clothes for Maria and snacks and drinks. Tanja looked at her watch and started placing estimates in her mind. If it really goes poorly, they would likely be back in 30 minutes, 45 if things go ok; 60 tops. She had to budget her time. Tanja really needed to tidy up the place; it looked chaotic. However, with the limited time and the possibility of interruption from Edita, she would just complete the 'going over' of the place that she'd planned for the preceding morning.

Edita was surprisingly amenable to the plan and co-operated; Tanja was able to make the place look reasonably presentable by 1 pm. Now, Tanja put her mind to the next chore which was nap time. She took Edita into the master bedroom and completed the usual routine of nursing and singing Russian lullabies and gently rocking. It only took a few minutes before Edita dozed off; Tanja put her in her crib.

Perfect, Tanja would just close her eyes for a few minutes and await the impending tidal wave that was the other two. She lay on the bed and fell into a very deep sleep. She dreamed that she was flying over clouds and could see the city of London below; she was flying over the Thames. She awoke, it had been a very deep sleep, she felt rested. She looked at her watch, it was 1:45. Tanja was impressed; her mother-in-law was really putting some effort into it and now, the place was tidy, Edita was down for her nap and Tanja had managed to sneak in about a half-hour kip.

When Tanja looked at her watch again, it was 2 pm and she began to worry. She'd just watch some television while she waited for Edita to wake or for the tribe to return. She couldn't remember the last time she'd watched television.

At 2:30, Edita awoke and Tanja went to attend to her. Tanja thought she was precious. They spent some time cuddling; then she put out a blanket on the floor and gave Edita some 'tummy time.' Tanja liked to put her on her tummy occasionally during the day so she didn't get bed sores.

By 3 pm, Tanja now needed to come up with a plan. At what point should she call the police and what could have happened to them? Tanja began to pace and pace. She was nervous. She would give them till 3:30, then she would call the police. When 3:30 came, she thought she'd just give them a few more minutes; then 3:45 came, she would have to call; she would call at the stroke of 4.

She was relieved to hear the key in the door shortly before 4.

What transpired in those next few minutes could only be described as surprising. Tanja expected the usual cacophony of sound and chaos, but when the three entered the apartment, each one of them seemed tranquil; each had a smile on their face. Tanja still wondered if there had been some sort of incident.

"You gone long time," Tanja commented.

"Yes, we had a very nice walk then Vlad suggested we take Maria to a ball room. He's a very considerate uncle, your brother. Maria had so much fun, then we went for muffins. I guess time got away from us. I hope you weren't nervous."

"No, no," lied Tanja.

Tanja couldn't get over the disposition of Barb's two charges. Vlad had obviously been treated to a round of compliments. He seemed to be trying to impress the old lady with his gentlemanly habits; he helped Maria out of the stroller and held her hand as they made their way to the sitting room. Maria also looked relaxed; she never attempted to toss even a single item as she wandered around the sitting room. She was at such ease; she'd obviously got her energy out at that ball room. Tanja began to feel a little guilty; Maria wasn't getting much quality attention from her these days. Maybe, that's why she was getting into the habit of throwing things around – maybe it was a cry for attention.

Tanja looked at Barb. For an instant, she saw something in the woman that she hadn't seen before. There was something in her behaviour or in her disposition or in movements that reminded her of something. Then, it came to Tanja; it turned into a sad reflection – she reminded her of George.

It was Christmas Eve morning in the cell. George knew it was Christmas Eve. One of the English lessons had been about date and time and Julie had told him the date. George thought that the relationship between Julie, her father and George had really evolved over those several weeks. The father would arrive every evening with his lighter and George would enjoy an evening smoke. When one packet was complete, another would be placed on one of the meal trays.

Julie had more tests and written assignments. They had all gone well. As time progressed, she revealed more and more of herself. He was gleaning bits of information from the conversational classes; he was in Lebanon. He knew that now. They had been talking about culture one afternoon. George started by saying that "In England, we like to drink tea" and then he asked her to talk about her culture. She started by stating, "In Lebanon, we…"

Whenever there wasn't a pressing test or paper, George would often talk about culture and exploring the world and the various places he'd lived and worked – Europe, the US, Britain, Australia. It seemed to impress Julie; well, at least she asked lots of questions. They were questions typical of a 16-year-old girl who hadn't travelled much – she was curious about how young people made friends, where they would go together, if teenagers danced, what people wore.

If George understood his current predicament, he was being held by a Lebanese family, which seemed curious. His holding cell had been professionally built, he had combed every inch of the cell in search of a vulnerability; the only way out appeared to be through the door, but even if he accomplished that, what was beyond that cellar door at the top of the landing?

That Christmas Eve morning, George heard the door being opened very carefully on the landing. It wasn't the correct time for either the lesson or a meal delivery; it was too early for lunch. He sat on the bed.

Then, he heard the door close, but, again, it was closed very gingerly. He then heard quiet footsteps; he began to think he knew what it was all about. As he predicted, Julie soon came into view and seemed to tip toe toward the cell door.

"George," she whispered, which was odd as George was pretty sure no one could hear anything that happened in that basement.

"Hi Julie."

"Should you be here alone?" George asked. It wasn't the first time she had been to the cell alone; she had come after passing her verb test.

"Well, father don't like it, but I'm soon 17."

"Doesn't," replied George, "and I'm pretty sure your dad would not approve of you letting me know that he's your father."

Then, Julie did something that was quite disturbing. It was so disturbing that George closed his eyes and tried to erase the vision that he had just seen. It was a sight that could very easily cost him his life. He kept his eyes closed; firmly closed. While she stood there, Julie had just removed her burka.

"Julie, please put that back on. I shouldn't see you."

"Why? I never wear burka except when I come to you. No one wear burka here."

"It's not that," George kept his eyes closed. "If I see you, I can identify you."

"You won't say anyone; you my teacher."

It was pretty clear that the teenager wasn't going to retreat. George was conflicted, but opened his eyes. Her face looked much like her hands; George would describe her face as 'cute.' She had soft brown eyes, chubby cheeks and beautifully tanned Mediterranean skin and long dark hair; she was going to be a beautiful woman.

"You're very pretty, Julie." George regretted saying it; he had been struck by her beauty, but it wasn't appropriate for him to say it to a teenage girl, especially a teenage Muslim girl as he assumed that's what she was.

"My name is Lamia."

"Lamia; again, you are very young; you should not tell me these things. I also want to protect you and your father, so the less I know the better."

George was surprised by the words he'd just spoken. He was not so surprised that he said them, but that part of him believed those words. He was falling into the Stockholm Effect; he was beginning to sympathize with his hostage-takers.

George continued, "Shouldn't you be in school?"

"No school today; it's end of term; Ramadan start next week, but today is special day for you. No?"

George smiled; the giggling school girl had come to wish him a happy Christmas. It was a sweet gesture.

"Yes, you are correct. You are very kind, Lamia. It means a lot to me."

"I tell to father that he must to buy you a present."

"You *told* your father and thank you, but that is not necessary."

George was originally disturbed by Lamia's visit, but as the conversation progressed, he felt more comfortable. It was nice to have a free conversation without the intrusive ghost behind his student. She was a sweet girl caught in a political game; a game she wasn't interested in playing. In some ways, George was gaining a new respect for her. She wasn't going to let the current state of affairs get in the way of her conversation.

The chat lasted about 15 minutes, then Lamia said she'd have to leave, but added one final request. "Oh, when I come with father, please you call me Julie."

It was Christmas Day and after breakfast, about mid-morning, George heard the door being gingerly opened again. Julie made her way quietly again down the stairs and walked to the cell; she wore her burka, but promptly removed it as she neared the door.

"Merry Christmas," she said with a smile.

"Thank you, Lamia, it's very kind of you to come. Is father away this morning?"

"They both away in mornings; they work."

Lamia didn't seem to care about divulging information. George couldn't believe that she could have been unaware of the importance of the information that she'd just provided. On the other hand, did it really matter? There didn't appear to be any way out of the basement.

George smiled at her, "What are you going to do today?"

"No school, no work, I chill."

"That's cute, where did you learn that?"

"I like music; my father don't like; *doesn't* like it. Do you get you present?"

"Not yet. Again, I don't need a present."

"He buy you a present. Maybe later."

Lamia was always very abrupt, but she seemed to hesitate before asking the next question. George detected it; it was the type of hesitation one uses prior to asking something difficult.

"George, why you are here? Did you fight us? Did you fight Hezbollah?"

George contemplated before answering the question "I would never fight you. I think they are looking for a ransom. Looks like no one wants me back." George tried to laugh; it was a difficult thing to say; it was more difficult because it could very well be true.

"Do you have a wife?"

"Yes."

"Childrens?"

"When I left, I had one daughter. Now, I hope I have two *children*."

"What she like?"

"Oh, she's beautiful. When I left, she had just learned to walk."

"No, you wife."

George now had to pause again; no one had asked him anything about his life in close to half a year. It made him feel sad; it made him miss those two women.

"She's wonderful," George could feel a tear coming to his eye, so he tried to appear stoic; as if the question hadn't fazed him.

"When they let you go?"

"I don't know; I was hoping your dad might know."

"I don't think he know. I can ask him; I can ask father."

George wasn't quite sure how to reply, it sounded like a question, not a statement. He was now really pushing his luck; he could very well end up dead if anyone found about the secret liaisons with the teenage girl. On the other hand, he could very likely end up dead in any event.

"If you feel comfortable."

"What that mean? I do it?"

"Yes, but don't tell him I wanted to know."

"Of course not."

The two spent about 20 minutes talking about George's life, then about Lamia's life before she made her way up the stairs. It was a quick Christmas gift but George enjoyed seeing her; it not only gave him something to do, but the girl was making him more and more curious. She had a much stronger personality than Jihad Julie, who had hesitantly been forced into English lessons only a few months ago.

Lamia had been true to her word. That evening, before dinner, her father arrived with a tray. The tray contained a pair of scissors, a razor, a tiny mirror and a can of shaving cream. Lamia's father signalled that George should complete the operation now, while he watched.

George took the mirror and walked over to the metal sink. It was a small mirror held up on a little plastic handle. George looked at his reflection in that mirror; he couldn't identify the man. This man had a long beard and long hair; he looked unkempt. He also looked much older than his 28 years; in the space of six months, George had progressed from young man to middle age. He didn't like the man that he saw in the mirror and yet, it was the man he had become.

He took the scissors and cut as much excess hair from the beard as possible, then he turned on the tap and, clasping his hands together, used them to propel the cold water onto the face. He shook the can and administered the cream; then he took the razor and completed the job.

The ritual was therapeutic; it reminded George of when he was someone. It may have seemed therapeutic, but the result looked odd. His face looked pock-marked; the long hair looked strange on the newly shaven face. He had become a kind of animal in that cage; he wondered if he would ever be human again. Yes, he would be. Next Christmas, he would be home with Tanja and Maria. Next Christmas, he would be free.

Barb could only be described as the ideal house guest. Each day, there was an outing for Vlad and Maria. Two of the outings were to central London where they met up with Barb's brother. Each day, Barb insisted on washing dishes, setting the table and helping around the house. However, it wasn't the household and domestic duties that surprised Tanja - it was the outpouring of absolute love that seemed to be on offer for all of them. Vlad was constantly showered with compliments; Barb sat through his trilingual interpretations of the Flintstones. Maria seemed to be enamoured with the woman; she had gone from ignoring the old granny to clinging to her constantly. Tanja was surprised one morning when Maria woke up, made her way out of her room and immediately hopped on her grandmother's lap as Barb drank coffee at the dining room table. Even Tanja was feeling the love. It was all about compliments and condolences for having lost George.

Tanja couldn't quite determine how Barb's personality had changed so much and so quickly. Tanja thought that maybe the events over the last few months had changed her or maybe she used to be very kind and now she was returning to being very kind. Either way, this new Barb was someone Tanja wanted to be around.

Christmas dinner was the highlight. Barb had insisted that she prepare a turkey and do all the cooking. It was a welcome offer; George always did the turkey at Christmas. Tanja had never cooked one; it wasn't a Russian tradition. Barb had bought a number of bottles of wine, which she was busy consuming while she cooked. Tanja didn't quite know how to understand that; drinking alone seemed to be kind of a dark thing. While Barb cooked on Christmas afternoon, Tanja had time to take all the children out for a walk; it was good to walk on Christmas Day; it was not a particularly friendly neighbourhood, but today, many people said 'Merry Christmas.' It was an interesting cultural experience.

When Tanja returned, the smell of the turkey was wonderful. Even though the pots and pans were under full deployment for the accompaniments, the kitchen looked like it had been tidied along the way. By Tanja's estimate, it looked like Barb had completed about a bottle and half of wine at that point.

"Care to join me, Tanja?" Barb held up a glass.

"Ok, but very small."

Barb carefully poured out a half measure into a crystal wine glass that had belonged to Tanja's mother. Tanja loved those glasses; they were filled with memories.

Barb handed the glass to Tanja, then raised her own glass.

"To our husbands."

The toast caught Tanja off-guard; she thought it might have explained all Barb's drinking that day. Tanja suddenly realized that she would never have another Christmas with George. She would never see him again.

Tanja put down the glass on the counter and started to cry.

"I'm sorry dear," said Barb, who quickly put down her glass and embraced Tanja. "I didn't mean to hurt your feelings."

After a minute or so, Tanja was able to compose herself. She felt badly for reacting that way; she'd lost a husband, but Barb had lost a husband and a son. Tanja raised her glass from the counter and looked at her mother-in-law's eyes.

"To our husbands," said Tanja and they both toasted together the men that had loved them.

When December 31, 1997, came round, the place was back to its usual chaos. While Maria tossed items onto the floor, Vlad sat watching cartoons and Edita occasionally protested for nursing, nappies and attention. Tanja had to admit that she missed her mother-in-law. It had been a good Christmas, better than she had ever expected. She'd enjoyed her time with Barb; she'd actually enjoyed being with her. In all the commotion, there was only one thing she'd forgotten to tell her. Whatever spirit had driven her to award that middle name had also driven her to another decision. This would be her last Christmas in England; Tanja was going home.

CHAPTER 4

Budget Clarifications

January turned into February, then into March, then into April and now April had bled into May in the little cell in the basement.

George used to look forward to the lights going out at the end of each day, it meant the end of another day. But on that early May evening when the lights went out, he felt much sadder lying on that bed; his life was ticking away, it meant the end of another day; another day, locked in a cellar. Concessions were coming more frequently now; he was allowed to shave twice per week; it was something to look forward to; after requesting them, he was even allowed those dull scissors a few times and attempted to cut his own hair. He was allowed cleaning supplies, but only under the same conditions as the razor and scissors – the man would watch him when he used them, then remove them at the end. Sometimes, after his evening smoke, George would light a second or third Marlboro using the hot tip of the first or second respectively.

He looked into the darkness on that May evening - 'Why wouldn't they pay?' He just couldn't understand it. And if the amount was too high and no one else would pay, why wouldn't they settle something with Tanja? She had access to thousands of pounds. And if that wouldn't suffice, his parents might be able to round it up for them. It would pay for a good stock of munitions, if that's what they wanted to buy.

He lay there on the bed and stared into the darkness and reflected on all the months that had passed. It just didn't make sense. After the Christmas Day meeting, Lamia asked her father why George had been taken captive. Lamia had reported that her father explained that he was a middle man and was only told what he needed to know, it was safer for everyone that way. Lamia had encouraged him to make an exception, she was curious and wanted to know if the devil resided in the basement and was teaching her English. The father told her that curiosity kills cats; he was only to contact his handler in an extreme emergency; otherwise, they were only to contact him. It was an interesting glimpse into the world of hostage-taking protocol, but it didn't help George in the least. George continued lying there on that May evening and thinking about those months that had passed.

Lamia came solo to his cell regularly now, at least several times a week. The process was always the same; it was usually mid-morning, which coincided with a school recess. He'd hear a quiet opening of the cellar door; she would come down with no gloves but with her burka, then she would remove it; for these one-on-one visits, she usually stood near the bars rather than sit in her school chair. The school chair seemed reserved for her lessons when her father stood behind her. The conversations were about general topics; they talked about how young people lived in Lebanon versus the West, about Lamia's school, George talked all about his life; about growing up in America with English parents, about moving to Britain as a young man and his time at Sheffield University. He talked about teaching in Lithuania and meeting Tanja and how they didn't share a common language and used sign language to fall in love. Lamia was particularly impressed with the latter story and would sometimes ask George to repeat it. Sometimes, he would repeat it and she'd ask different questions than she'd asked before, as if she'd studied the story in her head and wanted to fully understand it. It was sometime in early spring, when George started to redirect the conversations; he started to exert pressure.

He hadn't originally intended to use Lamia; she was young and innocent and he'd grown affectionate toward her. He would not use her overtly anyway. He carefully noted all the information that spilt out of her mouth. He tried to figure out how to use it; there was only one problem, he couldn't figure out a way from that room.

As time progressed, his desperation grew. He needed out of there and would lobby Lamia to make it happen. By late April, he finally asked her directly for help. He had the plan all mapped out in his head. They could stage it. While her parents were out, Lamia could bring down the keys and let him free; George would stick some plastic utensils in the cell lock to make it appear that he was able to pick it. Lamia would then hear banging on the landing door and would make the mistake of opening it; he would then overpower her. That's the story she could tell. It would work. George looked to her as a lawyer looks to a jury when he's just delivered what he believes is the perfect argument – a case that is rock solid.

And that day, George learned what it was like to look at a jury when they absolutely did not subscribe to his argument. Lamia looked blankly back at him then noted that it would never work. Firstly, she didn't have access to the keys. Her father carried them everywhere he went. Secondly, if that scenario were to occur, her parents would be held accountable. She wanted to help George while not getting her parents killed or hurt. She assured George that it was all going to work out, but that patience would lead them to a solution.

When she said it, George looked down. He didn't know if he believed her about not ever being able to access the keys. He thought; her father must sleep at some point, there must be some way. However, he thought it was the second argument that was likely the more powerful one in Lamia's mind. Her loyalty was to her parents; George hated it but begrudgingly accepted it. Lamia also had a funny way of saying things to him, she would say things to reassure him like 'all going to work out'; it was just words, George knew it, but somehow, they were delivered with such sincerity that he took some comfort in them. Or maybe, what choice did he have? He wanted to take comfort in something.

As those months passed, the conversations covered an array of topics. Lamia's English had really improved. George decided that she just needed a bit of confidence; she was actually much smarter than she or anyone knew. And now, with her 17th birthday behind her, she seemed so much more self-assured. George thought about her first English lesson with her father coaxing her to the chair. She had seemed so juvenile then; things had changed; she had grown.

George remembered a recent conversation on religion. George had started it; he had said something like 'it's a pity that religion had made them enemies.' The pronouncement had been met with a stare. She paused for a second before replying.

"It's not about religion." She seemed to just stop there but George looked at her with an inquisitive stare.

"It's about…" She stopped for another second as if she just wanted the right word or maybe she had the right word and didn't know it in English. "It's about us… living."

George became curious. It felt like she hadn't been pleased with the choice of word. He could glean the gist but was curious if he fully understood it. The teacher would offer some possible alternatives.

"What do you mean? Survival? Self-preservation?"

Lamia seemed to grab on the word. "Yes, it's about survival. I don't care about Christian or Jew; I care that they want kill us."

George was now very curious. He leaned his body forward toward the cell door; he didn't want to miss even a single word of what was about to be said. The monologue was about to be a surprise; a surprise that was not only to change his views on Lamia, but also his world view.

Lamia started downloading, in intricate detail, about the 1967 war, the slaughter and occupation of Palestine, the slaughter of the Christian militias, the Israeli occupation of her own country and the slaughter of her own people by that Israeli army. And then she moved on to talk about the West who encouraged it; like a crowd encouraging a bully to beat the victim.

As George listened, it seemed like the more Lamia spoke, the more passionate she became. The more passionate she became, the more her English seemed to improve. She spoke for several minutes; it was likely 10 minutes or even more. The address was provided with such historical detail and with such emotion that it was hard not to be mesmerized by the young woman's arguments. At the end of the speech, George was the juror whose convictions had now changed; he would now acquit; no question. The accused wasn't a murderer, she was a victim.

And now, George sat in the cell on that May night and continued to think. He continued to think about all the conversations with Lamia. It was so complicated; she seemed to care for him, but also for her parents and for her people and for their cause. George then thought about the future and thought about what might happen on his first day of freedom. It must have been the wee hours of the morning now, he was anxious to shut his brain off. He wanted to stop it; he thought about the next day, maybe she would come; that would be something to look forward to. He prayed she would come.

George's prayer from the wee hours was answered. About an hour after breakfast, Lamia quietly made her way down the staircase. However, this wasn't going to be the happy meeting he'd prayed for; this was very bad news.

As George stood there, she delivered the news carefully but clearly; summer break would start at the end of the month, she would go to the countryside to help her grandmother at the farm, she'd be back in August.

George started to cry. He hated showing this type of emotion in front of the teenager; it wasn't right, he was the teacher, she was a girl. However, it hadn't been the first time that he'd broken down in front of her. His psychological health was poor. At first, he'd been physically imprisoned in a cell; now he was a prisoner in his own mind; he knew he was depressed and couldn't get his mind to stop thinking about it.

Lamia reacted by offering her right hand through the cell bars. He held it, she then put her left hand over both of the clasped hands. It wasn't the first time she'd done it, she did that each time he broke down. George loved the touch of her skin. It wasn't like the first time he'd touched her hand. That first time, he'd felt guilty about touching her; about having an inappropriate thought about her soft skin. Now, it was much different. It was almost like Lamia had progressed from schoolgirl to woman to something else. Her touch was almost messianic. He was becoming to recognize that he was reliant on this girl for everything – for his spiritual health, for his mental health, for a lifeline to the world beyond those bars. And now, he would be alone; completely alone for months.

Lamia gave a soft smile; he could see tears forming in her eyes as well. She began to speak. She began to comfort him.

"I will miss you too, but don't worry... patience. It is only for a short time. But, if you have luck, it will be a long time before you see me."

George looked dazed at her; what did that mean? Was there a chance she wouldn't be back in August? His gaze was met by what appeared to be a triumphant smile.

"I talked to father; I talk every day; he is bored of me. He loves you too. He will call them. He will tell them you are not the devil. He will make you free."

Ibrahim was surprised to get the call; Jamal used the coded term requesting a meeting. Ibrahim knew it was not going to be good news; the Briton was either dead or very ill. He doubted the former; Jamal and his family were very reliable and it would have taken a great deal of creativity for the hostage to have killed himself with anything in that room; still, it could happen.

Ibrahim had to disguise himself; he had a wig and fake moustache and beard that he used for such occasions; he used a neighbour's vehicle for these types of emergency visits. As he drove, he tried to play the scenarios out in his mind. It must be something really serious. He hoped the Briton did not need medical treatment. It would mean introducing someone else to the arena, but it must be something serious; Jamal wouldn't have called for the flu or food poisoning. As he made his way, he pulled off the highway several times and drove around small villages. If they were trying to follow, he would know about it.

When he arrived, he parked the car in the drive; as was the protocol, no other car was permitted in the drive when he was called out. He turned off the ignition and walked toward the door. As he came up the steps, the door was opened for him. It was then swiftly closed after he entered.

To an outside observer, the next minutes would have seemed quite odd. Ibrahim greeted the man but did not use his name. He came close to Jamal and kissed him three times on his cheeks. He then used his hands to frisk the man from top to bottom. Jamal complied and, after Ibrahim completed frisking his front, Jamal turned round so he could frisk him from the back.

"Anyone else here?" Ibrahim asked.

"No."

Without being invited, Ibrahim then made his way through the house, he started with the main floor and then worked his way to the upper floor where the bedrooms were located. Jamal did not follow; he knew not to follow. Once the inspection was complete, Ibrahim waved Jamal up the stairs and into the 'special' room. There was a bedroom on the upper floor, which was not to be used as a bedroom. It was the size of an extra-large closet; it was never to contain furniture. It had no windows; it was a very difficult room to bug or watch.

Once the two men were in the bedroom and the door was closed, Ibrahim could now speak properly to his subordinate.

"What's up? Is he still alive?"

"Oh yes," said Jamal.

"Is he ill?"

"No, he's fine."

And then Jamal got right to the point. He told Ibrahim that there was something not quite right about the Briton. He didn't act like a spy; he had been there for nine months and hadn't made a single attempt to escape. He spent his days reading the Koran and desperately trying to speak with him.

Jamal left out the part about the English lessons for his daughter and lending him scissors, cleaning supplies, razors and giving him cigarettes. That is the type of information he would keep to himself.

Jamal then continued; he made it clear that he wouldn't normally say anything. He was a devoted party man and he was happy to continue to do his duty; the Briton could stay as long as required, but he was having misgivings about the situation and believed that Allah had raised those concerns in his mind.

Ibrahim didn't know what to say. Had it been a more junior subordinate, he would have chastised the man for calling him. He had taken a risk by coming to visit and now, Jamal was questioning a decision. He opened his mouth and then closed it again. He didn't know if Jamal was telling him the whole story. Jamal had always been loyal to a fault; perhaps he was trying to warn him about something. It was odd to bring Allah into this conversation, maybe it was code.

Ibrahim looked at Jamal. "I don't know his background. There must be a reason for it. I will ask."

"It's nothing urgent; whenever you have a chance." replied Jamal.

Ibrahim thought that a very odd thing to say. Jamal had just called him out using the coded phrase, which meant he needed to make his way immediately to the spot.

"I have a meeting in August. Is that soon enough?"

It was an important question; Ibrahim was trying to determine if this was an important but not urgent issue or an urgent issue. He was also now very conscious that something was being left out.

"That would work fine." Jamal then offered his hand as if to end the conversation. It was very very odd.

As Ibrahim made his way home, he repeated the process of making various diversions in his motorcar. While driving, he played out the meeting in his head. He'd met his new superior a few times since the explosion, they had talked about a number of things. The new superior had mentioned the Israeli hostages by name, but never mentioned the Briton. Maybe, the Briton was a nobody – not worthy of a conversation, then why keep him? Then Ibrahim thought again – or maybe it was the opposite, maybe the Briton is so significant that he doesn't want to bring him up? Either way, the two would meet to discuss budgets in August, he would find a way to bring it up.

It was a beautiful early June morning in Canary Wharf and Tanja was busy packing. It was somewhat emotional. She hadn't yet done anything with George's clothes, but she couldn't take them to Lithuania. She folded them carefully and lovingly as she put them in big black plastic rubbish bags; they would be mixed with other items on their way to the charity shop. Tanja had also taken care of all the administrative duties; notice had been given on the flat, her landline and mobile phone would be disconnected; the utilities would cease billing.

Tanja had decided to start packing now; there was a lot to do. They still had the flat till month end; the idea was that Vlad would be able to finish the academic year. Tanja's best friend in Klaipėda, Asta, was now an estate agent and had arranged a rental for them. The digs would only be temporary as Asta would help the family find a place to buy.

Although it should have been a sad moment as Tanja packed those bags, Tanja couldn't help feeling optimistic. She'd felt a little better since the beginning of spring. The longer days and warmer weather had contributed to it. However, Tanja was now also buoyed because she had a plan. She was going home and it gave her something to look forward to. She had been busy with all the shipping and travel arrangements. She'd also finally settled with the life insurance company. George had been well insured and, as he was on company business at the time, she was entitled to additional benefits. The final settlement was well over two million dollars.

There was also other stuff in Tanja's life that was making her feel happy. She had started taking Maria to playtime several times a week. Maria was always so excited about it; it got Edita out as well, but getting a chance to get some energy out seemed to calm Maria who spent less time throwing stuff around the apartment. Vlad seemed to be growing up a little and was less maintenance than he had been. Giedrė was becoming more like a sister than a care aide for Vlad. She was someone Tanja could talk to. She was also very accommodating. At one point, Giedrė asked if it might be helpful if she babysat the entire brood once a week to give Tanja a couple of hours to herself. Tanja loved that time to herself. She would just walk round the Canary Wharf. If the weather was really miserable, she would go to an indoor shopping mall. She didn't want to buy anything, just look at the shops and keep dry.

There was one other point of happiness in her life and it was Barb. Barb called once a week now and Tanja looked forward to it. Sometimes, Tanja detected a hint of sadness in Barb's voice and she would ask her mother-in-law about it; but, apart from complaining about some headaches, Barb would decline to talk about herself. She always wanted to talk about Vlad, Tanja, Maria and Edita, which was nice as these were things Tanja cared about, but very few others seemed to care about. Tanja hesitated about bringing up the move. Tanja would be leaving the place that she'd lived with George. However, in the end, Barb was supportive, very supportive. Barb even said she was looking forward to seeing that part of Europe; Tanja invited her to come and stay and this time she meant it.

Tanja was disappointed when Giedrė relayed her decision that she wouldn't return to Lithuania with them. Vlad's school had offered her a permanent position; Giedrė was going to stay in Britain and apply for a full work permit. However, even that was good news, Giedrė had wanted to work there and it was a dream come true for her.

As she packed her past away on that June morning, Tanja thought to herself 'I'm glad I came; I'm glad I'm leaving.'

As they flew into the Klaipėda airport on that late June afternoon, Tanja was filled with excitement. As the plane began its descent, it dipped below the clouds and Tanja could see the miles of sandy beach which made up the Baltic Sea coast; she was going home; it was the beginning of a new life.

It was the first big decision she'd made since George's death. Come to think of it, it was the biggest decision that she'd ever made. Tanja was aware that there were people in Klaipėda who probably thought it was a joke; after all, she was giving up the comforts of the West to move her family to a third-world republic. However, Tanja thought differently. Not only would she get to be back home, but she reckoned that her pounds and dollars would go much further. She could likely live well and for the rest of her life on the money that George had saved and from the money from the insurer.

Tadas met them at the airport. Tadas had been her mother's boyfriend before her death and was the closest thing that Tanja had to a father. Her real father had left them when she was 12 and lived in St Petersburg now; he'd tried to contact her a few times once she'd moved to the West, but Tanja saw right through that plan and made it clear that he was no longer welcome in her life.

Tadas stood about 180 cm tall. He looked much older, it had been two years since she'd last seen him. He was greying now, but still had comforting blue eyes. He shouted out at them in Lithuanian; he was a Lithuanian and preferred it to the Russian he'd spoken with Tanja's mother. Vlad saw him first and dropped the bag he was carrying to run and hug the man. Tanja stood in awe as the two held each other tightly for a minute. Tadas was a good guy. He was kind and generous and loved them. Tanja thought that it was nice to be amongst people who genuinely loved them.

Tanja embraced him next. It felt like being draped in home. She had missed his smell. It was comforting to be with the closest family she had left. She had missed being with the one man in the world that gave unconditional love to her and her brother without ever asking for anything in return.

Tadas drove them the half-hour from the Klaipėda Airport at Palanga to their new rental in the centre of Klaipėda. When they arrived, Asta seemed to appear from nowhere. Tanja hadn't seen her in a couple of years. The old playground chums hugged and kissed. They even held hands as Asta dragged her into the rental suite. The family followed behind.

In Tanja's mind, the rental suite could only be described as 'functional.' Oh, it was nicer than the one she'd lived in as a girl and nicer than Tadas' flat. It was big enough; three bedrooms, a kitchen, a full-sized bathroom and a sitting room. It was also furnished, even if the furnishings looked a little worn. In general, the place was old and on the ground floor, which would be fine in the summer, but Tanja had lived on the Baltic coast most of her life, it would be damp and cold in the winter.

Asta saw the look in Tanja's eyes, she interjected immediately.

"I know, it's not great. Rental stock is hard these days. I could get my hands on Soviet stuff in the suburbs or this older place which is closer to town; I hope it will work. It won't be for long; there is some decent stuff on sale at the moment; hopefully, they'll be something out there for you. I know what you're looking for."

Tanja had made her requirements clear. She wanted something central with either a view of the river or of the sea. Her previous place had a view of the Thames and she had gained comfort from watching it. It felt like a passage through life; it gave her strength.

"I'd like to see them as soon as possible, Asta."

"I'll make it happen; we can start tomorrow."

Tanja liked that; it was all going according to plan. She was home, she had Tadas, she had Asta and soon she would have a home of her own. The first home she had ever owned.

Tanja was excited when she woke that next morning. Her new life had begun. Before coming to collect them at the airport, Tadas had been allowed access to the rental suite. He'd bought groceries and filled the cupboards and fridge. Tanja thought that this was a gesture that only an easterner would make and it was further validation of her decision to move. During that first evening in the flat, Tadas had also prepared the family dinner and the whole place suddenly filled with laughter. Tadas told old jokes to Vlad, who enjoyed them so much that even Maria joined in the laughter in solidarity. Even Edita was less demanding than usual; she was nine months old now and was growing so quickly.

Today, she would start putting down new roots. Tadas would be there at 8 am; he would do some child minding for a few hours while Tanja embarked on her house hunting. As was his custom, he arrived 10 minutes early. Every other Lithuanian person who Tanja knew arrived late, but Tadas was always on time.

"Thank you, Tadas. They've all been fed and Edita's been changed. I won't be long."

Tadas smiled, "take your time, sweetheart. It's not a chore to watch Vlad and my granddaughters."

At that moment, Tanja was overcome with a wave of affection for her stepfather. She had never heard him refer to her daughters as his grandchildren. Tadas had no children of his own. Tanja thought that Tadas was better than a father. He was like a grandfather, father and favourite uncle all in one. He gave constantly and never asked for anything in return.

She kissed him on the cheek and departed the flat to walk to Asta's office. She was alone now in those familiar streets, free of the children for a couple of hours, but more importantly, she was free in the city which she loved. She walked through the ancient passages, it was not like Seattle or Canary Wharf; she was in a European city with history. It wasn't on the way, but Tanja made a detour to the market and walked amongst the stalls. They were selling quite different stuff now; the last time she was there, it was mostly about beer, chocolates and cigarettes; along with the usual area for butchers and the area set aside for old babushkas selling vegetables. Now, it was quite different, the stall owners were just setting up; the beer, chocolate and cigarette area now had Lithuanian art and crafts, local honey, mead. They must be attracting tourists now, Tanja thought. There was something else that seemed a bit peculiar; there was less Russian spoken now; she wondered if some had gone home or maybe to western Europe.

She arrived at Asta's office promptly at 8:30. Every time Tanja looked at Asta, she could see the little girl she had known so well. Asta was the first girl whom she'd met when they'd moved to Klaipėda. It was then that a rather odd thought came to Tanja. When they'd first met, they had trouble communicating. Tanja could only speak Russian and Asta only really spoke Lithuanian. Tanja began to wonder if she had an affinity for people she couldn't communicate properly with!

Tanja surprised that little girl. Asta had her back to the door and Tanja sneaked behind her and hugged her from behind.

"Oh," exclaimed Asta as she turned around, "I was hoping you were a man."

Tanja laughed "I'm sorry to disappoint you, but let me tell you, they are all overrated. You saw the problems they created for me!"

Asta laughed at the joke about Tanja's children. She liked that about Asta; they had the same sense of humour.

The two ladies walked and gossiped as they made their way to the first showing. It was on the third floor of a newly-built seven-storey building. It had three bedrooms. Asta described it as ultra-modern, built in a Scandinavian style. Tanja described it back to her as lacking any kind of soul. It felt like it could be a social housing estate in Helsinki.

Asta laughed; it was a strange way to describe it.

The next place was an old Soviet bloc; it was going to be much cheaper. It looked similar to the building where Tadas lived. Tanja and Asta climbed up to the third floor and looked at the suite; it had been wonderfully restored inside and was spacious.

"I'm sorry Asta, we have both been there and done that. The suite is nice; the building brings back the wrong memories. I'm sorry to be so picky; you must have other clients to attend to."

Asta laughed again, "Tanja, you're a first-time buyer; people like you often think that they are going to spend a day looking at lovely places and then choose one. This is likely going to take weeks; I'll try to steer you from the dogs but I will show you places that have views of the water and are central."

Tanja was disappointed by the response. She was absolutely one of those first-time buyers. She really didn't want to spend weeks looking at places; her time was almost up for the day; she needed to relieve Tadas from his babysitting duty.

"One last one, ok?" said Asta.

They walked past the market square and made their way through the old town. Asta stopped in front of a door in a side street.

"What about the view?" asked Tanja.

"Oh, this is just the front entrance. Wait for it."

It was a three-storey building and the ladies climbed the steep staircase which was located at one side of the building. They climbed to the top floor. Tanja already knew that this wouldn't work; how could she get Edita's pram up and down?

Asta turned the key; it would be a relief to get out of the dark old staircase.

Once the door opened, a beam of light drenched that dark corridor. Tanja entered the room and directly in front of her, she could see the Danė River glistening in the hot late June sun. Tanja just stared in awe. It was the most beautiful view she'd ever seen in Klaipėda. The living room was spacious, there were four bedrooms, not three and it had been completely redone with modern appliances and a gourmet kitchen.

"So, Tanja, I hesitated showing you this one. I'm thinking it has Tanja written all over it, but it's the price point that is the issue. We haven't talked about your budget; this one might be a bit of a stretch."

Tanja began to worry; she'd banked on things being cheap; she suddenly started to panic a little. What did she mean by 'stretch'?

"How much are they asking?"

"Close to $200,000 USD."

Tanja let out a sigh of relief. "Oh, I think we can stretch."

The current owners were impressed with Tanja's offer, which was close to full price. She was also offering a cash deal; no need to wait on financing. Tanja had only two conditions to the offer. One was that, at her expense, she would hire a building inspector to review the property and ensure it was in good order. The other was that she wanted quick possession. If they wanted the sale to go through, they would give her possession within a fortnight.

Asta presented the offer and the sellers agreed quickly. The building inspector found only minor issues for a building of that age. So, on July

14th, 1998 at noon local time, Tanja became a property owner; after living in state housing and rentals all her life, she was now a landlady. She was also still very wealthy. After paying for the property, there was still just over $2 million left from the insurance.

Tanja was keen to get out of the rental accommodation, but she wouldn't move in immediately. There was furniture to be purchased, but more importantly, her new castle would need to be decorated. She knew that her decorating would mean remaining in a dingy flat with a teenage boy with Down Syndrome and two little princesses, but this was her first home and it should be perfect.

'Perfect' had a specific meaning to Tanja. This place wouldn't be like the 'Scandinavian' inspired flat that they'd seen earlier, which was now common round the world, or like the Seattle or London apartments. This new place was to look like a European apartment. If people saw photos of it anywhere in the world, they would know it was in Eastern Europe.

Tanja was able to get Asta's help in lining up the trades; the ceiling in the living room would have a mosaic; there were no craftsmen left in the West who could do that type of work but it was surprisingly easy to get artists in Klaipėda who had the skill. The walls were to be changed from their current white, except in the two bathrooms. Each room was to have three walls painted one colour and the 'feature' wall painted another. Window coverings were to be net curtains with proper heavy curtains that pulled back and were held by an ornate clasp; at night, they could be let go and provide the required privacy. Tanja went about buying paintings as well. She chose paintings with local animals, buildings, seascapes and landscapes. She only bought from local artists. Some of the trades and artists were surprised by her choices, the nouveau riche who used their services preferred their places to look more western, but not Tanja, she had seen that world and was coming home.

It was late August when Tanja looked around at her beautifully decorated 'European' apartment. She walked over to look at the view; she gazed at the river. There was a noisier road right beneath the flat and before the river walkway, but because she was on the third floor, you'd have to crook your neck down to see it and the noise was muffled. She loved that view and nothing could distract her from that river. Her life was changing so quickly. One year ago, she was in a den of despair; now, she had completed one of the most important projects of her 24 years.

Tanja looked over at Asta, who smiled.

"You've come a long way, Tanja. Remember how we used to play on a muddy playground in front of the flats?"

Tanja smiled but she wasn't in the mood to discuss childhood memories. Today was a special day and Tanja had two purposes for her site visit. One was to inspect the place and ensure it was ready for occupation. The other purpose was a bit more sentimental.

Tanja removed the framed photograph from a plastic carrier bag and carefully placed it on the mantle above the fireplace. She took her hand and touched the side of it. She gazed at the photo of her wedding day and stared at George's eyes. She thought to herself 'you made me so happy, sweet prince, don't worry about me, I'm happy again.'

Ibrahim had to be careful how he raised the issue of the Briton. He didn't feel comfortable questioning anything; he knew his duty was to execute orders – no question. However, Jamal knew that as well; there was something that wasn't right about that meeting. Ibrahim had decided that Jamal knew more than he was divulging; he wouldn't have raised the alarm for no good reason. At that August budget review meeting, Ibrahim knew he needed to exercise caution when raising the issue with his superior.

As the two men sat across from each other, Ibrahim discussed the money that had been used year to date and provided a summary of the money he needed to complete 1998. He read from a page, but there were only numbers and individual letters on the page. Ibrahim knew the various operations associated with each of those letters – A, B, C, D etc., but they were not explained on the paper. If that paper ever fell into the wrong hands, it would be worthless. They would need Ibrahim to interpret it.

Ibrahim pointed at some of the numbers and then got right to the summary. His new handler didn't seem particularly interested, he never asked any questions. Ibrahim had hoped today would be different.

"Very good, Ibrahim, you do such a remarkable job for us. I'll take that number away; I'm sure it will not be a problem. You're bringing in far more than you're spending."

Ibrahim understood the reference, which was about drug shipments. He couldn't let the short meeting end, he needed to keep the man talking.

"Any questions, Sir?"

"No, nice job."

"Fares always liked to deep dive into the operational numbers to ensure the money was being properly allocated."

"Fares and I are very different. You have proven yourself repeatedly to the operation. You have my absolute trust, Ibrahim."

This was getting frustrating; he was not going to get the information out unless he spat it out. Ibrahim decided he had no choice.

"I appreciate your kind words, which are undeserved. It is my pleasure to serve... If it's appropriate, may *I* pose a question?"

"Ibrahim, my door is always open to you, please don't ask 'is it appropriate,' we are a team."

"Thank you. It's about the Briton; he never seems to come up. It's expensive to hold him and it ties up one of our best people. I just can't figure the connection to the cause."

The man sat back in his chair; until that moment, he wasn't even aware that they were holding a westerner; they'd stopped that years ago – maybe it was an exception; yes, it may be an exception.

"He must be an Israeli agent."

Ibrahim wasn't satisfied with the verb, the 'must' inferred the handler likely didn't know for sure.

"I see," replied Ibrahim, "would it be desirable to ask for clarification?"

"Just treat him like an agent. No one is asking for him, so that can be the only reason."

"I understand."

With that, Ibrahim took his sheet of paper, carefully placed it in his bag, shook his handler's hand and bade him farewell. He left the August budget meeting.

George spent a good deal of time pacing these days. It was August; he didn't know exactly what day Lamia would return and he'd now been speechless and touchless for more than two months. He had paced before in that cell, but now he did it far more often. The routine was breakfast, exercise, pace, lunch, exercise, pace, dinner, smoke, pace, sleep. George now knew why the animals paced up and down at the zoo. He had thought they were just getting exercise. He now knew that wasn't true. They paced because they couldn't get out, they couldn't get free so something in their souls told them to pace. And that's what he had become. After a year of captivity, he was just a human animal stuck in a cage spending his days pacing behind the bars.

He desperately tried to hold onto reality. When not thinking about Tanja, Maria, his parents and friends, he thought of things he would do when he got out. He missed having a proper drink, an alcoholic drink. He would have a proper pint of bitter in an English country pub, he would take a bottle of scotch and sit on a Scottish hilltop and drink it. He would chill a bottle of vodka in the freezer and treat himself to a shot. Oh, that last fantasy was nice. He could almost taste the cold elixir going down his throat; he would consume it with oysters; that would be the perfect mix and the oysters would be fresh, uncooked and served with freshly grated horseradish.

He would also do much more walking when he got out; he would celebrate his freedom by walking a lot. Sometimes, he thought about where he'd go on those walks. He would walk through the forest or through the countryside. However, he more often thought of the city walks he would do. He thought of walks he could take in Milwaukee, in Seattle, in London. He would trace the walks in his mind and try to memorize the streets he could take. He could walk from Victoria Station, down Buckingham Palace Road toward the palace, then down the Mall to Trafalgar Square. He would go through the various maps in his head as he paced back and forth and back and forth.

How long could he go on like this? How long could he pace?

CHAPTER 5

Perspective

It was late August when Lamia finally made it back to the cell. George was so excited to hear the steel door open at the top of the landing - at an unaccustomed time and with unaccustomed gentility.

George reached his hands out of the bars; he was desperate to touch her. She removed her burka and then Lamia sandwiched both her hands around his hand; the way only a close friend would ever touch someone.

"I miss you, George."

"I missed you; hard to live without human contact."

"Sorry, I have been home since a week, but father said I can rest from English lessons and mother and father have been around all the time. Anyway, I have good news; father talk to the man in June; there will be a meeting this month to talk about you."

It was a ray of hope and George's face lit up a little; it was the first ray of hope in a long time.

"Any idea when in August?"

"No, maybe it already happen; but we not heard from them."

George just looked at her; her skin was tanned and some of the chubbiness around her cheeks had dissipated; she had changed so much in such a short period of time. She didn't look like a girl anymore; she was a woman and a beautiful woman. She had transformed from a cute cygnet to a beautiful swan.

"Your English is still really good, Lamia; did you practice?" George continued to hold her hands as he asked the question; she tugged away gently to return her hands to her own possession.

"Well, kind of; grandmother has a cow, two pigs, chickens and olives – and a satellite! Father put it there. I watch MTV, BBC."

George smiled at the thought of an ancient olive grove with a satellite dish; the world was changing.

"BBC news? Did you watch the news?"

"Yes, I know you ask questions. Don't worry; I even wrote some things down I wanted to ask you about, but let's do it another time. Ok? I want to see how you doing."

"I think your summer sounds more exciting. I'm glad you're watching the news; you're so clever. You have a bright future ahead. BBC is also a good network for news; it might be the closest thing to the truth."

Lamia paused a moment.

"From your side."

"Yes," George smiled, "from our perspective, I guess."

George continued, "So, are you excited about your final year of high school?"

"Oh, yes, there's going to be special meetings and parties."

"Then what is the plan? Marriage, college?"

Lamia went quiet a moment, then a question seemed to come to her.

"George, why did you ask me that question?"

"I am curious; I'm sorry, you've told me so much; I just assumed there was nothing I shouldn't know."

"No, not that, about marriage."

George was feeling a little awkward now, he'd clearly touched on a sensitivity; maybe her father was pushing her into something.

"I was just curious; it doesn't matter, I didn't mean to offend you."

"No, no problem… George?" Lamia paused. "Would you ask a British girl that question – or boy?"

George thought about the question, so Lamia continued, "or did you ask that because I'm a Muslim girl?"

"Oh no, I'm sorry; I was just talking."

Lamia smiled, she let it go and answered the question; she was hoping to get into university, her father's friend was even applying to some foreign ones for her, but in his mind, George was pondering that earlier question. She was right – he had just been taught a lesson on perspective.

In Klaipėda, Tanja felt things were progressing swimmingly. Tanja had hired two babysitters to help her. She hired one young woman to help out with Vlad and take him to and from the Children's Centre. And she hired one older lady to help out with Maria and Edita, so that Tanja could get some personal time. Now that she was safely in her new apartment; she needed time to consider her next step. She should obtain some sort of job or maybe volunteer at the Children's Centre. She'd worked there before they'd left for Seattle; she loved working with special needs kids.

After a couple of weeks, two things became clear about those hiring choices. The young woman wasn't working out and Vlad could walk himself to school. The other thing that was clear was that the old lady was a natural with children. Maria clearly loved her, the old lady clearly loved her back; and she seemed to love Edita and Vlad as well. Maria began to refer to the old lady by an English title, which she must have picked up from somewhere. She called her 'Auntie Luce.' It sounded cute, Maria's pronunciation of Luce was quite correct, like Lucy, but with a long e at the end – Luceee.

In addition to being a very competent caregiver, Auntie Luce also appeared to be a workhorse. When she wasn't engaged with the girls or Vlad, she was doing laundry, making snacks, cleaning dishes, she seemed to be constantly tidying things. It was also good to hear Maria now starting to pick up some Lithuanian words from her. She already could understand quite a bit of Russian and liked to watch the English language cartoon network, so sometimes she would repeat English words too. Tanja was suspicious that the cartoons may have been the origin of Auntie Luce's nickname.

Tanja came to a decision. Auntie Luce was only coming three days a week for four hours each time. She would ask her to come every day and stay most of the day; from 9 to 3 weekdays. She would then let go of the other lady and, if Vlad ever needed to stay home from school, Luce could help. That would work.

At first, Luce declined the offer. She was too old to work full time, she just worked for something to do and for some pocket money. However, Tanja thought she knew how to move beyond that objection. She offered her twice the amount of money and time off anytime; just give her some notice.

Tanja could see the old woman mulling it over. It was a cunning tactic, it would never have worked if the old woman didn't have children and grandchildren, but Tanja had already asked all about the widow's life and knew her background well. Tanja also knew that the old woman was never going to spend any of her wages; she was going to continue living in the same flat, eating the same food. However, the offer of all that money wasn't for her; Tanja knew how easterners thought, she was one of them. That extra money would be too hard to decline because Luce would give it all away – all to those children and grandchildren.

Luce contemplated for a minute before smiling and saying "ok." Tanja let the younger lady know that her services were no longer required, she didn't seem particularly upset.

The next project that Tanja directed her attention to was Vlad. In London, the special school had a rigorous agenda; Vlad's English improved quickly along with his executive functioning. The Children's Centre in Klaipėda seemed more about socializing. Vlad was having fun, but there were few expectations of him.

One morning, after Luce arrived for her 9 am shift, Tanja made her way over to the Children's Centre to discuss the issue with the headmaster. She liked the headmaster; she'd worked for him before and thought she had a good idea of how to broach the subject. She'd ask for more academic time and offer a donation to make it happen.

"Thanks Tanja," said the headmaster, "I understand your perspective; but, as you know, we are a therapeutic centre; not so much an academic facility. We train life skills here. However, things are changing. You're not the first parent to make this request. You're the third over the last year whom I can recall. Before that, no one asked about rigorous education for Down Syndrome children; it's a positive development."

The headmaster continued, "There's a young man, very young actually, he's still at university, he is studying special needs education and he tutors. The other two were impressed. I think he's fairly expensive. You could try him."

Tanja took down the name and phone number of the tutor and left the Children's Centre. Although it was late October, it was a surprisingly beautiful day; it was cold but the sun shone. Tanja was motivated; she had made arrangements for her girls and now she would get Vlad a proper education.

When she arrived home and climbed the stairs, she found the apartment empty. That's what she liked about Luce - if there was a semi-decent day, the girls went for long outings. Tanja decided to get right to business. From the phone in the kitchen, she called the tutor to ask if he might be interested in taking a student. They discussed price and it was decidedly not expensive. The tutor started talking about a time for a first lesson for them to all meet, but that wasn't good enough for Tanja.

"Is it possible for us to meet separately first? I'd like to meet you before Vlad starts - if that's ok."

There was a delay and then a methodical answer, "Well, I'm home now; can you come now?"

Tanja thought it a perfect response, just perfect. She would make good use of this day. It was a little far to walk, but she decided to walk anyway, she walked out of the beautiful old town, along the river and then eventually toward a block of Soviet flats near the stadium.

When she arrived, she looked up at the building. It was a very typical prefab Soviet flat block. It was 5 storeys high and made of concrete with absolutely no concession to architectural merit in the slightest. It reminded her of her mother's flat block and Tadas' flat block; they all looked the same. She opened the archaic door; it required quite a bit of strength to pull the steel door open; it had broken at some point and a homemade repair ensured it could still be opened, but would then need to be pulled shut. She obliged and was left in a dark dingy hallway with concrete steps. She climbed up the stairs to the first floor and rang the bell.

Mantas, the tutor, opened the door. Tanja thought he looked like a peculiar figure. He must have been 190 cm tall. He had an austere look about him. He wore glasses and was very slim, lanky in appearance. His clothes looked too big for him. He wore a shirt that was buttoned right up to the neck, but with no tie. He wore an old sweater and wool trousers. Tanja thought he reminded her of her old high school teachers, except he was so young. He was likely younger than her.

Mantas beckoned her in. It was a studio flat, a bedsit, but Tanja couldn't see a bed. He must pull the sofa out, she thought. The room contained a sofa, an old coffee table, a desk with a computer and chair, a small sideboard with another chair beside it and a wall filled with books. Tanja looked at the books, it was mostly academic textbooks about education.

Mantas waved Tanja toward the sofa and he sat in the desk chair. He adjusted his glasses.

Tanja continued in Lithuanian.

"Thank you for seeing me, Mantas. I just wanted to introduce myself and tell you about my brother." Tanja was surprised when Mantas retrieved a notebook and pen from his desk and began writing Vlad's name. She could see that his handwriting was very precise; yes, he was definitely a typical Soviet teacher.

Tanja explained all about Vlad and how the Children's Centre wasn't challenging enough and how they'd lived overseas and how he was good at languages, but got them confused; she wanted him to focus more on improving his communications skills as well as doing some social sciences – history and geography.

Mantas kept writing and didn't look up. "What about maths and science?"

"Well, not his strong suit; you could do some maths as well."

"Can he count money?"

"No, if there's time that might be a good place to start; again, not his strong suit."

At the end of the meeting, Tanja wasn't really sure how she felt about Mantas. He seemed so cold and regimented. She worried that a rigid approach wouldn't work for Vlad. However, in the end, she decided that she would try it - twice a week for 60 minutes per session, Vlad would attend tutoring with Mantas.

It had been a productive day; it had turned out slightly differently than she'd thought, but as Tanja climbed the stairs to her river view apartment, she concluded it had been a very successful day indeed. She was unaware it was about to take a turn for the worse.

It was a little after noon and Auntie Luce and the girls were still out. She might have taken a picnic, thought Tanja. Tanja began making her own lunch; she brought out some bread – good dark rye bread that was hard to get even in London. She was looking around for the cheese when the phone rang in the kitchen.

"Allo," said Tanja.

"Hi Tanja? Is that you? It's Gary. Can you hear me?" Tanja was confused; the man spoke in English; she didn't know any Gary, but she could hear him.

"Yes, hello, please I hear you." Tanja hated speaking English; she thought she always muddled it up.

"It's Gary; I don't know if you remember me? George's cousin?" Tanja was relieved; she did remember Gary; they'd met him once when she and George went to Milwaukee to visit her in-laws. He was one of George's favourite cousins; he was always smiling when Tanja had been with him. His voice sounded more serious now.

"Oh Gary, it is good to hear you."

"Tanja – I'm sorry; I'm calling with news. It isn't good news. Auntie Barb passed away yesterday; I'm sorry. It was very sudden; no pain. It was a brain aneurysm, a shock."

Tanja couldn't believe it and just went quiet; her mother-in-law seemed so strong; now she was gone, the third person to die in a row – and just when she'd gained a new relationship with her. But Tanja didn't cry. Pain was something she'd become accustomed to in her short life, she just paused and said...

"Oh God, she was healthy; we, we, she was with us for Christmas."

"Yes, she always talked about it. She was so proud of her girls. She was looking forward to going to see you in the summer. She'd even bought a book about Lithuania."

"Very bad luck," continued Tanja, "the family is cursed."

"I suppose so, I actually think Auntie Barb died of a broken heart; she was never quite the same after Uncle Doug and George died. I'm so sorry, Tanja."

"Thank you, Gary, you a good cousin, thank you for telling it."

"Tanja – there's one other thing. After Uncle Doug's passing, Auntie Barb was in a bit of a state. I helped her get all her financial stuff in order. I also helped her get a new will together with a lawyer. I'm the executor of the will; you're the primary beneficiary. The equivalent of about 10% is meant to come to me; the remainder to you. Auntie Barb asked that I be put in the will as an acknowledgement of the executor services. However, I'd be pleased to give that money to you."

"No, thank you, Gary. We don't need it; she want that you have it."

When the conversation ended, Tanja put down the phone. Tears welled in her eyes then one tear began streaming down her cheek as she reflected on the irony of the moment. She'd lost a woman who had come to mean so much to her over that last year – and gained another pile of cash.

In September, the English lessons reconvened with Lamia's father standing behind her. The lessons were still only 30 minutes; George looked forward to them. The secret meetings also continued; it was something else he looked forward to, but it wasn't enough. The pacing was moving from physical pacing to a kind of mental pacing – George was thinking the same thoughts over and over – Maria, Tanja, mother, father, scotch, walks, pint, walks, friends, Tanja, Maria, newborn, mother, hilltop. George regularly asked Lamia about the outcome of the meeting, but no one had been in contact yet.

It was late October when George felt that he might now be losing his mind and it was pretty obvious to Lamia. She'd come for one of her clandestine meetings, but was having trouble carrying the conversation. George kept talking about his homelands in the United States and Britain and how he belonged to both. He kept talking about different streets in London or Milwaukee, where he was born, and would sometimes cry for no reason.

"George – how do I stop you depression?"

George was impressed; he'd covered that word but didn't think she'd recall it.

"I just can't stand the boredom anymore. I have memorized the Koran, the New Testament and David Copperfield. I miss you; I appreciate your visits, but I think I need more of you."

Lamia thought for a minute; she was now coming almost every day; whenever her parents were out.

"How about more books?"

"No, I couldn't ask you to do that. If your father found them, it would be a problem."

"No, I won't bring them; I'll get him to bring them." Lamia went quiet for a moment as she thought it through in her mind. "When I come for my lesson, we will talk about books; I will say that we want discuss one, but you need read it. He'll bring it; he do anything for me."

It was a brilliant plan and brilliantly executed. During the afternoon lesson, they talked about authors and history in English. Then, Lamia turned her covered head toward her father and said something in Arabic. The father nodded his head. George thought his choice was a long shot, but he'd take anything in the genre.

When the dinner tray arrived the next day, there was a beautiful new paperback accompanying it. George looked at it with awe; it was exactly what he'd wanted. He looked at the cover several times and read it and re-read it. The cover said "Jeffrey Archer" at the top and "London" in the middle. It was the book he'd started reading before going on that business trip.

Three weeks had passed and now Tanja was getting angry. Her frustration was further amplified by the loss of her mother-in-law. Tanja was beginning to think she'd made a terrible mistake with hiring that tutor.

The first week produced very little, Tanja was hoping that Vlad would be assigned homework. He wasn't. During the second week, there was a lot of homework and it was complicated stuff and it was all math. Tanja tried to help Vlad with it but he got annoyed with her. The third week was more math and harder homework; Tanja was getting frustrated and Vlad seemed to be angry that she was frustrated. She had had enough. She called Mantas and asked if she could meet him at his flat the following day.

As soon as Auntie Luce arrived that following day, Tanja was off. She was angry and she decided to walk to Mantas' flat. It was cold and wet but she walked; she needed to calm down. She had asked him to keep maths light and now he was setting Vlad up for failure. She needed to be polite, but the lessons had to be redirected or she would have to consider firing him. It wasn't desirable, but she would have to teach Vlad herself.

She hesitated before ringing the bell at the flat door; she was still a little angry and needed to calm. She took a deep breath and knocked. Mantas answered the door; she couldn't remember exactly, but it looked like he was wearing precisely the same clothes with that buttoned up collar that made him look like a nerd.

"Hi Tanja, please come in."

The flat had been thoroughly cleaned and tidied; she could smell a bleach scent coming from the WC room. He was a neat freak as well.

Tanja sat on the sofa and Mantas sat on his desk chair. She needed to relax; she'd rehearsed; she needed to focus on the outcome, not on her emotions.

"Mantas, thanks for your help with Vlad. I just wanted to ask about all the math. I'm worried it might be a bit challenging for him."

"I thought you wanted me to challenge him."

Tanja was shocked at the impertinence; she needed to stay calm; he was a Soviet relic; she knew how to handle it.

"Yes, but he's stressed about it; I was wondering if you could switch the lessons up a little."

"He doesn't seem stressed about it; he had trouble with the money exercise at first, but I tried a few different approaches and he seemed to get it, but he needs to keep working on it at home and when you go out and buy things. I understand you've been working with him on the homework?"

Tanja was beginning to think Mantas was clueless, but she would keep going.

"Yes, that's right and well, he is stressed, so about changing direction a little…"

"Tanja – may I make a suggestion? Is there someone else who could do the homework with him? You may be a bit too close to him emotionally. How about your husband?"

Tanja was now beyond angry; it was hard to calm down.

"I don't have a husband!"

"Oh, I'm sorry, Vlad mentioned that he had nieces."

"He does; I just don't have a husband – he's dead."

"I see; well, is there another adult in the household?" Tanja couldn't believe it; she had just told him that her husband was dead and then he went right back to his demand, which included an inference that she couldn't do it. Tanja gritted her teeth.

"If *you* think it's worthwhile, I could ask his stepfather or our babysitter. If we try that and it doesn't work, can we try to redirect?"

"I can't see why it wouldn't work."

Tanja was now too angry. She needed out of there before she said something that she would later regret.

"Ok," she stood up and walked toward the door; she didn't look at him; she just walked to the door and said "goodbye" and closed it behind her. What a jerk, she thought.

Alone in the apartment, Mantas closed his eyes for a moment while sitting in his chair. She was so beautiful, the most beautiful blue eyes he'd ever seen; he could bathe in them. Her blonde hair was like gold, he thought, with a figure that was something from a Paris runway; you'd never know she'd given birth. And that accent, it just hint at her Russian roots, just slightly and, when she spoke, it sounded like his language was being sung to him; when she got angry, she would betray those Russian roots just a little more – incredible. He had fantasized about her since their first meeting. He just seemed so awkward around her; it didn't matter, they were from different worlds, it would never go anywhere but the fantasy was a wonderful one and now he had more information for that fantasy – she was single.

That evening, Tanja got Tadas to complete the money exercise with Vlad. Tadas had to pretend to be the customer and give Vlad a 20 Litas note for something that cost 18 Litas and Vlad would have to provide change. Then, there were 9 other similar exercises that got progressively harder. Tanja had to grit her teeth again; the exercise was going ok. He was doing the work correctly with Tadas; Vlad slipped on one question, but tried again, and got it. Tanja was pleased that it was working but was also irritated that the tutor's suggestion had worked.

Tanja decided that, as Vlad seemed to be learning, she would keep the tutor. However, she would take him there and back. She had been relying on Tadas and Luce. She wanted to keep an eye on things and the pickup would give her a chance to talk to Mantas. She begrudgingly understood that he knew what he was doing and, if there were an opportunity to learn a technique to teach Vlad better, she would learn it.

However, all great plans are susceptible to failure and Vlad's hijinks were just about to scuttle that plan. The next morning, Tanja got a call from the Children's Centre; Vlad had fallen off the playground equipment. It was nothing serious, but they had taken him to the hospital. It was a sprain; could she collect him.

When she arrived, she spoke to the doctor. It was a bad sprain; he should rest it for at least 10 days. It meant that Vlad would be at home for the next 10 days. Tanja knew that wouldn't be good; he would climb the walls and she would have to find ways to entertain him; he'd miss three tutoring sessions. She needed to find ways to keep him busy. They took a taxi home and Tanja helped Vlad up the stairs – she cursed those stairs today.

When they arrived home, Luce gave him lots of attention. He was taking the pain like a man; that was one thing, thought Tanja, but now she would need to find a way to fill the next 10 days. She could ask Tadas to help with homework. Then, she thought again; I wonder if the tutor could do house calls? She would call him in the morning, make it worth his while, she could pay for taxis, she would take any timeslot he would give her.

Mantas was surprised to get the call on that November morning. Tanja explained all about the accident and would there, please, be any chance he might be willing to do some house calls and would he, maybe, be able to provide some additional tutorials over the coming 10 days. She would pay for a taxi there and back; she would pay travel time; she would take any timeslot he'd be willing to offer.

Mantas thought for a minute; he definitely wanted to see her place; he wanted to see her again. It would add to the fantasies that he was having. He often fantasized about caressing her cheek and she would smile as he touched that skin.

"I'm ok with that, I can come tomorrow and we can talk about scheduling for the remainder of the period then. But I won't put you to the expense of a taxi. I love to walk and have a bus pass if the weather is rough."

"Great, God bless, you, Mantas. I tell you what; our place is a little tricky to find. I'd like to come and collect you tomorrow – if that's ok; we can walk over together."

"Yes, that would work for me, Tanja."

Tanja put down the phone. She was pleased with herself. She would get him relaxed and get a full half-hour to bilk him for information on ways to teach Vlad.

Mantas put down the phone. This was wonderful; he would not only get to see her place; he'd get a half an hour with her.

Lamia continued to put gentle pressure on her father, but he wouldn't call them again – no way. A 'no response' meant no. Her father didn't understand it but there must be some reason that they wanted him. He had thought it through; George was likely an Israeli agent. He watched the news and his name never came up; no one was looking for him – at least no one important in the West.

Lamia was finding it increasingly difficult to talk with George about it. She used to be excited to visit him for the private meetings; now it was sometimes a chore. He was so emotionally needy; however, she knew that it was her people that had made him that way and she felt guilty about it. He was more composed during their daily English lessons, but often fell completely apart during their private chats. As she made her way into the basement that November morning, she hoped today would be different.

"George!" She tried to sound bubbly as she neared the bars. He smiled at her; maybe today would be one of his better days.

"Lamia, thank you for the book."

Lamia had managed to secure another book; this time she used a book she actually needed to read for her English class. It was "A Christmas Carol;" it was supposed to be challenging to read and good exposure to English culture. After reading the first few pages, she agreed that it was both – particularly the challenging part. She needed to submit a book report on it before mid-December. Her father had also given her a copy of the London book and George and her had to discuss it during the lessons. She'd tried to read it, but it was too long and the vocabulary was difficult. So, George would just ask questions during the lessons while flipping through the book and she would answer with anything. Her father appeared none the wiser. It was more interesting to listen to George explain it; she now wanted to see London more than ever.

"You are welcome; I haven't started reading – just a couple pages. Is it good?"

"Oh, it's one of the most important books in the English language. I loved it as a child. It's about ghosts who change a miserable man's opinions about the world. He goes from a terrible man to a very kind man."

"George – can I ask something? It's hard question and you don't need answer; if you don't want answer, I understand."

George nodded his head; it was a pointless question; he would always answer her.

"I like the idea of the book; sometime people change. Do you change?"

"Of course."

"I mean do you… were you bad?"

George wondered if he were about to enter a philosophical conversation on the meaning of the word bad, Lamia detected the confused look on his face, so she decided to be more specific.

"My father don't… doesn't know why you are here. He thinks that you are…maybe a…spy - a spy against Hezbollah."

At that moment, George was surprised at his naivety. He'd been locked in a dungeon for close to 16 months and he was now just getting it. She'd asked him if he were an enemy once before, but he hadn't clued in till this minute. He thought this was about money; he'd also considered that he might be a barter item for a prisoner exchange. However, this made more sense; they thought he was a spy.

"Lamia – I can tell you that is absolutely not true. I am a shipping company executive. I have never been a spy."

"Hmm… have you been to Israel?"

"No."

"Do you know Israelis?"

George thought for a minute; he wasn't sure if he'd ever talked to any of the Israelis who worked with Trans-ship.

"I don't think so, I talk to all sorts of people in my job; it's possible, but I don't think so."

"You know anyone who work with army, you know, secret army?"

"Military intelligence? No," then George caught himself; no, that wasn't completely true. Darius had once confided in him that he'd worked with US and British intelligence, but that was in support of the Mujahedeen. George didn't think it relevant, but decided to talk about it anyway.

"Well, I had one friend; he was in the Soviet army, I'm pretty sure he collaborated with US or British intelligence, but it was during the Afghanistan war and it was to help the Mujahedeen."

Lamia let out a sigh, "I don't know, George. It doesn't make sense. I just doesn't understand. I don't understand."

Tanja was there exactly 10 minutes early. She arrived early intentionally; she might be able to sneak 40 minutes out of him, instead of 30. She knocked; he opened the door; it looked like he'd just shaved and smelled of a cologne; he was wearing newer clothes that were slightly more stylish. She thought him to be an odd duck; maybe he dresses up when he goes out; seems odd to do it before a kid's tutorial; maybe he's going out in the old town later. Anyway, it gave her an opening to start buttering him up; she needed to loosen his tongue a little.

"You look sharp, Mantas. You must be meeting a very lucky lady." Mantas blushed; damnit she'd pushed it too far with that last stupid comment.

"No, I'm afraid you're the lucky lady. I just got cleaned up a bit." Phew, she thought, he made a joke, she'll get there.

"Shall we go?"

The afternoon had turned overcast and it had started to spit rain. Drat; they would likely have to walk faster; she was going to lose her window.

They began the walk from the Soviet flat block. Tanja wanted to jump right to the point.

"It looks like you've had tremendous success in special needs – especially for such a young man. I'm curious, what kind of techniques have you been using with Vlad?"

At that moment, the skies opened. The rain poured so heavily that the two had to escape under the covering of the front door of one of the Soviet flat blocks. It was just as Mantas had hoped; his prayer had been answered.

"Tanja, I brought an umbrella. Please share it with me." In Eastern Europe, it wasn't an unusual offer to share an umbrella with a member of the opposite sex; it was more important to stay dry. The woman was expected to put her arm around the man's arm so they could both be protected from the elements.

"Yes, of course." Tanja was annoyed; her window was going to be lost; it was all going to be about dashing through the rain.

She placed her arm around his and moved closer to him as he held the umbrella above their heads. It was the first time that he could really smell her. He also felt her body which was nonchalantly bouncing so close to his own as they ran through the rain on the way to Vlad's tutorial.

It was a frustrating walk for Tanja; there had been no time to talk about learning strategies. She'd arrived soaking wet as well. As Vlad sat in the sitting room with Mantas, Tanja escaped to her bedroom to put on clean clothes. Tadas was there and had been minding the girls.

Mantas looked around at that apartment. She must have been married to a mafia man; those are the only types able to afford this type of luxury, but it added to the mystique. Tanja had insisted that he give her his wet clothes and now he sat beside Vlad in a pink fuzzy robe, but it didn't matter, just the memory of her wet body close to his was worth it. It was hard to focus on poor Vlad at times, but he was doing well. The money section was going really well; Mantas now asked him to go through the exercises; simple addition and subtraction would soon be the main focus and then telling time.

The rain was letting up as the lesson neared its end and then Tanja appeared.

"I am so sorry, Mantas, your clothes are out of the dryer now; I put them in the bathroom for you. I'll pay for a taxi back."

"No need, the rain has stopped; I'm going to walk."

"Sure, it's turning into a nicer evening; would it be ok if I came along?"

Mantas wondered if the fantasy was coming to life. She seemed interested in him, always giving compliments and finding reasons to be with him.

Tanja was hoping the rain wouldn't start again; she needed to bilk him for information; she was hoping to give it one more chance. She'd pre-cleared it with Tadas; he was willing to stay and mind the family.

The two started by walking along the Danė river; it was still drizzling; evening was setting in; it was slowly getting dark and the electric lights had turned on and illuminated the pathway next to the river.

"So, tell me, Tanja, where did you live overseas?"

Tanja needed to make the chit chat, but didn't want to prolong it. She gave an overview of her history and a quick reference to Seattle and London, then she quickly changed subjects.

"It is such a fascinating field, special needs education, I'm really impressed by you, Mantas. Tell me, what kind of approaches do you prefer?"

If there was a doubt in Mantas' mind, it was beginning to falter. She kept making compliments and getting him to talk about himself. He couldn't believe it; they hardly knew each other and yet there appeared to be a spark.

Mantas started talking about the various strategies he deployed; it was his passion, so it was easy to talk about it. He then talked about his university work and the various academic approaches he'd tried to deploy, but experience had weaned out a number of them. Vlad was responding to practical applications; Mantas had started with money and would work backward to simple addition and subtraction; it was the opposite approach deployed for neuro typicals. Mantas noted that his real love was child psychology. He was torn about whether to enter a master's degree in teaching or shift to psychology; the first was more practical, the latter was his true passion.

He couldn't believe it; she was trying to appear genuinely interested in the subject. She kept leaning in to listen and often interrupted with questions.

As they approached the flat, Mantas decided to try his luck.

"Care for a drink before you go home?"

It was cold and Tanja had water in her ear; she kept having to lean in to hear him. She needed to use a washroom to clear it; it would be vulgar to stick her finger in her ear in front of the tutor.

"Yes, that would be very nice, thanks Mantas."

When they arrived in the flat, Tanja excused herself to use the washroom. She stuck her little finger in her ear and tried to loosen the water, then she turned her head to the left and repeated the motion; thank goodness, she was able to drain it. She felt a bit odd that it had taken so long. She took a brush out of her bag; her hair was a mess from the drizzling rain.

Mantas was busy; he had put on some soft music; he turned on only a single desk lamp. It was dark now and he faced the beam of that single lamp toward the wall and closed the curtain. He had a decent bottle of single malt scotch that one of his student's parents had bought him and he had beautiful crystal glasses to serve it. It was odd that it was taking her so long, what was she doing in there?

As she came out of the washroom, Mantas understood the delay. She was trying to make herself look beautiful; she had combed that beautiful blonde hair. Mantas had arranged a small plate of peanuts and two crystal glasses with the bottle of scotch on the coffee table. He beckoned Tanja to sit beside him on the sofa.

Tanja sat and looked at the bottle. It brought back fond memories; it was one of George's favourites. It wasn't anything she particularly enjoyed and thought it a little odd to offer whisky to a woman, but it would warm her up and the smell would remind her of him.

"This is a single malt scotch from the UK. Would you like to try it?"

"Oh yes, sounds lovely, Mantas, you are a very good host."

Mantas poured two glasses and they clinked those glasses. They both took a sip of the whisky. He looked at her.

"Any other questions, Tanja?"

"Yes, we haven't talked about scheduling for the next week. I was hoping to see you more often. Would you have availability tomorrow, same time?"

"For you, of course."

Tanja liked the answer; the lobbying and sweet-talking were finally paying off.

"Would you like another?" asked Mantas.

Tanja was embarrassed. In her excitement about getting the concession and in her cold state, she'd downed her first drink.

"Just one more, thank you. So, tell me, of all the books on that wall, what is your favourite?"

There could be no doubt now; she was asking about his favourite things. He went and retrieved a photo book of local landscapes and the Baltic Sea. Mantas wasn't particularly interested in that book, but had noticed similar paintings at her place.

She looked through the book, "I like these as well; I bought some similar paintings a few months back; they're beautiful; you have good taste."

And then it happened, Mantas knew the signs were there. He leaned in and very gently kissed her on the lips; then he kissed her very softly again.

Tanja was shocked and wasn't sure what was going on. Did he just kiss her? Yet, it was unexpected, but also felt strangely nice. She realized that no one had kissed her in well over a year. She didn't want him to kiss her and yet she wanted to be kissed. She was surprised at her decision – she kissed him back. He then kissed her more passionately; she kissed him more passionately. He then teased his tongue with hers; it aroused her. The kissing session lasted about 2 minutes; Tanja had to give him a gentle push. She needed a scotch break. She took a drink; ok, this had been a mistake, but he was also Vlad's tutor.

"Mantas, thank you for a lovely evening." She stood up and he ran to get her coat. He helped her put it on and then the two faced each other.

"See you tomorrow?"

"Yes, looking forward to it." He then leaned in and gave her one final kiss goodnight while he clasped both of her hands with his own hands.

When Tanja returned to the apartment that evening, she was filled with a sense of shame. At first, she even had trouble looking Tadas in the eye when he asked how it had gone. The one man she trusted in this world and now she couldn't face him. She looked down; Maria was busy charging around the place pretending to be a princess slaying dragons and knocking stuff over in the process. She was even too ashamed to tell her off; how did she let this happen? She decided to keep her head down as she made her way to the sitting room; she finally looked up, but it was completely the wrong place to look up – her eyes looked directly at her wedding photo on the mantle. Now, she felt a new sense of shame; she'd betrayed the father of her children; she'd betrayed her children; she'd betrayed herself.

Then, her shame suddenly turned to anger. How could he do that to her? He was a freak and now he was going around assaulting women. No, that wasn't completely right; she hadn't said no. He had certainly crossed a professional boundary; he was a teacher – it wasn't right; well, he was a student tutoring her brother. He shouldn't have done that. He had no right; he had no right to make her feel ashamed.

That night, she tossed and turned as she tried to sleep, she needed to figure out a way to tell him not to do it again, while still ensuring that Vlad was not impacted by her decision. The whole incident had also stirred up strange feelings that she hadn't experienced before. She had to admit that she'd enjoyed being kissed, just not by him. She hadn't thought about it before, but maybe it was time to move on. George would have wanted it; maybe she should find someone to share her life with; someone who could hold her, someone to be a father to Maria and Edita. She was a single mother of two little girls and caregiver to her brother; maybe she owed herself some type of affection.

CHAPTER 6

Strange Liaisons

The next day, Tanja oscillated on the best approach for the Mantas issue. At first, she thought it would be wise for her not to be there when he was around; she wouldn't be there for the next several tutorials and then it would fade away. Then, she realized that she was running from the problem. Beyond the upcoming tutorial today, she hadn't negotiated a schedule for the remainder of Vlad's recuperation period with Mantas; she certainly didn't want Vlad lying on the sofa for the next week without any work to do; he could become quite difficult when he had nothing to do. So, she decided on a different plan. She would be there when Mantas arrived, she would be professional and polite; she would just let him in and hand him over to Vlad; she would have a quick conversation at the end of the tutorial to establish a follow-up session and then see him out. That would do nicely.

At tutorial time, she tensed when she heard the buzzer from the ground floor. She pressed the entry button, but left the front door to the apartment closed. She was going to prepare Vlad and ensure he was ready in the sitting room. Maria was dressed in a princess costume and was running around with her sword; Tanja wouldn't remove her to the master bedroom until the tutorial had commenced; Maria would be a diversion for any unwanted conversation.

Finally, there was a knock at the door. Tanja took a deep breath before opening that door. Then she opened it and looked at Mantas. She looked at him in horror.

He was carrying a large and quite beautiful bouquet of flowers. Tanja blushed and gave a contorted smile to mask her emotions; this wasn't going to be as easy as she'd hoped. She was trying to think of something to say, but couldn't think of anything that would put an end to it.

"These are for you," said Mantas. Mantas was pleased; she blushed when he gave them to her.

Tanja said nothing for a moment; she just nodded and then said thank you and ushered him into the sitting room. She then grabbed the princess's hand and removed her to the master bedroom where Tadas and Edita were practising walking. As Tanja closed the door behind her, she looked at Edita who was walking quite proudly with Tadas around the bed. She sometimes lost balance and needed to grab the bed, but she looked so overjoyed. It should have been a happy moment, but Tanja stood there with her bouquet of flowers and felt so upset and angry.

Tanja tried to entertain Maria by playing castle, but Maria got too excited and made too much noise. Vlad had trouble concentrating at the best of times and didn't need the distraction of a toddler niece trying to slay dragons in the next room. Tanja had ensured that one of Maria's favourite books was in the bedroom just for this eventuality. She retrieved it from the bedside table. She was about to invite her to hop on the bed when Maria took flight. Maria opened the door and ran into the sitting room. Tanja scurried after her; Maria ran right toward the tutorial and, as she passed close to Mantas, he stood up and grabbed the toddler with both hands and, with a big grin on his face, he gave Maria a swing through the air. Maria was impressed; she stood in front of the tutor with a big smile which seemed to implore another swing. Mantas duly obliged and gave her another swing through the air.

"You're quite a little princess." Maria didn't say anything but was clearly pleased with the compliment.

Tanja thought to herself – darn it; this means I need to talk to him.

"I apologize gentlemen; Vlad's niece is sometimes enthusiastic."

"No trouble at all," replied Mantas. "I love children."

Oh brother, Tanja thought; now, he's taken the opportunity to show his paternal side; I just want this to be over.

Tanja smiled and grabbed the toddler and began reeling her back to the master bedroom. After closing the door, Tanja tried to read the book to

Maria; it was a gong show. Edita wanted Tanja's attention as well and she was no longer satisfied walking round the bed with Tadas. Tanja looked toward the flowers, which just sat wrapped in the original cellophane on her dresser.

"Tadas – would it be ok for you to watch the kids for a bit? I just want to clarify a few things with Mantas after the tutorial."

"Of course, my dear."

Tadas was always so accommodating. She needed to scrub her original plan; Mantas wasn't going to get it. Tanja had unexpectedly smiled when receiving the flowers and she didn't want him to think that she'd orchestrated the disruption with Maria; she wasn't giving him the opportunity to prove his paternal proclivity. She would have to do what she absolutely did not want to do; she would have to be very clear and set him straight in person – that was the right thing to do. She would be diplomatic; she would just say that she was not looking for a relationship at the moment and leave it at that. It would be professional and polite.

Tanja waited for the session time to be over. Originally, she was going to interrupt five minutes before the end, but now she decided to just wait; she would walk Mantas part way home and they could cover the timing of the next session first, then she would move onto the conversation where she would dump him. If it all failed, at least Vlad would get those five minutes of tutorial time.

At session end time, Tanja appeared and closed the bedroom door behind her, which was a fruitless thing to do. Maria immediately opened it and dashed past her. Vlad and Mantas were still finishing their work, but Maria didn't care, she ran right toward the tutor, who complied with her apparent wish. Mantas grabbed her and did the swing through the air. Tanja was about to shoo her off to close the situation; to get him out of there, so she could talk to him. Then, Edita started shouting in the master bedroom. It was apparent that Edita felt that she was being left out of the action. Tadas then appeared with Edita holding his hand and wobbling toward the group. Any chance of professionally evicting the tutor was now lost; she had let him see the chaos which was the life of Tanja.

"Mantas – maybe it would be better if we discussed the next session outside. Would that be ok?"

"Of course." Mantas gave her a knowing smile. It was creepy.

Mantas said a quick goodbye to Vlad, shook Tadas' hand, gave Maria a final swing and patted Edita on the head. He then grabbed his coat and put on his shoes and waited by the door. It was as if he were waiting for his date and he'd gotten ready too quickly. Tanja decided to scurry; she put on her heavy winter coat; she wanted this over with.

Tanja closed the apartment door and Mantas began the descent down the stairs with Tanja following. He seemed to still be in a hurry; he opened the ground floor door and kept walking. Tanja hadn't said anything about walking him home, although she had intended to walk him part way, but he seemed to have that as an assumption.

Tanja got annoyed with that assumption. She just stopped at the front entrance; Mantas looked round and seemed to get the hint. She wanted to talk at the front door, he turned and walked the few paces back toward her.

"Mantas – would you have availability for tomorrow? Could we do the same time?"

"Absolutely, you're my priority; I'll be here."

"Um, thank you, just also; I wanted to talk, well about, last night. I'm sorry I may have given you the wrong impression; I am not looking for a relationship."

Mantas knew right away what this conversation was all about. He'd studied the theories of regret in psychology at university; this one was commonly referred to as 'buyer's remorse.' He'd also studied oppositional defiance strategies when working with Down Syndrome children; he thought to himself; yes, he should try it.

"Oh, that's fine Tanja, I am not looking for a relationship either."

Tanja thought that an odd comment. He'd kissed her the day before and brought her flowers today.

"Ok, I'm glad you understand. You're a great guy; just I am not ready for anything right now."

"I completely understand; would you like to walk a little?"

Tanja was in two minds about the thing; she'd delivered the message that she'd rehearsed, but the response had been a surprise. Maybe, he was taking her seriously or maybe he really didn't want her. She had to make sure he got it, she would walk for just a few minutes so that it was clear and there were no hard feelings and that it was over.

It was a very cold evening, but Tanja had her warm coat; it was nice to be out of the looney bin for a few minutes. She nodded her head 'yes' to the invitation and began to walk.

"Again, I'm sorry, Mantas, I hope you understand. I didn't intend to lead you on. I'm sorry."

Yes, he thought to himself, it was very typical buyer's remorse.

"Oh, you didn't, Tanja, it was my fault. I suspected that someone as beautiful and clever as yourself wouldn't be interested in someone like me – I'm a nerd really."

Tanja grimaced at the word; it was exactly what she thought. Then Mantas continued.

"I know you're very worldly; I know you lost your husband; I thought you were just looking for some physical comfort. I know you must be lonely; when I say these words, I really do feel guilty; I guess I was taking advantage of you. I hope you will forgive *me*."

Tanja kept walking; she went quiet for a minute. That's exactly how she felt when it happened; that's why she hadn't stopped him.

Tanja continued. "That's ok; I am responsible for my own actions; I shouldn't have let it happen."

Mantas paused for a second before continuing.

"You're kind of a superwoman, aren't you Tanja? I've never met anyone like you. You're a single mother; you're absolutely devoted to your brother – running around the city finding him tutors and making sure he has an education. I never had anyone speak to me the way you did about him; most people are just happy that their special people get any kind of education, but you, you were so passionate about it. You know what you want. You're tough."

Tanja blushed. With the possible exception of her mother-in-law, no one had ever said anything quite like that to her. She worked so hard for all those children, but no one recognized it. He is a bit of a freak, but he is perceptive.

Mantas checked Tanja's face; she was registering; she was hanging on his words; he would continue. He laughed before he said his next words.

"I didn't think someone like you would be interested in someone like me; we're from two very different worlds. I just thought; well, I thought…" He intentionally went quiet.

"Yes?"

"Well, it's just, when I, when I tried to kiss you, you seemed to reciprocate; you seemed to enjoy it. I… I… oh, it's silly."

"No, no, what, what were you going to say?"

Mantas looked at her; it really did seem to be working. The tables really did seem to be turning.

"Well, I had this impression; you're kind of a modern type of woman and you've lived in the West. I thought maybe you'd enjoyed it and maybe that's what you wanted – some type of physical reassurance. You seem like the type of person that gets what she wants. Again, I'm sorry, Tanja."

They were more than halfway to Mantas' flat now. Tanja looked down at her watch and thought about poor Tadas. She was exploiting him these days, but she wanted to keep walking. Mantas was right in many ways – she had enjoyed the kiss and it was reassuring; she hadn't been touched romantically by anyone since July of 1997. She was a modern woman; she'd just made a controversial decision to move her whole family to a backward country to give them a better life and it was working. She just walked in silence and Mantas stayed silent for close to a minute before he interjected again.

"Anyway, I know you have other things on your mind. Did you want an update on Vlad's session today? It went well."

Tanja replied that she would be interested and Mantas began a long overview of how the money exercises were going; they had used part of the session to start work on simple addition. This was going to be harder; Vlad seemed to respond to practical applications, but he had a few techniques that he thought might work.

Tanja wasn't really listening; she was just replaying the earlier comments in her mind. She was lonely and she wasn't a little girl anymore and she had enjoyed someone touching her; she wished it wouldn't have been him, but he wasn't actually a terrible choice. He'd be a terrible choice for any type of relationship, but it would be nice to have someone to talk to who wasn't a child or Tadas or Luce – someone her own age. He was really smart and great with Vlad; he had seemed pompous and arrogant, but he was actually quite kind and said all those nice things about her.

About 10 metres from the broken door to Mantas' building, Mantas turned to her and extended his hand for a handshake. He continued.

"Anyway, Tanja, again, apologies, I'm really hoping we can be friends. You're a very special person."

Tanja accepted his handshake, but didn't release right away. She then gently moved toward him and gave him a soft kiss on the lips before saying 'goodnight' and beginning the journey home.

As she walked home that night, she thought about the situation and she began to smile. In an odd way, she felt slightly triumphant, even empowered. She was taking control of her life, she had found someone to talk to, someone who interested her. It wasn't going to be a romantic thing, but she had felt lonely and her self esteem was low, now she felt so much more confident; she had someone who liked her. She must have surprised him in the end; he looked shocked. Tanja thought to herself – I am a young single European woman; I should have men in my life and he could be a friend who could maybe offer some physical support. It would be fine; it would be fine for now. In fact, she felt happy; it was the first time she'd felt happy in a couple of days.

Mantas opened the door to his tiny flat. It had worked. It was very typical buyer's remorse. He would have to brush up on his reading on overcoming oppositional defiance. In fact, he would find that book tonight and review it.

It was early December and George's mood had improved a little. It was all about access to books; it had been a difficult thing at first to get access to books and there seemed to need to be a reason to have any particular book, but Lamia had negotiated with the father. She claimed that the teacher seemed a bit depressed at some of the lessons and could he give George more books.

In the end, Lamia's father had agreed as he saw no harm in it. However, there were to be rules. When he brought his first book after A Christmas Carol, he signalled to George to surrender a book. He would only be allowed five books at any time. George surrendered David Copperfield, he kept the Koran and London and the New Testament and A Christmas Carol. Every time, he was finished with a book; he left it beside his tray; the man in black would then take it away along with the dirty dishes and plastic cutlery. A little while later, another book would be delivered along with another meal. Mostly, the books were used books, but George felt like they were gifts from heaven. He was able to cut down on some of the pacing. At one of their private chats, George asked Lamia if there was a way to ask about pen and paper, but Lamia thought that a poor idea – pens could be used for two things – communication and as a weapon and neither would sit well with father.

When he heard Lamia that morning, he sat upright. He sensed that his sombre mood was also affecting her; he could not risk jeopardizing those secret liaisons. She was his only friend in the world and he needed to pretend to be happy. As he was determined to demonstrate a happy disposition that day, he actually felt happier while pretending to be happy, so it was a winning situation.

He put his hands out to touch her. This was now their tradition. She would hold his hand and place her other hand over the top of the two clutching hands.

"How's your day, George?"

"Very well; the new book club that you arranged for me is working out; I feel much better; I'm grateful. What have you been up to?"

"All good. I watched BBC news again last night. I am understanding more and more; you are a good teacher."

George blushed, "You are a great student."

Lamia paused a moment before asking her question, "George... why they never talk about you on the news?"

"I guess I'm not important enough."

"They talk about the Israeli captives sometime."

George didn't quite know how to respond; he just looked blankly toward her.

"George – you told me you born in America. Are you a *real* American?"

"Well, I was born there; I grew up there; I think I am."

"I mean; do you have a USA passport?"

"I do."

"My father always talks about you as British." She paused a minute. "Maybe we should talk about you being an American at our next lesson. I can then explain it to him later."

George looked at her. "I think that's a bad idea; if they lock up a Briton indefinitely; I can't imagine what they'd do to an American."

"You might be right." Lamia looked down toward the ground and seemed to be thinking about something.

George continued, "Why did you make that suggestion?"

"It's just that my father won't call them. Maybe, if he had some new information; maybe he would call them. It might be an excuse to call them."

George nodded his head, "Let me think about it; it might not be a bad idea."

"George... has anyone ever said Hezbollah to you – I mean anyone except me?"

"No." It seemed like an odd question; she had clearly thought about the questions she was asking this morning.

"So, when you were first taken, you said it was a couple of men, then there was a crazy man, then some other men, then my father; if I didn't say to you, would you know that you were with Hezbollah?"

"Well, I became suspicious when I got beaten by the crazy man and, more so, when I saw this professional cell, then even more so when I got a copy of the Koran from your father."

"I see... Have you ever hear of Al Qaeda?"

"No, what is it?"

"Well, you are not in the news, but they are on the news always. They issue a hunt of Americans. They attack US embassies." Lamia paused and now seemed so deep in thought that George felt he should not interrupt; she was clearly planning something. Then she began to talk again.

"Imagine if the crazy man; imagine if he said something about Al Qaeda."

"He didn't."

"No, no, imagine that he told you that you were a prisoner of Al Qaeda and that is what you think now; that you are prisoner of Al Qaeda."

"What difference would that make?"

"If my father think there was a connection between Al Qaeda and you; maybe he would call. Also, if they thought you thought you were Al Qaeda prisoner, maybe it would be more easy to let you go."

George had trouble following the plan; he had worked on large strategic shipping initiatives but this was confusing. Lamia went through it again; as she understood it, Al Qaeda was a bunch of people from different places, but mostly Saudi Arabia, but were now based in Afghanistan. They were a Sunni Muslim group; Hezbollah was Shia, like her. With all the recent events, the father might call them – if he believed there could be a connection.

In the end, George agreed to the plot. What choice did he have? There seemed to be risk, but he was very likely to die anyway; this might just expedite the inevitable.

The two agreed a plan - at the next lesson, George would talk about his life story – well bits of it anyway. He would talk about being an American. He would tell her that he knew he was being held by Al Qaeda; he knew that because the crazy man had told him. He was to try to use the word 'Al Qaeda' frequently. That way, Lamia might not even need to raise the question; the father might ask her about it after the lesson.

By early December, Tanja could only describe the relationship that had developed between her and Mantas as unusual. They were from very different worlds, but she enjoyed hearing about child psychology and special needs education. That is mostly what they talked about. Tadas would allow Tanja a 'break' for a few hours for a couple of evenings a week and she would go over to Mantas' flat. Their physical relationship was limited to kissing and cuddling. Tanja wasn't interested in anything more. At one point, she was sitting on his sofa; he had his arm around her waist and they began to kiss. He tried to work that hand up to her breast, but Tanja gently pushed it away and he seemed okay with that. Mostly, she liked the cuddling; he would put on soft music and put his arms around her and he would stroke her hair. It had been a long time since anyone had done that. He would also shower her with compliments – she was an incredible mother and devoted sister; she was brave and beautiful. Tanja wasn't sure if anyone had ever done that.

By early December, a couple of things became clear to Mantas. The first thing was that he was deeply in love; he couldn't have imagined being with a woman like that; she was incredibly beautiful; she was devoted to her family; she was so filled with life. He could see why the American millionaire had fallen for her; what man wouldn't? She was the complete package of beauty and kindness. The other thing that was now painfully clear to Mantas was that her opinion of him was quite different.

He knew now that he had misinterpreted those early signals. During that first kiss, she had genuinely come to his place to discuss Vlad's education. She'd told him that one day with a smile. She wouldn't hold his hand in public and hadn't discussed their relationship with anyone. He was not allowed to touch her intimately; this seemed a relationship she wanted to have in order to rebuild her self confidence. He was a dirty little secret and would likely be kicked to the curb when the next foreign millionaire came along. Unless he could come up with a plan.

It was in his flat on that December evening when he decided to at least test run his plan. He held her in his arms and stroked her hair; he knew she liked that.

"Tanja? Do you find me attractive?"

"Of course I do, why would you ask that? Your dress sense needs a little work," she laughed with her head on his chest, "I could help you with that if you like."

Mantas paused. "Tanja – if I did that, would you hold my hand in public?"

"Mantas – don't spoil the mood; I have two little girls at home, I don't want the town discussing us. It's only our business. Besides, it's more romantic this way."

Mantas went very quiet, then continued.

"So, you don't want people to know about us, but you find me attractive?"

"Yes."

"So, can I ask you something? I find you incredibly attractive. After my confusion over our first kiss, I don't want to make any assumptions. I know you lost your husband. It's been almost two years. If we can't display this relationship outside this flat; can we, at least, be intimate? I mean would you at least consider it? I just feel that you don't want to really be with me."

Tanja looked up and looked at his face. He looked sad.

"Oh, silly boy; you're very attractive to me, but I'm just not ready; it's too soon for me."

"I understand. I can wait for you, but will you think about it?"

"I will, but I think you can do better than me. You should find a college girl; someone who is more clever than me."

Mantas went back to stroking Tanja's hair. He had put the idea forward; that's all he'd wanted to do. He would now need to keep gently working on it. It would take weeks or months; he needed to be patient.

A week had passed and Mantas kept raising the subject but also reassured her that he understood the situation; she would know when she would be ready. He would resign himself to the cuddling and listening to her talk about her day. In many ways, it was just nice to be with her, to smell her; even if he knew he'd have his work cut out to keep her long term. He would just have to continue his charm offensive, continue to woo her.

He decided that he would at least try to gain a concession around the 'being seen in public' rule. He invited her to one of the best restaurants in Klaipėda to celebrate Christmas a little early. He was surprised when she said yes. It seemed to bend the public rule, but then Tanja explained that having dinner together was not the same as showing affection in public. It would have to do; it seemed to represent at least some progress in the relationship.

Mantas had dressed nicely for the dinner. He'd bought some new clothes; Tanja had recommended colours and type of clothes he might look good in and he tried to use that advice when he'd purchased them. He had cleaned the flat in the hope she would return to it before going home. He had strategically chosen the restaurant. It was close to his place. It was tricky to get a reservation; it was one of the few good restaurants in the area; the other good restaurants in Klaipėda were all in the old town.

They met outside the French restaurant at 7. Mantas arrived 10 minutes early; he didn't want to keep her waiting. When she arrived, he was not disappointed. After entering the restaurant, she removed her long winter coat to expose the most beautiful dress he had ever seen – or maybe it was so beautiful because it was on her. It was a black dress, a simple affair with a plunging neckline that just hinted at the outline of her breasts; it was cut high at the back. The dress bottom was also cut low; it wasn't a mini skirt but was cut a few centimetres above the knee, enough to expose a pair of beautiful legs. She also wore a simple silver necklace which looked so elegant with the dress. Tanja also carried a plastic bag along with her handbag. After giving the maître d' her coat, she removed a pair of high heel shoes from the bag; she removed her heavy winter boots and exchanged them for those shoes, she then gave the bag to the maître d'.

"I have to admit, Mantas, I'm a little excited. I can't even remember the last time I was in a restaurant. We haven't been to one since we moved her; too much work with that tribe. It was nice to dress up."

"You look stunning," said Mantas.

Tanja blushed, "You don't look bad yourself; I see you took my advice."

Dinner was an exquisite affair. With the clothes, it was going to cost him months of tutoring, but he didn't care tonight.

Tanja looked at the menu. She looked at the prices and suddenly felt a little uneasy. Maybe, she should pay for the dinner; this was going to cost. No, that could offend him. She'd just find something cheap on the menu, it was just nice to be out amongst adult company; that was the main thing.

"Tanja – can I order for us?"

Tanja didn't like the suggestion; she could order for herself, but Mantas detected the hesitation and continued.

"It's just that this is a kind of anniversary for us. It's been a month since our first kiss. I think I've learned a lot about you and, if I let you order, you will worry about the bill and order something inexpensive. I want to make this a treat for you; you don't get out; you have your girls and Vlad. I want to treat you tonight."

Tanja blushed; it was a beautiful argument; he had a very kind side that Tanja liked. She conceded to the request.

She was surprised at what he ordered. For a starter, he ordered two shots of vodka and a dozen raw Baltic oysters. It was a surprise because of the expense, it was also a surprise as it was one of George's favourites, but she wouldn't bring up the latter.

When the oysters were served, Tanja interjected. "Mantas – I'm just happy to be here with you. This is going to cost you a bomb; please please consider something more modest for the main course; or let me pay, I've worked in the West."

Mantas told her that he was insulted by the offer and that he didn't want her to talk about money anymore.

The two enjoyed the oysters with fresh horseradish. The vodka was served in intricate little shot glasses. Tanja sipped at hers, but Mantas encouraged her to take it quickly with the oysters as it improved the effect. She tried that approach and agreed it did work better. He then ordered another round.

After oysters, Mantas had arranged braised pork with pearl onions and grapes and side potatoes. It was an unusual dish for Lithuania. He ordered a bottle of French Beaujolais to accompany. Tanja was feeling a bit giddy; Mantas didn't usually have much of a sense of humour, but tonight, he seemed quite funny and charming. She also thought she should be careful with the drinks. She wasn't much of a drinker; she'd recently gone over a year without almost any drink while nursing Edita, and she'd only had a couple here and there since that time. But, tonight seemed like a night to celebrate. The food was wonderful, the drinks were going down nicely and she had someone to laugh with - and it wasn't regarding the latest escapades of a certain two-and-a-half-year-old princess.

Crème brûlée was for dessert with coffee and cognac. Tanja just wanted coffee, but Mantas insisted.

It was a magical evening; Tanja detected that she was slurring her speech a little. It was close to Christmas and now she was starting to get into the spirit of it. It had been a tough year, very tough, but it was almost over and next year would be better.

As they were leaving the restaurant, Tanja had a little difficulty removing the high heels. She was a little embarrassed about it, but Mantas helped her to a nearby bench where people normally waited for tables and helped her remove them. When the shoes were off, Tanja leaned forward and kissed him. "Thank you, this was magical." It was the first time that Tanja had ever shown any affection in public toward him.

She put on her boots; then her big coat and placed her heels in the plastic bag. It took longer for Tanja than for Mantas, but she eventually got completely dressed for the cold.

And it was very cold as they stepped outside, Tanja put her arm around his arm so she wouldn't lose balance. There was a dusting of snow on the steps. The two walked down the steps arm in arm together.

They walked across the road from the restaurant. There was a little park there on a hill. The couple could see the lights of the old town in the distance. Facing her, Mantas hugged her, then looked down at her blue eyes. She giggled a little more then reached up and gave him a kiss on his lips. He hugged her some more and danced with her a little while he serenaded her with 'lady in red' except he changed the chorus to 'lady in black.' Tanja was moving her body with him and giggling; it was like the weight of the world didn't exist that evening. It was fun; fun to be free and dancing in a park in winter boots at night.

"Want to come over for a nightcap?" he asked.

"I am sorry to say I will come over but definitely not for a nightcap. I should have peed before leaving the restaurant." She snorted with laughter.

They ran quickly toward the flat. Tanja was relieved, in so many ways, to get there. She ran right to the WC to relieve the pain that was in her bladder. In the meantime, Mantas went about the usual arrangements – soft music, lamp pointed toward the wall.

Tanja was still giggly when she appeared from the washroom. Mantas was expecting her to sit beside him on the sofa, but he was in for a surprise. Facing him, she climbed onto his lap and knelt with his legs between her knees and she began kissing him. He could feel her body gently moving as she kissed him; she was likely unaware but some of those movements were directly touching his groin area. He could begin to feel himself becoming extended. It was going to be frustrating after she left.

She kept kissing him and stroking his cheek and moving around. She stopped occasionally to look at him and say something funny. Then, at one point, she looked confused and announced "I'm sitting on something." She used her hand to search around for the item that was poking her. Then, she put her hand on it.

Tanja looked at him and began to laugh. "I'm sorry, Mantas. My, that's a surprise. Did I do that?" Mantas didn't know how to respond. He just nodded his head.

To his surprise, she now started slowly stroking his trousered groin area and seemed to think that his erection was worthy of some humour, but the stroking wasn't funny to Mantas. He knew she was going to end it there; it was frustrating. He was in for a surprise.

She continued rubbing the area and then noted, "You know something, Mantas. That was a very nice Christmas dinner present. Would you like a present? It won't be quite as expensive, but I think you deserve it." Mantas wasn't completely sure what she meant until she started unzipping the fly on his trousers. She giggled some more and looked at him in the eyes. He looked confused; she liked that. She kissed him passionately. She then slithered onto the floor; undid the button on his trousers and pulled them down to his ankles and then off completely. She threw the trousers onto the desk chair and laughed when she did it.

She then looked at him in the eyes. She liked it; she felt like she had control of the situation; he was just waiting there with anticipation. She would make him wait. With his underwear in place, she massaged his erection over the undergarment; she stroked it softly, then a little more firmly. All the while, she stared at him in the eyes. He felt uncomfortable about the staring, but wondered if she was going to stop. No, she couldn't stop now; why would she go this far?

Tanja gently tugged at the waistband of his underwear. She tugged only enough to expose the top of his waiting member. She took her finger and gently stroked the tip. Mantas thought how different it felt when it was skin to skin. Mantas felt like he was on fire; he yearned for her to touch him with those beautiful lips. She must have read that thought as she briefly raised herself off the floor and kissed him on his lips, but that's not exactly what he'd hoped for.

She returned to her kneeling position and completely removed the underwear. It was thrown at the same chair and with the same laugh. She continued stroking him, but now moved her hand a little faster and then wrapped her whole hand round while she stroked it. He closed his eyes; he thought this might be the closest he would ever get to heaven. He was wrong.

While his eyes were closed, she very gently kissed the tip. She then repeated the process a few times, but the kisses were a little firmer each time and she worked her way down and then back up. She then started to tease him by gently licking it. Then, she opened her mouth and slowly enveloped him. Mantas could only describe those next few minutes of fellatio as the most erotic few minutes of his life. At times, he had to think about child psychology and oppositional strategies so as not to explode – after a few minutes, he realized that he shouldn't worry about climaxing, this was as far as things were going to get. And then, he had an idea.

He pulled her away from her task and pulled her closer to him. He kissed her passionately; he wanted to see how passionately she responded and she did respond. He slipped his hand under one of the strings that held up her dress. It fell down her shoulder. Then, he attempted the same manoeuvre with the other strap and it fell. He then grabbed her and kissed her again and fidgeted at the back of the dress – he was frustrated that he couldn't find the zipper and then he did; he gently unzipped it. He did it slowly and deliberately, if she wanted to object, she could object. She didn't object.

He tugged gently at the dress and it fell to the floor. He continued to kiss her; now, he was determined to arouse her. He kissed her neck – very gently and then slightly more roughly, then he took his hand and gently caressed her breast just over her bra. That seemed to really arouse her, she moaned a little. It seemed to be permission. He started the process of removing her bra using the same strategy as he'd deployed with her dress. Once complete, he tossed it onto the desk chair where his own clothes had been tossed. To his surprise, she continued to kiss him and pulled at the buttons of his shirt then took off his undershirt; all were tossed onto the chair.

Wearing only her panties, she then climbed on top of him facing him; the same position she'd had at the beginning of the evening. It was his first opportunity to look at her without her top. She was magnificent; like a model. Her breasts and figure were like something he had never seen before. She continued kissing him and gyrating on top of him. He wondered how far this was going to go. He was pretty sure it would come to an end soon. After the 'I'll think about it' conversation, he'd gone to the chemist shop and bought protection on the off chance, but he was never expecting to use it tonight. She kept kissing him and seemed to be satisfying herself by gyrating on top of him and moaning. Mantas wanted to see where this evening was going to go.

He stopped kissing her and asked, "Tanja – would you like your present now?"

She giggled, "What is it?"

He pushed her off him and lay her on the sofa. He started by climbing on top of her and kissing her on the lips; he then worked down and kissed her breasts. This made her moan again and move around under him. He got down on his knees and very gently tugged at her panties and removed them. She giggled when he did it.

He then very gently kissed the hair on her groin. Then he kissed her inner thigh; she giggled; and then her other inner thigh. She giggled again. And then he very gently took his finger and touched her. It didn't take much; she was very aroused; his finger met no resistance and gently slid part way inside of her. She moaned and seemed to gasp for breath.

He needed to be careful. He worked very gently and slowly; he used his finger to gently arouse her for several minutes before beginning the act of satisfying her orally. Once commenced, she screamed at times and grabbed his head to move it into different positions. She pulled his head forward inside of her; he was using his fingers as well as his mouth now. Mantas pleasured her for several minutes while she gyrated and moaned. He was quick about running to the desk drawer. He then returned to her and continued the process.

He looked up at her and smiled and said "Please – one more present?" He then produced the condom for her to see.

"You're a very sneaky Santa and I'm pretty sure I've fallen for some psychology trick, but I don't want it to end. Just be careful, piglet."

George began the afternoon lesson by telling Lamia that he wanted to talk about where he was from and then ask her questions to see if she understood. The man in black stood in his usual place behind her.

"I am an American citizen and I was born in Milwaukee. I love America and would like to return to the USA someday. I remember my childhood in the United States; I had lots of fun. One time, for my birthday, my father took me to the Wisconsin Fair; it was the biggest fair in the United States. Ok, Julie, now, I will ask questions. Ok?"

She nodded her head.

"Where was I born?"

"United States."

Where was the biggest fair in the United States?"

"Wisconsin."

"What country do I love?"

"United States."

"That's good; I used the word America instead of United States, so next time, try to use the same word that I used. Do you understand? So, the United States can also be called?"

"America."

George then looked at the two covered in their black burkas.

"Now, let's make it harder. I want to tell you the story of how I became your guest. I will tell you the story and then ask questions."

"One evening, I was in a taxi near the centre of Beirut. I was in the backseat of the cab and I was returning to my hotel. When we stopped at a red traffic light, I was surprised when two men jumped into the backseat with me. One man sat to the left of me and one man sat to the right. They took me captive. After a few days, I was then taken to another man at a different location. I say a couple of days because I was drugged and it was hard to keep track of time. The man at the second location told me that I was a hostage of Al Qaeda. This surprised me as I had never heard of Al Qaeda, but he kept repeating that I was a hostage of Al Qaeda and I was to do as he told me. The following afternoon, another man came and guarded me and he was relieved by a final man. Eventually, I was brought here. That is how I know I am a captive of Al Qaeda." George punctuated the last sentence by pointing at the both of them.

"Now, where was I when I was taken captive?"

"Taxi."

"Good, in a taxi. There were five men involved in the story. The third man at the second location told me something. What did he tell me?"

"You with Al Qaeda."

"Yes, he told me that I was a hostage of Al Qaeda."

"In a full sentence, tell me how I know I am currently a hostage of Al Qaeda. It must be a full sentence – begin with 'you know you are a hostage of Al Qaeda because'."

Lamia paused a minute. "You know you are a hostage of Al Qaeda because the third man tell to you."

"Very close, your verb choice is not quite right. Let me correct it and then you repeat back. You know you are a hostage of Al Qaeda because the third man *told* you."

Lamia repeated. "You know you are a hostage of Al Qaeda because the third man *told* you."

When the lesson was over, father and daughter climbed the stairs. Once passed the door, Lamia began walking toward her bedroom and removing her burka.

"Psst," said Jamal, "Wait - let me lock this; I want to talk." He bolted the door to the basement, removed his burka and signalled her to follow him to the sitting room. She sat on the sofa and he sat in an armchair facing her. Then he seemed to speak in hushed tones.

"What was he saying?"

"About America?"

"No, he kept saying Al Qaeda and you kept repeating it. Does he mean *the real* Al Qaeda or does that word mean something in English?"

"He was talking about the man who took him hostage. He was Al Qaeda."

Jamal went quiet for a second, "How could that be? Was he in Lebanon at the time?"

"He said he was in Beirut."

"It doesn't make sense. Why would they operate here? Why would they take a hostage in Lebanon?"

"They hate Americans. He's an American, you know. You keep calling him British, but he was born in America. He says he's an American citizen."

Jamal sat back in his chair. He couldn't compute the information. He thought – 'how could Al Qaeda be involved? Why had he been told he was British?'

"Why did he start talking about Al Qaeda today? Has he talked about it before?"

"I don't remember if he did before. I think he may be realizing that he's never going to get out of that basement. Maybe, before, he thought he should keep quiet about it."

Jamal just looked toward the blank television screen and continued pondering 'why would they hold an American Al Qaeda hostage that no one ever talked about?'

Tanja never expected the dinner to end that way, but it was perfectly fine. In fact, she'd enjoyed it and was glad about it. She hadn't really thought about having relations with Mantas until he started raising it. Then, she thought that she wasn't a little girl and what exactly was she saving herself for. Besides, she'd only had full sexual intercourse with one other man and that was her husband. The sex with the tutor was somehow different. She couldn't quite put her finger on it, but it was rougher somehow. When there weren't serious emotions involved, it felt somehow freer to her. She would need to be careful. She sensed he was getting emotionally involved. She wasn't against being with him again, but it wouldn't be a regular thing. In fact, she would need to start thinking about a strategy to end the relationship; she worried that it could drag on. She had decided that she would like to find someone else to be with, someone to be a father to her children and, having Mantas around meant that future candidates would be dissuaded from pursuing her. So, she decided that she would end the relationship by Easter. She had recently bought a new wall calendar for 1999; she looked at March, then flipped to Easter. Easter Sunday for Catholics would be April 4th and Orthodox would be a week later. She decided that it wouldn't be nice to end things on an Easter weekend; so, she decided that her deadline to terminate would be no later than March 31st. She would need to be careful how she ended it because of Vlad, but now she was happy with herself. She would enjoy the winter romance and move onto new things in the spring. It felt good to be in control of her life.

Mantas still couldn't believe his good fortune. He hadn't expected it and hoped it was more than a one-time thing. In his earliest fantasies of her, it was never that erotic. He was upset when she left. She only stayed for 10 or 15 minutes afterward; she said she had to get back to the children. Mantas was well aware that the evening was either a concession for him or something she decided she wanted as well, but for her, it was only physical. He had originally engineered the relationship, but now he realized that he was a plaything to her. Unless, he could make his plan work.

It was Christmas Eve evening in the cell. Lamia had been there earlier; she had reported on the progress of their subterfuge regarding Al Qaeda. In the end, her father decided not to call them. Lamia said she started with just hoping he would think of the idea himself and then she asked about calling and then she suggested that he call, but father thought it wasn't his business. They wouldn't send him a hostage without knowing the background; he had already used up his emergency call and there had been no response. Besides, there was no proof that the hostage was telling the truth; he may be trying to confuse them.

While George reflected on his second Christmas Eve in the cell, the lights suddenly went out and bright light was turned into absolute blackness. He reflected on the last Christmas Eve he'd had with Tanja; it was such a powerful memory. They had made love in their new London bedroom as Christmas candles burned on the night table. He wondered about his new child; Tanja thought it was going to be a boy. 'I bet it's a boy,' he thought.

As he sat in the dark, he thought about where Tanja might be now. She is probably in the Canary Wharf apartment; Maria is likely already asleep. He wondered if he thought clearly enough if maybe he could communicate with Tanja. He would try and, when they next saw each other, he would ask if she could remember having any unusual premonitions on this Christmas Eve night. He closed his eyes and prepared to communicate telepathically with the love of his life.

"Tanja, I'm here and I love you so much; I will be home soon. I think about you every day. You keep me going; without the knowledge that I am coming home to you, I would have forfeited this life. It wouldn't be worth fighting for. We will be together soon."

The children were already in their beds, Tanja was alone now. It was Christmas Eve night; they had lit a fire in the fireplace to memorialize it.

She looked at the flames which gave an orange glow to the room. She listened to the sparks from the crackling wood. She looked at her wedding photo on the mantle above the fireplace.

She smiled; she stared into the eyes of her husband. She wondered if he might be able to hear her in heaven. She closed her eyes.

"George, I love you so much. I think about you every day. I see your eyes when I look at the eyes of our beautiful daughters. You gave me such happiness and love. You will always be in my heart; we will be together again one day."

On Christmas Day, Mantas began to deploy the plan. He referred to it to himself as the 'Christmas Offensive.' He was hoping that he could get a chance to make it work before the Christmas break was over. If it needed more time, that was also okay.

As Mantas' parents lived in a rural area far away, Tanja had invited him to spend the day with the family. He normally would have travelled to see his parents, but he had been hoping for the invitation. Mantas arrived at 10 am sharp that morning, but he didn't come empty-handed. For Vlad, he had purchased a video game, "The Legend of Zelda;" Vlad had mentioned it in one of the tutorials, it was newly released and difficult to acquire. For Maria, he had a giant castle, which she could stand in. It was harder to choose something for Edita; so, he got her a game where she could push different shapes through holes which were cut to only fit each of the particular shapes. The last gift wasn't expensive, but the first two were very expensive and Mantas had to take a taxi to get there as the castle was huge and difficult to carry. He had had to borrow money from his mother to cover the cost of the gifts, but he was hoping it would be worth the investment.

It was Tadas who waited at the top of the stairs for him on that Christmas morning. Mantas knew that Tanja had told Tadas about the two of them now, which was some progress. Tadas had a big smile when Mantas appeared on those final few steps carrying the castle.

"You're going to be very popular with one little Princess." Tadas smiled and helped manoeuvre the castle through the apartment door. It turned out to be much more difficult than either could have imagined. They had to try several angles to get it through.

When Mantas finally got through the door, he was struck by the beauty of the sitting room which was like something out of a fairy tale: a wood fire burned in the hearth, a Christmas tree sat to the side of it and piled beneath were unwrapped new toys and clothes. Throughout the sitting room were reminders of the season – stockings hung near the fire, a painting of St Nicholas graced the wall.

Vlad stood up from an armchair and waved from the sitting room. Edita stood beside her uncle balancing herself on his armrest. It suddenly struck Mantas how fulfilled he felt at that moment; he didn't just have the most wonderful girlfriend in the world, he also had a family, a rather beautiful family; he would get to love them; they would get to love him too.

Then the fantasy was interrupted. Maria tore from the kitchen area and then stood there with her mouth open. Maria rarely stopped moving and Mantas was pleased when she just stopped and gawked at the castle.

"Happy Christmas, Maria," said Mantas as he knelt down to offer a hug.

Maria wasn't interested in the hug. She approached the castle as if it might contain opposing knights inside. She pulled at the door and gently opened it and stood inside it. She now continued to stand in awe as she just stood inside of it inspecting the internal perimeter.

Tadas had found the whole incident rather funny. "It looks like you've managed to surprise our Maria into silence; now, you know how to choose a gift, Mantas!" The two men laughed.

While Maria digested her new castle, Mantas removed his winter boots and coat and made his way over to Vlad.

"You've done so well with your work this year, I thought you deserved something special. Here…"

Now it was Vlad's turn to be quiet. At first, Mantas was concerned that Vlad didn't like it, but Vlad had mentioned that game at one of the tutorials and said it was impossible to get in Europe.

"Vlad – it's the game that you mentioned; it just came out in Europe; I thought you'd like it."

Vlad said nothing. Then, he put his arms around Mantas; he just stood locked in that position until Tanja arrived in the sitting room.

"Oh my, you have a fan, Mantas."

"Yes, I think your brother liked the present." Vlad held up the game and Tanja smiled, then she looked at the giant castle which now blocked the exit to the front door.

"Oh my God, now the princess has her own place?" Maria ignored the commentary; she was busy moving her most important toys into the castle. A sword went first, then a couple of her dolls, then a book that Giedrė had sent her about princesses.

Mantas thought to himself that it was working; the charm offensive was working.

While Tadas and Mantas played cards, Tanja was busy trying to figure out how to cook a turkey. She had decided that she would continue with English Christmas traditions as she now lived with two of them; well her daughters were half English. She would celebrate Christmas on December 25th and do something small on Orthodox Christmas. There was just one thing she regretted about trying to stage an English Christmas and it was the food. She'd had trouble getting the bird in the first place; it wasn't a local tradition; now, she couldn't figure out what temperature to use and how to prepare it for the oven. In the end, she called Auntie Luce to wish her a merry Christmas; then slipped in a question to ask for some advice. It was a good job she had called early; it was going to take much longer to cook that bird than she'd thought.

Once the turkey was finally in the oven, the rest of the day was spent with games and a short walk. To Mantas, he was in a dreamworld of domestic bliss. He loved playing father to those kids; he was going to fit in nicely. Vlad was already a fan; Maria had been easily swayed by the castle and he'd have to work on Edita.

Dinner wasn't bad. It was supposed to be served around 3 pm; it was served at 5. The turkey was dry and the gravy was really salty, but the rest of the food was fine.

After dinner, Tadas insisted on doing the dishes. It was the first time that Mantas would get some alone time to talk with Tanja. It had been a perfect day. Maria was busy with her castle, Vlad with his new game and now, Edita was sitting on his lap. It was perfect.

"I bought you a present, Tanja."

"You didn't have to do that; dinner at the restaurant was the present."

"Then I bought you two presents, but it's at home; I was hoping you could come over sometime and I could give it to you?"

"Sounds nice." Tanja was distracted as Maria began to send volleys of dolls over the castle walls. "Please stop that, Maria."

"I also got you something, Mantas." Tanja got up from her chair and made her way into the master bedroom. When she returned, she was carrying a bottle of scotch with a bow on the top of it.

Mantas looked at the label. 'Highland Park 18-year-old Single Malt'

"It's a good one, Mantas; my husband used to drink it."

Mantas could have done without the reference. "So, what about New Year's Eve?"

Tanja looked confused, "What about it?"

"To come over for the present."

"Can we play it by ear, Mantas? Tadas and I have some family stuff we wanted to do with Vlad and the girls."

The comment was like a dagger through Mantas' heart.

It took a few phone calls to gain the concession, but Tanja agreed to come over for a few hours on December 30th. Tadas would watch the children; she would come over for dinner and they could listen to some music. Mantas was slightly disappointed by the arrangement; he had originally asked about New Year's Eve, but Tanja said she preferred to spend the first New Year's Eve at her new apartment with her children and Vlad; they'd had a tough year and she wanted to be with them on that night.

Mantas had never been much of a chef, but this night had to be exceptional. In order for the plan to work, it would have to be as special as the evening at the French restaurant. He started by stocking up on drink – he bought two bottles of champagne, two bottles of merlot, a bottle of vodka and a bottle of cognac. Alcohol had worked as a wonderful aphrodisiac previously and he bought a wide selection to ensure there would be something she could enjoy. He would also start by offering that scotch that she had bought him; that would be a nice touch.

He then went about intricately planning the food menu. It had to be something remarkable. He called his mother for advice. It was good advice.

After explaining all about Tanja, which was a story that he loved to tell, Mantas' mother suggested that he should try a traditional Lithuanian New Year's Eve menu. His mother reasoned that, if the woman left the country and elected to return, there is a good chance that she was homesick, which also likely meant that she'd missed the food. In response, Mantas planned several herring dishes to start as an appetizer, along with some mushroom dishes. He knew that the quality of mushrooms was weaker in the West and it was an eastern obsession. He would have a good quality rye bread to serve with it, the perfect accompaniment for vodka. The main course would be cepelinai, a kind of giant dumpling stuffed with meat. It would be hard to make but his mother assured him that he could call her and she would talk him through it. For dessert, he would make it easy on himself, there was an old woman in the building who made cakes to order; they were always delicious and he could request it to be made on the morning, so it would be extra fresh and moist.

He also thought about the ambience; this evening had to be something special. The lamp pointed at the wall wouldn't suffice. He bought some candles to provide softer mood light.

On the evening of December 30th, Mantas was excited. He'd cleaned the place from top to bottom, spent most of the day chopping and cooking; had intricately set his coffee table with all the appetizers and had lit the candles. She was going to be there soon; there was only one more thing that he needed to do.

He went into his desk drawer and found the box of condoms. There were five left in the pack. He removed one of them by gently tearing the serrated edge that connected it to the other four. He already had the pin ready; he'd poured some boiling water on it earlier. With the pin, he gently pushed it through the middle of the package. After removing it, he inspected the package; it was impossible to tell that it had been tampered with.

When Tanja arrived, he was a little disappointed. She removed her coat; she wore a nice red dress, but it was nothing like the dress she'd worn at the restaurant. Mantas was originally excited to see the plastic bag that she had with her, but was disappointed again to find that it contained a bottle of wine and a pair of slippers. Mantas thought she looked odd in the dress and slippers, but Tanja explained that his floors always got so cold.

He kissed her cheek and invited her to the sofa. Tanja looked at all the plates of appetizers.

"Oh my, you've been busy; is this all for us?"

"I thought you might like some traditional food; I wasn't sure what you'd like, so I tried a whole bunch of stuff."

"Wow, well, I think you've done incredibly well. I like the look of all of them."

Mantas smiled and opened the bottle of expensive scotch. Then Tanja did something unexpected and discouraging. As Mantas was about to pour the scotch into her glass, Tanja put her hand over her glass.

"I know your tricks, Mr Mantas. Honestly, the other night was an exception. I'm not much of a drinker and I had to nurse a terrible hangover the next day. You do not want to have two toddlers and a headache on New Year's Eve."

Mantas couldn't help looking dejected, but Tanja continued.

"However, if this was intended as a romantic lubricant, I don't think you need to worry about it. I enjoyed our time; I wouldn't mind being with you again – although, if I eat all this food, it likely won't happen."

Mantas decided to bring some humour to the comment by pretending to remove several of the dishes. It made Tanja laugh. Then she continued to talk.

"Mantas – I don't know what you think about me? You always call me a modern woman. To be honest, I am kind of traditional. I've only been with one other man. I don't want you to think this is a regular thing, but it's New Year's; if you're into it, we can celebrate a little tonight. Ok? This will be our New Year's Eve together. Well, except I'll need to be home by 11, so I'm afraid there won't be a countdown."

Mantas was relieved and allowed himself a laugh, "Oh, so would you like your present?"

"I would."

Mantas scurried to his desk drawer and removed a crushed velour box. He then presented it to her with such pride.

"Jewellery?" Tanja asked.

Mantas didn't reply; he just looked expectantly as she opened the box.

Tanja gently pulled out the silver chain with an amber cross pendant. She looked at it then looked at him with her mouth open in awe.

"Mantas – this is too much; it's beautiful; I don't think I can accept it. I think our friendship is putting you into the poorhouse. Again, I'm a traditional woman; I don't need these things."

Mantas smiled – she liked it; she really seemed to like it. "I insist, I want you to have it."

"Can you put it on me?" Tanja stood up and turned her back to him. He placed the necklace around her and clasped it at the back; he then very gently kissed her neck. She ran to the washroom, turned on the light and, with the door open, admired it in the mirror. Mantas watched – she was even more beautiful when she wore it and she really seemed to like it.

Mantas thought that it had been a magical evening. They had so many laughs. In his opinion, the food worked out quite well. For a first-timer, his cepelinai had been quite ok. The old woman's dessert was perfect – moist and soft. Tanja only had one glass of champagne, but that was ok, she'd made it clear that she didn't need an elixir.

Mantas thought that the lovemaking that followed wasn't quite as erotic as it had been the first time. As Tanja was the pursuer during their first encounter; it seemed that she expected him to take the lead this time. That was okay; it had been magical nonetheless.

After she left, he carefully inspected the prophylactic that he'd carefully placed in a tissue on the floor beside the sofa. He felt the tip; it was impossible to tell if it had worked; maybe he should have used a bigger pin. Next time, he would definitely use a bigger pin. It would likely take several attempts to get the timing right.

As Tanja walked the 30 minutes home that cold night, she contemplated the evening that had just transpired. Mantas was getting serious and she was leading him on. The necklace would have cost him a fortune and he must have spent days preparing for the dinner. The lovemaking wasn't as good as the first time. After some thought, she realized that, although it was liberating the first time, now she really didn't enjoy it; at least, not with him. It was time to remove her body from the relationship. The next time they met, she would have to tell him that she didn't want to be physical anymore. If he were okay with kissing and cuddling, she could tell him that she might think about becoming physical again in the future. In the meantime, March 31st would soon be upon them and then she'd move on.

As she walked, she then considered adding a new date to the equation. She still wanted to be his friend and she still wanted him to be there to support Vlad. She couldn't just terminate the relationship – that would be hard on him. She decided that she would start weaning him. On February 21st, she would start being less available and indicating that she wanted to be more of a friend, but she would continue to see him. Yes, that would work; she hadn't chosen that date at random. It would be exactly one week after Valentine's Day; they could enjoy Valentine's Day together and then she would begin the weaning process working up to the final termination date which must occur by the final day of March.

CHAPTER 7

Surprises

It was February now; the days all seemed to morph together. George had his books and the twice-weekly shave and the cigarettes and the English lessons six times a week and the secret visits several times per week. Apart from that, there was nothing to look forward to. There was no spring or summer or Christmas or Easter in the cell; it was just one day after another. The monotony wasn't quite as bad now since the book regime had commenced, but he was still a prisoner.

George thought that the only positive thing that had come from his incarceration was Lamia. He was impressed with his teenage student; her English was leaping forward and she had taken on an interest in current affairs. It was an interest he thought that he might have stirred. He was also impressed with her strategy about introducing Al Qaeda as a topic. The scheme hadn't worked but the idea was rather clever and the planned deployment was excellent. He thought he was helping to build a bright young woman; he smiled when he thought about what he first thought he'd be creating – Jihad Julie.

He was excited when he heard the landing door being very softly opened. She was coming. It would relieve the monotony for a little while. He held his hand out the bars and felt her soft hands caress it.

"How was school?"

"Fine, we have a longer recess today; I can stay longer. I had English first lesson, my first day in advanced."

George smiled as he released his grip and reclaimed his hand. She'd been promoted to the advanced class for the current term - not bad for a girl who struggled with basic verb tenses less than 18 months ago.

"How did it go?"

"Teacher only speaks in English now; kids are very smart in the class."

"You are very smart; you belong in that group."

Lamia looked down and looked a bit sad, so George decided to continue with his support.

"I mean it; look at how you've grown; your English is excellent; you know lots of things about current events; you have a really strategic mind – remember the Al Qaeda plan. I wish the people who reported to me at the shipping company were as intelligent as you. You are also kind and caring; who else would care for a miserable man stuck in a cage? There is nothing in it for you. You belong with those smart kids; get used to it; any university would be lucky to get you."

George thought that the pep talk should have worked well, but Lamia seemed to look even more dejected after it. She waited a second before talking.

"That is the problem, George. My marks from last term are good. I think I go to university… but that's… I…I don't know how to help you. I thinking about taking the key. I checked; it's in his pocket in trousers at night and he hang them in…" At that point, Lamia began to sob. George reached his hand out of the bars and she grasped his hand. "It's, I don't know what happen to him if I do it."

A sudden wave of paternal energy seemed to surge through George. Lamia was considering placing herself and her family at risk to get him out of there. A few months ago, he would have leapt at the opportunity, but things had changed.

"I wouldn't let you let me out. I would just stay here with the door unlocked and I would wait for your father to come back and lock it again. I will not have you risk yourself or your family. This is a matter of patience; I will get out of here when your father opens that door with whoever's permission and not before. I don't want you to think about it anymore. You need to focus on your studies. I will be fine here. You found a way to get me my books, so I'm ok now; I will find a way to carry on."

Lamia just kept looking at the ground. She wasn't sobbing anymore but still looked dejected.

"I am not happy with this. You are like a father to me, my father in a cell." She firmed her grip on his hand and gently kissed it. George recognized the gesture; she was showing respect, extreme respect.

"Anyway, let's stop talking on this subject. Let's talk about something that makes you happy."

Lamia looked up at George. She let go of his hand and tried to wipe away the tears. Then, she cleared her throat.

"Maybe, I could try... but that get father in trouble too."

"Again, it's time to change the subject. I will not let you endanger your father or mother or you. Let's talk about the new English class; tell me all about it. I want to hear everything."

By February, Mantas' master plan had become delayed. Shortly after New Year, Tanja had told him that she wouldn't be intimate with him for a while. She wanted to be affectionate with him, but she still had some emotional baggage to process. She hoped he'd understand. And Mantas did understand, it just meant he was going to have to wait a little on his plan. Valentine's Day was coming up; holidays seemed to put her in a happy mood; he'd work on something. In the meantime, he was very much focused on the second part of the plan. His Christmas charm offensive would continue. He no longer had Vlad's tutorials at his flat. He would teach Vlad at Tanja's apartment and he had increased his sessions to five days a week, Monday to Thursday and Saturday. He would arrive early on weekdays sometimes before Vlad had returned from school; sometimes even Tanja wouldn't be there, but that was okay, Luce would let him in. He would bring chocolates and books and little toys for Edita and Maria. He would encourage them to jump on his lap and he would often grab either of them and swing them through the air. They were falling in love with him; he was sure of it. Vlad was an easier target; any effort in the tutorials was rewarded with the highest praise. Vlad was also doing extremely well; Tanja had said he'd never learn maths and yet he had mastered money, time, addition and subtraction. Mantas was considering moving to science; he needed to keep showing the magic. He knew she loved that.

For Tanja, February seemed to bring renewed hope. For some reason, it felt like spring. The weather wasn't springlike, but her optimism felt like fresh air to her. It started with the headmaster at Vlad's Children's Centre. She had approached him about volunteering opportunities for the next academic year and, to her surprise, he offered her old job back. She could start in September. Tanja hadn't said 'yes' yet, but was definitely planning to say yes. Now, with all the techniques that she'd learned from Mantas, she could really make a difference with some of the higher functioning kids. In fact, one of the reasons for taking a little time to consider the offer was that she was thinking of going back to school as well. If she could work part-time at the centre while taking a few courses on supporting special needs kids, she could really make an impact. By September, Edita would turn 2; she would be old enough to leave all day with Luce. And Luce – Luce was no longer a caregiver; she felt more like Tanja's aunt as well; Tanja suspected that if she didn't pay Luce, she would still show up to be with the girls. She loved her. Luce was no fan of Mantas; she had told Tanja that he kept showing up when neither Vlad nor Tanja were even home. Tanja agreed that he had become too clingy; she always wanted Luce to be happy, so she confided in her about the plan to terminate him. The weaning process was due to start soon, but she decided it would be wiser to start it now. She wanted to symbolically move to a brand new chapter; it was time to move on.

Valentine's Day was on a Sunday. So, he invited her to the same French restaurant for dinner on Valentine's eve. It was hard to get a reservation, but he'd gotten one for an early 5:30 seating. He was disappointed when she declined; she said she just wasn't feeling herself these days. However, it wasn't all bad; she'd agreed to take a long walk with him on the Sunday; then she called on that morning and asked if she could put it off till tomorrow. She wasn't feeling well and could they postpone till Monday. It wasn't convenient; he'd have to skip a class, but he agreed. However, on Valentine's Day, 1999, Mantas worried about the cancellation of that walk. He was right to be worried.

Tanja had played the talk through in her head; she was planning to deliver it on the Sunday as Mantas had school on Monday. Then, she decided that she couldn't do that, not on Valentine's Day; she told him that she didn't feel well, which wasn't a complete fib; she was feeling a little tired these days.

On Monday, he arrived 10 minutes before the agreed 10 am meeting time at the apartment. He was anxious to know what was going through her head. As they walked, Tanja explained, in very carefully chosen words, that she'd come to a decision. She explained that, at one point, she had told him that she wasn't ready for a relationship. She was so happy that she'd changed that view; Mantas had opened her eyes; she was ready to have relationships and that buoyed her to realize that she was ready to start a new phase of her life. However, she also realized that they were very different people; she wanted to continue to be friends but she didn't want to be lovers. She then went on to praise his intelligence and tenderness and told him that, one day, he'd find the perfect woman and that, when he did, he would know it. Tanja had that experience once in her life and believed it happens to everyone once in their lives.

For Mantas, each step on that cold February morning seemed to be one step closer to hell. He had to be careful what he said. She'd clearly thought the speech through. If he protested or pushed, it was going to backfire. His only hope was to keep quiet now, accept her decision, and maybe, maybe he'd get a chance to change her mind. Maybe, she'd get lonely; maybe she'd find someone and it wouldn't work out and he could get another chance. No matter how upset he got, he needed to keep quiet. He would take that offer of friendship; he would take any offer that would keep that window open a crack.

George looked down at the simple heart that had been cut from thick red crate paper. It had an arrow drawn on it and, in very precise handwriting, in the middle of the heart, it read "I love you." It had been a gift from Lamia for Valentine's Day. George had brought it out and looked at it everyday, several times a day, for the last fortnight. He loved it; he loved how neatly the arrow had been drawn; how perfectly cut the heart was; it must have been cut free hand and yet it was perfectly shaped. Sometimes a tear would appear in his eye when he would quietly mouth the words on that heart – "I love you." It was the first present Lamia had ever given him. She even gave him an alibi if he were caught with it; it was stuck in one of the books. She had intentionally spent time on the handwriting so it wouldn't appear to be hers. She also suggested that, if he had time to do it, and, if he needed to do it, he could rip it up and flush it down the toilet. George hated the thought of doing that, but admitted that he might have to. He looked down again at the heart. He had two girls in London who loved him and he had Lamia; he hoped that Maria would be like Lamia; brave and clever with a beautiful soul. Then he smiled, of course she would be, she'll be like her mother.

He stood up when he heard the gentle opening of the door on the landing. Just in case, he put his heart in his copy of the New Testament, but it was nothing to worry about, it was her and he put his hand out the bars and she grasped it.

Today, there was a big grin on her face and she seemed to be almost giddy. "I have news for my teacher, good news."

George smiled and released his hand from her grip.

"I got a place, a university place and guess where?" George looked at her, but she wasn't going to tell him. "Guess!"

"Beirut?"

"Better."

"Outside Lebanon?"

"Yes, now guess."

"I don't know; you never told me where you applied."

"I never know where I applied – long story – keep guessing."

"England?"

"Better."

"USA? Is it America?"

"Better."

"You're killing me with this, Lamia. Will you tell me?"

"I thought my game was fun, but I tell you. I am going to Canada."

"Canada? Lamia... I am so proud of you. You'll love it there."

"Have you been there?"

"Many times. I love it there. It's like America without all the bad stuff." Lamia smiled. George continued. "Where are you going; what university?"

"Trent University."

"I never heard of it. Where is it?"

"Ontario."

"What city?"

"Just Ontario."

"Lamia – Ontario is a province and it's probably the size of 100 Lebanons. Don't you know the city?"

"I find out, but are you happy?"

"It is the happiest news I've heard in many years. You're going to do so well. You should be so proud of yourself... It'll be expensive. Who's going to pay? Your father?"

"No, the party give me a scholarship."

"Hezbollah has scholarships?"

"Well, Lebanon has some special thing with that university. The university don't know about Hezbollah. Hezbollah gives money to Lebanon government to give to me."

George put his hand out the cell again, but this time to offer a firm handshake; she would need to learn how to do things in a western way now.

After she left, George sat in the cell and felt so proud of his student. Then, he reflected on the irony of the situation. He was pleased for his captor; he had completely succumbed to the Stockholm Syndrome. He smiled, and then an odd feeling came over him, he had a disconcerting thought. 'I never heard of that university and the River Trent runs through northern England.' He wondered if she had confused something and then he wondered whether someone had offered her a place at a university that didn't really exist.

"No, it's not possible," Tanja firmly declared. "It isn't possible."

The young lady doctor was so young that she looked down, she seemed to lack confidence, "Well, ok then, we'll run some tests and see what else could be going on. It's just, with a woman your age and with the firmness in your lower tummy, the darkened areolas and the fatigue and period symptoms you described... are you and your husband using protection?"

"I don't have a husband; he's dead."

The young doctor looked to the ground again and looked slightly ashamed that she'd asked that question. "Well, ok, I'll give you a requisition for a urine test; we'll start there and my assistant will call you for a follow-up."

Tanja nodded her head and the doctor excused herself from the examination room. Tanja just sat on the examination table a moment. She would have to proceed with the urine test, but it wouldn't matter. She had been pregnant twice before; the juvenile doctor was right – now she was pregnant for a third time.

How could it have happened? They used protection both times and, both times, she'd seen the condom afterward. There didn't appear to be any damage. It must have been the night with all the drinks. Stupid girl, she thought. I need to stay away from drinking; something must have gone wrong. But had she really been pregnant for 2 ½ months? The symptoms seemed so mild – a bit of spotting during the last period, a little fatigue, some tenderness. She wondered if the symptoms were reduced as she became more accustomed to being pregnant; she'd been pregnant for a sizable chunk of the last four years.

Tanja just kept repeating the word 'pregnant' in her mind. Until today, it was a word filled with such joy. This was her second 'unexpected' pregnancy. The timing around Edita's conception was unexpected as well, but this current one was not only unexpected, it was unwanted. She remembered looking at the plastic pregnancy test when she discovered that she was pregnant with Edita; the initial worry about the timing dissipated in seconds, then she was filled with joy. She was going to be a mother again; it was a gift from heaven. She looked down at her tummy; this was no gift from heaven; this was a gift from somewhere else.

Tanja decided she wouldn't discuss it with anyone now. She would do the test and wait for the confirmation.

It didn't take long; she got the call on Monday morning, March 1st. It was the young doctor herself who called – it was confirmed and she was about 8 weeks; the baby would likely arrive in late September. The doctor wanted her to return for another check-up; Tanja agreed and put down the phone.

She then stood in the kitchen of her apartment and listened to the girls playing with Luce in the next room; they were laughing and shouting with enthusiasm. She needed to compose herself before she went out to the sitting room. She reflected on the irony of the call that she'd just had. Firstly, it was at the beginning of a new month; a month that should have been filled with new hope as spring would soon be there and Tanja could begin on her plans for the future. She also thought about the irony of another September baby. Tanja thought that she should not only give up drink, but she should definitely celebrate Christmas more modestly in future. Her next companion would get socks. The joke made her feel a little happier; she used to tease George about Edita with that joke.

Tanja stood there. She took her fingers and pulled on her bottom lip. She hated the thought of it; she'd always wanted to be a mother; she'd begged God for Maria, but it didn't make sense. Maria would be 3 in May and Edita wasn't even a year and a half. She had no husband, no boyfriend, she needed to get on with her life.

Tanja stood in the kitchen. She would have to terminate it; she didn't even know whom to call about it. Then, she realized that the doctor would know. She hoped that the young doctor would be sympathetic; there was a renewed religion amongst the young people; she might be Catholic. It was going to be embarrassing.

Luce came into the kitchen with a smile on her face.

"You look like you need some cheering up, Tanja. You should come out to the sitting room. The girls are playing pretend; Maria is pretending to be the princess in her castle and Edita is pretending to try to sneak into it. We shouldn't leave them too long; Maria sometimes takes make-believe too far."

Tanja decided that she needed to talk to someone and who better than Luce. There were only two adults in this world whom she could really trust and they were Luce and Tadas. As this was a pregnancy thing, it seemed wiser to talk to a mother, a mother who always gave her good advice.

"Luce – can we talk just for a minute? It's important." Luce walked toward the kitchen door and looked over at the children. They had lost interest in the game. Maria was reading her princess book and Edita seemed busy studying the castle.

"I'm all yours, my dear."

"Luce – I'm pregnant."

Tanja was surprised by the reaction. Luce came and embraced her and kissed her forehead. She then looked at Tanja's stomach and made the sign of the cross over it. Luce then went on to say how happy she was for her.

"Luce – I'm not keeping it." Luce was quiet, but took Tanja's hand and held it. Tanja continued. "I don't have a man; a child needs a father; I'm ashamed, Luce, really ashamed."

Luce paused a moment before comforting her. "Well, you shouldn't be ashamed; things happen. And you do have a man in your life – you have Tadas and you have me as well. You make the right decision but don't base it on how other people might see it or because you don't have a man. You didn't have a man when you had Edita."

"That's different; I had a husband and he died."

"Exactly, Edita doesn't know any father, she has her grandfather, her sister, her uncle and a great mother. Do you think she is missing out on something in life by not having a father?"

It was a rhetorical question so Tanja didn't answer it. The reality was that her mind was made up; she would call and ask to move her Wednesday appointment to tomorrow; the longer she waited, the more painful it would become.

It was a stressful night. At first, Tanja had trouble getting to sleep, then she had a dream that disturbed her. She woke up and lay in bed looking at the darkness. She closed her eyes again; it would be a big day tomorrow. She needed to move quickly with the abortion; she wondered how long it would take to organize, then she fell asleep again.

That next dream began in such a beautiful way. Tanja sat in a meadow under a tree. There was long grass all around her; there appeared to be wildflowers mixed amongst the long grass. The spring sun shone and she felt so content under that tree. A little boy ran toward her, he must have been about 4 years old, Tanja put out her arms and the boy ran into them. She cradled him on her lap and he looked up at her and said, "My name is Ata." She smiled at him and then his face changed; his body remained the same but it wasn't his face, it was George's face.

Tanja woke up and bolted upright in her bed. The dream was over but there was something weird going through her head. The baby wasn't the tutor's baby; it was George's baby. The tutor was just the conduit. It was a bizarre thought; then she started weaving together the coincidences. The baby was conceived near the same time as they'd conceived Edita. She'd never really been attracted to Mantas and they'd used protection, but she'd conceived anyway. George had wanted a boy; they had thought Edita would be a boy.

She scurried out of bed to the bathroom to put some water on her face. She was sweating now from the dream. She looked at herself in the mirror and was about to clean her face when she thought she saw the boy's face in the mirror and it changing to George's face. She blinked and it was gone; her mind was playing tricks as a result of the powerful dream.

After washing her face, she went back to bed. All sorts of thoughts were racing now. She thought about that strange name, Ata, she'd never heard it before; it didn't sound European. There were thoughts of her two daughters and how much she loved them. There were thoughts about wanting to be a mother. She'd told George when they'd married, that she wanted lots of children. George died and then she miraculously conceived a baby; it felt like he would be replaced by him; is that what the dream meant?

Then, she thought about Luce and her talking about Edita not having a father; Tanja had never thought of it that way, but it was true. And she didn't need a man; she hadn't had a man to really support her in a year and a half. She loved being a mother, it was something she was good at.

Tanja didn't bother trying to sleep anymore that night. It was dawn when her mind went to another unusual thought. She had a book of names that she'd purchased after she'd gotten pregnant with Edita. She'd kept that book; it was interesting; it was a dictionary of given names, their origins, the meaning for each of the names and the countries where each name was used. She tried to think where it might be; she knew she packed it when they moved from England.

A few minutes later, she got out of bed and rummaged through the various books on the bookshelf in the sitting room and found her copy. She turned to the page that contained the name Ata. It was Arabic in origin, meaning 'gift'. There was an extensive list of countries where it was in use, but Tanja's eyes set on only one of those countries – Lebanon.

Tanja believed in fate and the strange dream and all the unusual thoughts that followed had already started to cause her doubts about her earlier decision. But, the reference in the name book was the coup de grace.

She looked toward heaven and tears started to come to her eyes. "Ok, sweetheart, I hear you. I will wait for him – and I'll name him Ata."

Lamia decided not to tell George about her plan. It was unlikely to succeed and she was tired of raising his hopes. The plan could get her into trouble – and maybe her parents too, but if she approached it correctly, she might be able to ensure that only she got into trouble. If she were really careful, she might be able to keep that trouble to a minimum. As there appeared nothing else to try, she would attempt it. Her teacher was worth it.

Lamia's plan all revolved a single person - "Uncle Imad." Uncle Imad wasn't her uncle; he was the uncle of one of Lamia's best friends. She only even knew of the existence of Uncle Imad due to a peculiar incident that had occurred when Lamia and her friend, Gamila, were 10 years old.

At that time, Gamila was not only a close school friend, but both their grandmothers had farms within a kilometre of each other near the same village. This was a wonderful coincidence for the two friends. They played together in the schoolyard, then would look forward to even more playing during the summer holidays. They would both be shipped off to their grandmothers' farms and the two would spend their days roaming in the fields and by the river together.

One day, the 10-year-old girls had been playing at Lamia's grandmother's farm and decided to go to Gamila's grandmother's place. Gamila's grandmother had a new calf and Lamia and Gamila loved to look and pet her. When they arrived at the farm, Gamila's grandmother wasn't there. So, the girls petted the calf and then went into the kitchen to find a snack.

It was then that they experienced a bit of a fright. A produce lorry pulled into the long dusty drive and drove toward the farm. It was likely to collect or drop off something, but the girls were too scared to deal with it, so they made their way to their secret hiding spot. There was a little ladder that pulled down from the ceiling. They would escape up there and pull the ladder up into the attic. They could then see all the adults through some wooden slats that made up part of the ceiling. It was a great prank and, so far, the adults hadn't figured it out.

They could hear someone approaching the front door; they both assumed that he would knock and go away. He did knock but then, he waited and then, he opened the door and walked right in. The man was looking around; they were terrified; he must be a robber. Then another man appeared and then another one; there were at least six thieves moving round in the house now. The two girls were terrified and clutched each other's hands. Lamia wanted to cry but knew she had to stay quiet. And then it happened – in he walked.

Gamila screamed with excitement from the rafters "Uncle Imad." He looked up to see who was calling. Gamila put the ladder back and climbed down; Lamia followed. Gamila hugged the man; he smiled at them both then thoroughly chastised a man for not knowing there were children in the house. And that was Lamia's introduction to Imad Mughniyeh – one of the most powerful men in Lebanon; one of the most powerful men in the middle east.

Even at the age of 10, Lamia knew who he was. She'd seen him on television dozens of times. He was a Lebanese folk hero; admired around the Muslim world – and despised everywhere else. He led Hezbollah's military intelligence and had a reputation for extraordinary success. Lamia looked up at him. He was very very tall, with a thick beard and glasses; slightly rotund, but that just added to his presence. She wasn't in the presence of a mere mortal – she was in the presence of a God.

The visit was a short one. They both waited with him for Gamila's grandmother's return. After an initial introduction, Imad told Lamia not to ever say that she had seen him. It was a request that Gamila's mother repeated to her when they returned from the farms later. Lamia had promised both of them and only told her parents about meeting him.

After that accidental meeting, Lamia met Uncle Imad twice more over the years. As she now knew the secret, Gamila's family didn't try to shield her from him. On Gamila's 13th birthday, there was a big party with all the school girls. The next day, Lamia was invited back for dinner with the family – it was a family birthday party and she and Gamila were so close that she'd been invited too. As they were about to sit down to eat, a woman dressed in black knocked on the door. Gamila's mother let her in; the woman closed the door quickly, then began frisking her. Then, she moved quickly around the house looking around and then she waved her hand from the front window.

In normal circumstances, Lamia would have been terrified by these actions, but she wasn't, she was excited, she thought she knew what was about to happen. Within a few seconds, men started appearing from a panel van and then entered and made their way round the house. One man was in charge of frisking all the men at the party. The woman went about frisking the women; even Gamila and Lamia were frisked; it wasn't terribly intrusive; it was just a pat around their bodies. Once an 'all clear' hand signal was made from the window, in came Uncle Imad.

Lamia couldn't believe that he remembered her. After embracing his relatives in the sitting room, he asked her if she remembered him from the farm. Lamia was more than impressed and blushed when she said that she did. It was so strange to have Gamila's birthday dinner with a man like that. Lamia wished that she could tell the world about it, but she only ever told her parents, who were very impressed about it.

There was one final time when she saw him – she was about 15. She was at Gamila's grandmother's farm. This time, Gamila told her that Imad was coming and asked if she wanted to stay a little longer to see him. Lamia confirmed that she absolutely did. He arrived in a similar fashion, lots of security, he greeted her by placing his hand on his heart and commented on how much she'd grown. He even said "one day soon, you'll be old enough to join the struggle." Lamia couldn't find any words, so again, she just blushed.

Lamia's plan was a simple one, but was fraught with risk. She would try to find a way to meet Imad. She would tell him about the British hostage. If there was one man in Lebanon who could liberate him, it was definitely Imad. She needed to be very careful about what she said. She knew he believed in secrets and she was going to tell one. It was a faint hope strategy. Maybe there had been a mix-up, no one seemed to know or care about her teacher. They didn't even know he was really an American. She wouldn't tell that part to Imad; as she would then have to explain how she knew that. She would position it carefully – if she could get a meeting.

At first, Lamia approached Gamila and queried if she could ask about a meeting. Lamia explained that Imad must have helped with the scholarship and she wanted to thank him. Gamila said she would, but a couple of weeks later, Gamila just returned with a message that no thanks were required, Lamia had achieved the honour on her own merits. Lamia decided to try again and came up with an alternate plan. She would confide in Gamila and tell her parts of the story. Gamila and Lamia were so close that they already knew some of the family secrets. Then, Lamia thought better of it; that was outright telling a secret; an important one. So, Lamia came up with a third idea.

She asked Gamila if she could meet Imad because he was her hero. That was the real reason that she wanted to meet him. She was going away to Canada and wanted to help tell the real truth about Hezbollah. She wanted to tell people that he wasn't a murderer and that he was just standing up for the oppressed. If she met him, she could tell people that she'd met him and that he was kind and wanted peace.

This time, the ploy worked. Within a few days, Gamila received a positive response. He'd be happy to give her 10 minutes. She was to appear at an office in a few days across town at 9 am sharp and ask for Mrs Abbas. Lamia was excited, and a little scared. She was even excited that he'd be in the same town. None of the townspeople would know that. It was an honour.

When she arrived at the nondescript office block on that morning, she was surprised at the lack of security. It seemed like a regular day there with a single guard carrying a shotgun outside the front doors. Then, she thought that that made sense. His security was likely hiding. She walked past the guard and opened the door. Another security guard sat at a desk and Lamia asked for Mrs Abbas.

She stood there waiting for Mrs Abbas. There were no chairs, she looked around the office reception area. There wasn't much to look at - just bare walls, a typical civil service building. It wasn't long until Mrs Abbas appeared. She was a middle-aged woman dressed in a long black frock with her head also covered by a black hijab. The woman greeted her warmly and asked her to follow her down a maze of hallways.

Then, things became a bit odd. Lamia was asked to sit on a bench in a small room with no windows. It had no other furniture; Lamia wondered if they conducted interrogations there. She sat on the bench, Mrs Abbas excused herself and said she'd be back in a minute. It was hard to figure out if she would meet Uncle Imad here or whether they would take her somewhere else in the building. Neither was actually correct.

A few minutes later, Mrs Abbas appeared with another much younger woman who was dressed in similar attire. The young woman carried a strange object in her hand. Mrs Abbas asked Lamia to stand. Lamia complied and Mrs Abbas completed a frisk. But then Mrs Abbas asked Lamia to remove her clothes, except her undergarments. Lamia felt ashamed; she didn't want to do it, but what choice did she have? She obeyed; she took off all her clothes, save her bra and panties and placed the clothes on the bench beside her shoes. The young woman then took the object in her hand and started moving it over her clothes and rummaging through them. Lamia now knew what that object was – it was a metal detector.

After the clothes were inspected, the young woman turned toward Lamia. She didn't like the look of it and her worst fears were about to be confirmed.

"Put your hands on the wall and spread your legs," the young woman commanded.

Lamia was now so scared that she just did it. She stood there with her legs spread apart and a sense of humiliation came upon her. The young woman passed the metal detector over her body. She spent a long time holding it just above her bra and completed the humiliation by placing it just above her groin area. Lamia could even feel it touching her there; it was creepy and it felt disgusting to be searched that way.

"Ok," said the young woman, "put your clothes on." Lamia scurried to get her clothes on; she was done with that humiliation. She wanted to get to the meeting and get out of there. It wasn't going to be that easy.

Mrs Abbas asked her to follow. They walked through a hallway, down a staircase and kept walking down that staircase. They walked right to the bottom of that staircase – to an underground car park. Lamia was about to ask what was going on, but decided she wasn't brave enough.

Mrs Abbas made her way past the various cars and vans in the car park and then stopped at one and knocked on the backdoor; she knocked in a pattern, three knocks in a row. The back of the van opened; there were two men inside, both wore balaclavas. Lamia was getting scared. Mrs Abbas beckoned Lamia to follow. She was glad when it became clear that Mrs Abbas would sit beside her on the bench on the opposite side of the men; she didn't want to sit with the disguised men wearing military uniforms by herself.

There were no windows in the van, but they must have driven for close to an hour. Lamia was looking forward to getting out of the van. When they finally stopped, there was one more surprise. Mrs Abbas turned to her.

"I'm sorry, Lamia, there is one more thing. I will blindfold you now. This is for your own protection as well as ours. If you are ever questioned, you'll have no information to give. I hope you understand."

Lamia complied; they didn't seem to walk that far with the blindfold; there were doors that were opened and closed; she could hear that and then she was gently pushed into a chair and she just sat there. She was told to keep the blindfold on; then she heard Mrs Abbas walk away and then a door closed. Maybe, she was now alone, then she heard the familiar voice.

"Welcome, Lamia, you can take it off." Lamia pulled off the blindfold.

"Uncle Imad!" She then felt embarrassed again; that's what she called him when talking with Gamila, but it wasn't her uncle and it wasn't respectful, "I'm sorry... sir."

To Lamia's relief, Imad had a big smile on his face. "I prefer Uncle Imad; when I think of you, I think of my dear niece. I am honoured that you think of me that way."

Lamia let out a gasp. He was putting her at ease; she needed it. It had been a very stressful day and she hadn't even started to talk about the secret yet.

Imad continued, "I'm sorry, Lamia, I can only give you 10 minutes; I know you wanted to meet me formally; I'm honoured by that too. I also want to say that we are all very proud of you. You will do well in Canada – just make sure you come back; we need strong women like you."

Lamia blushed, but now she knew the clock was ticking. She would have to cover the foil topics first; then she would have to cover the real reason she was there.

Lamia had rehearsed. She asked for advice on courses she should take and how she could help stem the misinformation in the West. Imad talked about the importance of English and how they needed more people who were fluent; he then suggested also taking Political Science. He talked about how they needed people who could understand the political language of the West – understand the language; understand the politics.

He also cautioned her not to be too aggressive in telling the story of her people; they mustn't think she was sent as a spy or had any connection to the party. He suggested that she just spend the first two months listening and then slowly begin talking about facts when misinformation was presented as truth.

Lamia hadn't come for the advice, but some of it was quite useful. She liked the part about just listening for two months. It made a lot of sense.

Imad finished his speech and looked down at his watch; she was running out of time.

"Uncle – thank you so much for meeting me and for everything you do for us. You have honoured me and my family by meeting me. I will try to represent us well in Canada... Uncle – I had another question; it's a side issue really; I don't know if I should bring it up."

"Well, I still have a few minutes." It was the invitation that Lamia had waited for.

"Well, it involves a secret. So, we live in one of the houses that was renovated during the war."

"I know where you live."

Uncle Imad's face changed; the smile was gone and he now wore a frown, but Lamia had gone this far, she couldn't turn back now.

"Yes, so you know my father is a party man."

"I know all about your family," replied Imad.

Lamia was now feeling ashamed. Uncle Imad must now have figured it out, this final part of the conversation was the real reason she was there – not to talk about him being a hero, but both were true but now he wasn't going to believe that. She hesitated, maybe she should stop, but then she'd waste all this time for nothing.

"It's well... my father has a British guest there; you know, and... and no one seems to know about him and it seems odd that, well maybe he's an agent for someone else, I just thought you should know. You know; we could use the space for other guests; um; if you know what I mean. I just want to do the right thing. I just wanted to make sure that you knew."

Imad leaned forward. He didn't look quite as stern, but he was about to launch into a lecture. "So, Lamia, I know you well enough. You wouldn't have been allowed here had we thought that you weren't loyal and didn't come from a loyal family. However, be aware, you live in dangerous times, secrets are secrets. If your father told you something, you are obliged to keep it secret – you are not to talk about it. Have you talked about it with anyone else?"

"No, no, uncle. I understand the secrecy; I guess I didn't think it breaking a secret if I talked to you about it. I'm sorry."

"It's ok, Lamia, as you grow older, you will understand why we do things the way we do. Our enemies are everywhere; I hope you understand. All secrets must be secret – from everyone. Do you understand?"

"I do." Lamia started to stand up. That final rhetorical question seemed to be a signal that the meeting was over and that she should leave.

"Lamia – one more thing. Can you refresh my memory? When did your guest arrive?"

"Two summers back; in 1997; I think late July; maybe very early August."

"Ok, God be with you, Lamia, we are all very proud of you."

Lamia was now standing, but then Imad told her to sit. Someone would collect her and repeat the process to bring her back. Imad got up and left the room.

Lamia just sat there in that office. The plan had failed and she'd managed to take a happy conversation with an idol and turn it into something else. He must hate her; probably thinks she was trying to use him for something. She would be happy to be home and was hoping he wouldn't say anything that would get her parents in trouble.

It had been a long afternoon of meetings for Imad, but it was that morning meeting that he kept replaying in his mind. He wasn't aware of any British hostage – and he was aware of all hostages. He even knew the names of all of them – both Israeli and members of the South Lebanon Army. He didn't necessarily know where they were all kept. It was possible that Lamia's father had misunderstood something or maybe he had told Lamia a fib to impress his teenage daughter. Lamia might well have an Israeli in that basement. He would order someone to investigate and report back to him.

Imad sat back in his chair and thought about it. It wasn't her words that bothered him so much, that could be a mix-up in communication between father and daughter. It was the timing that was compelling. There had been other odd things that had emanated from that period. It all revolved around a single date. A date that had been etched on Imad – August 4, 1997 – the attack at Kfour.

The warm April sunshine made Tanja feel so happy this morning. There was much to be happy about. There had been a surprise call from Gary the previous evening. He was finalizing the sale of Barb and Doug's house. Once sold, Tanja's total share of the estate would be over $600,000. It was much higher than she could have ever dreamed. And now, she was walking along that beautiful Danė River toward a park that looked over the Baltic Sea – with her three favourite ladies in the world – Edita, Maria and Luce. There was now something for the whole family to look forward to – a new gift that would arrive in September. She'd told Tadas and he was very excited; he didn't seem the least concerned about the unorthodox circumstance. She hadn't told the girls about their new sibling; they were too little to understand it and she didn't want to have to explain if anything went wrong. She also hadn't told Vlad; he had a big mouth and the news would spread faster than printing it in the Klaipėda newspaper. Even if she swore him to secrecy, he would definitely blab to Mantas, which she did not want at all. In fact, she had made a special point of avoiding the father of her unborn child. He was still tutoring at the apartment, but he was timelier now and didn't stick around or arrive early. Tanja always made sure that she was out when he came over; she just didn't want to deal with him. She knew that they were supposed to remain 'friends', but she wanted to keep a little distance while she got her head together. She was showing a little now, but not enough for people to notice - especially if she wore bulkier clothes; she'd consider telling him when it was more obvious.

As the girls played in the park, she sat on a bench with Luce and put her hands on her belly.

"Can you feel him moving?" asked Luce.

"Not yet, but I definitely know he's there now."

Luce laughed, "We keep calling him 'he'; what if it's a girl? Dreams can be wrong."

"It won't be; and just in case, I'm going to ask for the sex at the ultrasound at the end of the month. If it's a girl, I'll just have to look up the Arabic for the feminine version of 'gift.' Either way, she'll be precious." Tanja smiled toward Luce; she was glad that she'd told her about the dream. Luce just seemed relieved that she'd decided to keep the baby; it was clear that she looked at the world from a mother's perspective.

"When are you going to talk to Mantas?" Luce enquired.

"Not sure; when I can't keep it a secret anymore. I don't want him to hear it from someone else and bikini season is coming soon."

Luce laughed. "This is baby number 3; you may have to forego bikini season indefinitely."

Tanja reflected a moment. "Luce – is this too weird; I mean I'm having a baby; I haven't told the father; I don't particularly want him in our lives. I decided to have the baby because I had a weird dream about my dead husband."

Luce's face suddenly went very serious. "Actually, Tanja, I think the opposite. Mother nature often gives signals to us. When you're pregnant, those signals are much stronger. I remember vivid dreams and nightmares when I was pregnant. Let me ask a question – do you usually recall your dreams the way you remembered that one; I mean when you weren't pregnant?"

"Well no. It was so memorable, it seemed to continue even when I was awake and looking at the mirror."

"So, if Mr Mantas were here, he would really disagree with what I'm about to say. He would dismiss it to hormones. However, my belief is that those dreams are mother nature's way of preparing us. The nightmares are a way of reminding us that we have a sombre responsibility; we must be prepared for bad things and to prepare us to protect our children. Your dream was different; I think the universe was telling you not to interfere. You're carrying precious cargo, maybe someone important. Most women also say that they can remember their dreams more clearly during pregnancy; it's mother nature's way of ensuring that we don't forget the message."

Tanja sat and thought about what Luce had said. Old Lithuanian women seemed to have an odd way of mixing religion with old pagan-like beliefs about things. George had once commented that he thought it was because the country was very agrarian and peasant beliefs still circulated. However, it didn't matter, the main thing, Tanja thought, was that everything Auntie Luce had just said rang 100% true.

It was a few days after her meeting with Imad and Lamia had just arrived home that afternoon from school to find her father reading the newspaper in the sitting room. He looked up at her and smiled.

"So, close the door; I have some news for you. Your wish finally came true. My boss came round today. He called this morning and came by this afternoon. Lots of questions about George."

"So," enquired Lamia, "Is there some sort of mix-up. What did he ask?"

"Not much. He asked if I thought he was an Israeli. I told him 'no'; I also told him that I don't think he's British, I think he's American and that he thinks we're Al Qaeda."

"So, you told him about the lessons?"

"No, not exactly. I just said he said 'I am American'; I can understand that much English. And I said he pointed to me and called me 'Al Qaeda.' I don't want to bring up the lessons; mind you, at some point, they'll likely interrogate him; I'm surprised they haven't already; and he'll likely tell them. That's ok. I'll tell them the full story. I tried to give my daughter a valuable skill to help with the struggle. We never identified ourselves; he even thinks we're Al Qaeda. Don't worry, your Uncle Imad would approve."

Lamia flinched at the reference. She hadn't told her father about her most recent contact with the man – and she was hoping he wouldn't find out.

Jamal looked at his daughter. "I think the next thing will be that they'll send someone around to interrogate him; I think that's next... there's just one odd thing. I told them almost a year ago that I thought something wasn't quite right. This conversation seemed to be a follow-up from my earlier concern. I wonder what happened for them to become interested now."

Lamia just stared back. She had a pretty good idea about the catalyst.

Imad listened carefully to Bashar. He had much respect for him; he was a loyal agent, who seemed always to be able to get to the truth. Imad sat back in his chair and listened to every word in that preliminary report.

"We seem to be holding a dead man and for no reason. He is British. The Lebanese authorities issued him a death certificate; he died in July 1997. We had someone search western media and look at our newspapers around that period – nothing. We had someone visit his warden. The warden said strange things – the hostage told him that he was an American; the man also told the warden that he thought he was being held by Al Qaeda."

Imad just sat there; he was thinking deeply. Bashar sat quietly; he had more to say but he had worked with Imad for a long time, he knew that the leader liked time to process.

"So, what about the cause of death on that certificate?"

"Homicide."

"Police report?"

"A joke; said he was killed by a taxi hijacker; there was a photo of him. It looked like he was dead in that photo. He was photographed with a copy of Al-Ahd newspaper from July 25, 1997."

"Can we make out where the photo was taken?"

"We have a photocopy of the original, so no, it just looks like it was likely in Lebanon."

Imad stroked his beard before continuing.

"Why wouldn't the British demand more follow up? It seems odd that he'd know the name Al Qaeda. They wouldn't have been known much in the West back then; unless someone has told him something in that cell or unless he was some type of agent. Could there be a connection to Al Qaeda? And what is our connection? We would have had to be talking to them."

"It's hard to know; things were different between us then; if we were talking to them, it would likely have been via Kfour and there'd be no evidence now. Well, except... initial contact would likely have been via email; we could check the back-up servers, but I'm not sure it would tell us much. It would be a coded message requesting a communications protocol. If we found something, I'm not sure we would be able to identify it. We send out hundreds of those messages everyday and most of them are completely phoney. They're decoy messages. I can ask around; we invited a couple of their fighters to monitor some training about five years ago;

maybe some on our side would remember something. I will do that. Do you want me to have the Briton interrogated? I would let you see the list of objectives and questions before we do it."

"Ok," replied Imad. "But please prioritize enquiries around any communications between us and Al Qaeda; if there's a connection, I want to understand it."

Bashar summed up the meeting. "Of course, leave it with me. But the solution looks like it is going to be pretty straightforward. We'll just have to make the current situation reflect what everyone already believes."

Lamia couldn't wait to get into that cell for a private discussion. She arrived home for recess that morning, but her father was at home. She would have to wait. It had been hard to sit through her English lesson the previous afternoon without giving George a hint – some bit of hope after close to two years. Lamia decided to skip an afternoon class – it was Lebanese history; she'd already read ahead anyway. She was hoping no one would be at home. She approached her house carefully; if she saw movement inside, she would scrap the plan and return to school. If she entered and someone was home, she would just say that she didn't feel well and wanted to stay at home for the afternoon. Her mother was normally home at this time, but not always.

After seeing no movement, she crept on the front step and listened for a minute. She put the key in the door and turned it. She entered the house and called out for her mother, then her father. No response. Then, she locked the door behind her and put on the deadbolt. She would have to leave the door open to the basement; if someone were having trouble with the house door, she'd have time to escape the dungeon and let them in; she could say that she must have put the deadbolt on by mistake.

Lamia softly unbolted the basement door and crept down the staircase to the familiar hand that was outstretched from behind the bars.

She grabbed the hand. "George – I don't know how much time we have. I spoke to someone important and they send someone to talk at my father. Listen – I think they may interrogate you – father told them that you were American and that you thought we were Al Qaeda. I am happy – maybe some change."

"Who did you talk to?"

"Don't matter. The main thing is that something is happening." Lamia paused for a second. "George – if I don't come for a time, don't think it's because I don't love you – or if English lessons stop, don't worry. Now, things may change. Ok?"

"I understand," replied George; he nodded his head, not really knowing if the development was significant.

"And George, maybe don't put your hand out when I come. Just wait on the bed till I come and remove the burka; that will be signal. Ok? Oh, one more thing, I worry about if they send a man to talk to you. Things are different now."

"How do you mean different?"

"Many things have change since you were here. Now, some people have computers in pockets and cameras are now even on our town's streets; new ways to watch us. We need to be careful, and I need to go. I try for tomorrow. Ok?"

George sat in the cell and listened as she scurried up the stairs. He heard the door close and the bolt being replaced. He was alone again, but it sounded like good news; something, anything that would happen now must be good news. There'd been no news in close to 20 months. He fumbled a pack of Marlboros while he considered the implications of that conversation. It was hard to follow; maybe Lamia had put pressure on them to settle a ransom demand or clarify that he wasn't a spy. It was difficult to believe she could have done that without admitting to the clandestine meetings. He closed his eyes; maybe it was the beginning of the end; the first bit of progress toward going home. But, it was hard to be optimistic.

It was Asta who first asked her about the bump. Tanja knew her days of hiding behind baggy clothes were coming to an end. She confided in Asta but asked her to keep it to herself. It was a secret that was now spreading amongst people she trusted; it wasn't going to be long till it would spread outside that group – she knew that. However, before telling Mantas, she wanted to buy just a few more days. She wanted to complete the ultrasound. She decided that it was still cool enough to wear a very baggy sweater that she'd owned for years; it would be very hard to detect anything – although, it was going to be a hot couple of days for Tanja in that sweater.

Tanja was a little disappointed that the ultrasound technician wouldn't tell her anything. She said that she wasn't qualified to interpret anything. So, Tanja just stared closely at the television screen and particularly focused when the probe was pointed toward her unborn child's groin area. She thought she saw an appendage but it was difficult to understand; it seemed out of focus somehow.

Tanja had to wait an additional two days before her obstetrician appointment. The old male doctor confirmed that things looked good but was reluctant about telling her the sex; he kept asking if she was sure she wanted to know it. Tanja thought to herself; she hadn't known in advance for the girls, but this was baby number 3 and she was beyond the novelty of 'surprise.' She wanted to know and told him. In the end, the old doctor looked at her with a smile and said… "Congratulations, you're carrying a boy."

Tanja made her way quickly home that afternoon; she wanted to talk to Vlad before his tutorial. She was ecstatic. The dream was correct; she wasn't losing her mind. It was also time to share the news with Vlad; she was going to attempt to swear him to secrecy. She thought the odds of him keeping it a secret were slim, but she would try nonetheless. Just to ensure she could deal with the situation properly; she'd asked Luce if she could take the girls out that afternoon – so she could be alone with Vlad and then alone with both Vlad and Mantas during the tutorial.

Vlad was ecstatic with the news. She didn't tell him about the baby's gender; that would be a surprise for September. Tanja noted that Vlad didn't really ask about the father; maybe he'd figured it out or maybe he didn't care or maybe he didn't understand it. Tanja thought for a minute; she'd never discussed the birds and bees with Vlad before; she would have to cover that over the next few weeks. She also made him swear not to say anything to anyone; she would let him know when he could talk about it.

When Mantas arrived for the lesson, he was surprised when Tanja opened the door for him. She looked like she might be coming down with something; her skin seemed pale and she was dressed in an overly baggy sweater; as if she were having trouble staying warm. Still, it was good to see her again; she had clearly been avoiding him; maybe that drought was over.

"Nice to see you again," said Mantas and kissed Tanja on the cheek. Tanja did not give any emotion away.

"And you, Mantas. Vlad is ready for you in the sitting room. I was hoping I could get a few minutes of your time after the session. Would that be ok?"

"Absolutely." Mantas said the word enthusiastically, but he knew something was wrong. She was going to tell him something he didn't like, but what more could she do to him? Then, it dawned on him; she was going to fire him. She wouldn't need his tutoring services anymore. Then, the plan would really be dead; she could firmly shut the window on him and leave no crack open.

Tanja left Mantas with Vlad in the sitting room and made her way to the master bedroom, leaving the door open just enough to hear the tutorial. It was a wise decision. Within the first 30 seconds, Vlad blurted out that he had a secret. Tanja ran into the room on the pretext of going to the kitchen. Vlad looked at her and looked down. Tanja glared at him "You should get started," said Tanja as she retrieved a glass of water from the kitchen and went back to the bedroom. The tutorial continued. About halfway through, there was a break; Vlad went to get some milk and then started to talk about a secret again. Out came Tanja from the master bedroom; Vlad looked down again and drank his milk. She decided since, she hadn't really had a reason to be in the sitting room, that she'd fill the time with asking about Vlad's progress and get a bit of a status report. Mantas gave an overview of the work they were completing today on science and noted that Vlad was doing ok.

It seemed to take forever for the final part of the tutorial to complete. Tanja now stood close to the door; listening carefully to every word. She desperately wanted it to end, so she could get this over with.

Mantas was surprised when Tanja came out of the room exactly at wrap up. He hadn't even stood up yet; whatever blow she was about to deliver; she had been planning it; probably listening for the tutorial end from the bedroom.

"Mantas, let's talk outside; Vlad's ok by himself; he can watch his cartoon programme."

Mantas nodded his head; he put on his coat and shoes and Tanja opened the door for him. While he began the descent down the stairs, he could hear Tanja locking the apartment door. As he heard the key turn in the lock, he felt like a lamb slowly making its way to slaughter. The fantasy that had somehow slipped into reality would now slip quietly back to where it began – a mere fantasy of that beautiful Tanja and that family that he had wanted to lead; now he would be removed completely from it.

Mantas stood in the street while Tanja pulled the main door shut. It was time to accept the lecture.

"Mantas, let's walk a little; just over to the river; somewhere more private." It was an unwelcome comment; she wanted to do it in private; maybe she thought he would cry or make a scene; he wouldn't give her the satisfaction.

In order to get to the river, they had to use a crosswalk which crossed four lanes of moving traffic. Mantas was beyond frustrated, the cars were meant to stop, but this was Lithuania and they often didn't. He wanted to take his frustration out on one of those cars – maybe kick one who refused to give way. When they finally arrived at the river walkway and got to the river, Tanja faced him; she leaned on a railing. She looked down at first then back up.

"Mantas – I'm not quite sure how to say this; I'm pregnant."

Mantas' spirits had just been lifted from complete despair to the glories of the heavens. The scheme had worked; he just needed to keep playing his cards; he would be with her. The fantasy was real again – very real. However, he was careful not to show too much emotion; his first impulse was to ask if it was his child; no, he couldn't do that, she wouldn't tell him this way if it wasn't; his next question would be if she was going to keep it, no, he shouldn't ask that now. Then he had an impulse to hug her.

Mantas put his big arms around her and hugged her. She didn't hug back or push him away; she just stood there limp. Mantas wanted to ask if he could touch her belly, but decided the timing wasn't quite right.

When the clumsy hug was complete, Tanja continued, "Thanks for being supportive, Mantas. You must have a lot of questions. So, yes you are absolutely the father; I don't know how it happened, but it must have been the night before New Year's Eve and I haven't been with anyone else since my husband died. Anyway, it doesn't matter. I'm keeping the baby. There are no expectations of you – George left me enough money and I have the supports that I need. We're still friends, it doesn't change anything. If you want, you can visit the baby; it's your choice. You can also walk away completely; it's your choice and I'll understand."

Tanja had rehearsed the speech carefully. She had been sure to include a reference to her dead husband. In her heart, that was the only person that would be a father to her children; that's what the dream had been about.

Mantas was taken aback; the speech had clearly been rehearsed and delivered with such 'objectivity' as if she were giving him an update on an experiment she was running. It couldn't be true; she wasn't the type of girl to bear a child without a father. He had overcome objections before; he would try again. He would raise the ante right from the start; maybe those words were only words – maybe they were intended to give him a way out – he didn't want a way out.

"I see; my choice is to be very much a part of your lives." He took her by her hand. "I love you, Tanja, I love Vlad, Maria, Edita. I love you all. I will be there for you. I'll be there at the appointments; I can move into the apartment and help; I'll be there every day; I will be the best father you've ever seen."

It was at that point that Tanja stuck in the knife. She removed her hand from his. The message was delivered so callously that it was hard to believe that they'd been lovers only a few months before. When they'd broken up, she had told him that she wanted to be friends, but the words about to be spoken were anything but friendly.

"It's a kind offer, Mantas, but that won't be necessary. I have alternate plans for his upbringing; I'm accustomed to being a single mother. I don't want the baby to be confused; I'm doing this as a single mother. Your contribution is complete; I'm taking it from here. I don't want you to move in or attend appointments. You're just the donor in this scenario."

A sudden rush of anger came over Mantas; he couldn't help himself. How could she sum up their relationship as him being a 'donor'?

"But I'm the father, I have rights!"

Tanja thought that could come up so she gave a knowing smile. She had enough resources to bury the student in court.

"I'm sorry you feel that way; certainly, if you pursued that angle, I'd understand, but I made an offer for us to be friends and for you to visit the baby; if you make this a legal thing, I would have to rethink that offer. I'm sorry, Mantas, I can see you're a little emotional; let's cut it here for now; we can talk another time about it."

At that point, she did something odd. She offered him her hand and gave him a firm handshake as if they'd just completed a contentious business transaction; one in which he'd lost and she'd won. She turned round and walked toward the old town.

Mantas just stood at the railing overlooking the river and couldn't believe what had just transpired. Every step of his plan had worked and then it had just all collapsed on the banks of the Danė River on the final day of April. He really had lost.

George knew that it wasn't Lamia on that May morning. It wasn't a tray time and it wasn't Lamia's recess and the door was opened in the way that he'd become accustomed to when Lamia's father opened it. He sat on his bed; maybe today would be the day; something would happen. It might be a happy day, then George looked at the man who appeared at his cell door.

He wore the traditional black head to toe with a burka and seemed particularly tall. His visit should have represented progress, but remembering his previous black-clad captors, George felt a wisp of cold air down his neck. He was about to be interrogated. George just gasped at the realization; he was hoping the man would not open the cell door. It was the first time that George had ever wished that the door should remain locked.

In the end, the door was left closed and locked. The man questioned him, in quite reasonable English, about his background at Trans-ship. George talked about his position freely. He asked about his nationalities. George was pleased to hear the question in the plural. He talked about being an American, who was also British and how he lived in London. George also offered to help him with any ransom; if they were willing to share information with him, he could help with advice. He talked about the day he was taken hostage and the transfer to a second hostage-taker and then his final move here. It was quite a civil conversation, George thought, it lasted about 30 minutes, then the interrogator asked one final question. He asked, "Where do you think you are?" George knew the phraseology wasn't quite right, but he would help the interrogator along.

"I don't know exactly where I am in the middle east, but I know you're Al Qaeda; I hope it's ok to know that."

"How do you know that?"

George went on to provide the familiar lie about the second location that he'd been taken and how the man had told him.

Bashar continued with the update as Imad listened intently. "The interview with the Briton went well. We kept it very diplomatic. Our man said he was co-operative; even asked if we wanted help with a ransom. Poor dolt – he thinks there's a ransom demand pending. Anyway, he is claiming to be an American; we can corroborate it if you give me a little time. He also thinks that we are Al Qaeda, so his warden was right on all fronts."

Bashar paused for a minute to allow time for Imad to think, then continued.

"So, we made some progress on communications. We found someone who had been at the meetings at the training camp; he knew the protocols. We searched the servers; there was communication after he would have been taken. The key words were Istanbul, but misspelt, and cairo. Their word was Istanbul and that was the first message through. It looks like we later sent two separate messages requesting more contact after that point."

Bashar looked at Imad, who posed the question, "Any chance we could recover any of those discussions?"

"No, it's an old webmail trick; there would be nothing left to find."

Imad just went silent again, so Bashar decided to move from analysis to outcome. "So, we can do more investigation if you like. There might have been an Al Qaeda connection, but no one seems to have been in touch for close to two years, the Lebanese civil authorities say he's dead, the British don't seem upset about it; we've never heard from the Americans. Do you want us to finish this off? It's costing us resources and time."

Imad sat back in his chair and pulled at his beard, "Not yet... but he has cost us and we have wasted a lot of time on him. Is there any way to recoup our investment without it blowing up in our face?"

"We could try the British or Americans, but then we'd have to admit that we took a hostage. We could try to blame it on Al Qaeda, then we'd have to admit that they took him on our territory, and we would then risk riling up Bin Laden and company."

Imad and Bashar just sat in silence for a moment before Imad continued. "You are right; we can't talk to either of them at this point – I think I need more time to think it through."

"Of course."

Imad stroked his beard. Bashar sat; he knew the stroking of the beard meant Imad was still thinking; Bashar had not yet been dismissed.

"Bashar – do you think Bin Laden would want him?"

"Not sure, but it would mean contacting them. Do we want to risk it? I thought we were keeping our distance."

"Well, the last time we talked to them, it seems we didn't even remember that we talked to them. Maybe we could try it again on the quiet."

Bashar let out a laugh, "Very true."

Imad leaned forward, "Do you know the full communication protocol that was originally agreed?"

"Yes, we have it."

"So, maybe we could feel them out; could we send a message requesting contact?"

Bashar took a deep breath; he usually thought of all scenarios, but hadn't thought of this particular one – he thought that was one of the reasons that Imad was so successful, he always thought of things that others didn't. "It was two years since we last tried it. They may not be out there anymore; their servers would have been updated; they may not even look for the cairo phrase anymore. The webmail account is likely dormant. We might be able to request an account with the same name – if no one else has taken it. I could start there and work backward to the email. Would you like me to proceed?"

"Just find out if you can resurrect the webmail account; don't send any emails. I need more time to think; I need to think if it's wise; I wonder how much he might be worth to them and whether we want that money."

"Is it money that we want from them?" asked Bashar.

"That's a good question. Another thing to think about."

Mantas was upset and called his mother to tell her the story – and she was upset too. How could he become involved with a woman like that? He had rights. It was confirmation, confirmation that he was right. When he put down the phone, he thought it through again. He still yearned for her when he thought about her, but his obsession about being in her life was now turning into something else, he almost felt obsessed about getting access to the child. It was a peculiar thought; he'd only wanted to conceive the child to be with her, now that she had taken that away, he wanted the child itself. He didn't like to have these thoughts. He was a person who loved psychology; he should be thinking logically.

He sat at his desk and tried to think logically. He could fight; he could make it clear he wouldn't be treated like a donor. When the baby was born, he could petition the court for formal access and a guarantee that the child couldn't be removed from the country without his permission. That would teach her. Then, he thought about his master's degree; he may have to delay starting it to focus on the dispute. Also, there was the money; Lithuanian justice wasn't something that necessarily championed the poor. Her rich former husband's money could bury him in debt – and he could still lose. She could even turn round and demand child support payments in exchange for any court concession. All the logical positions that he mapped out in his mind led to the same place – he would lose.

She was quite correct to shake his hand at the end of that conversation. He had lost; she had won. If he thought logically, the only way forward was to accept that premise. He would have to accept that he was the loser and she was the winner.

He hesitated about calling her; the next tutorial was the following day. He would phone in the morning and ask for a meeting after the session – maybe another walk to the river of doom to negotiate whatever concession she would be willing to offer.

The following morning, Mantas called Tanja and she agreed to the meeting but only after Mantas made it clear that he would not be seeking legal redress; he just wanted to discuss the arrangement; he wanted to discuss how their friendship would work, how often they would see each other, how he could help with the baby without overstepping any barrier.

Tanja put down the phone and liked the words that she'd just heard;

she was glad that she had been tough; he was now negotiating from her position. Any concession would be just that – a concession from the framing of the relationship that she had articulated. If he ended up being a part-time father and playing a role in Ata's life, that would be fine, but she would decide on the terms and ensure that he knew that any concessions would come through her.

When he arrived for the tutorial that day, only Vlad was there. They conducted the usual review and dove into the world of science, but Mantas' heart wasn't in it. At break time, he asked Vlad where his sister was. Vlad said that she'd left with Luce and his nieces just before tutorial time, so that he could focus on his studies.

When the tutorial time was over, she still wasn't there. It made Mantas upset; she was going to make him wait. She held the control now and she was going to humiliate him.

About 10 minutes later, Tanja, Luce, Maria and Edita all came through the door. Mantas wondered if she was going to force him to ask about the meeting that they'd agreed upon. In the end, she didn't. Shortly after entering, she kept her shoes on and apologized for being late and said that they could walk down to the river as Luce could watch the family for 'a few minutes'.

Mantas fixed on the words for 'a few minutes.' Maybe, he was being overly sensitive, but it sounded like his paternal rights would be settled in 'a few minutes.'

They made their way down the stairs and into the street and down to the crosswalk. It was even harder to cross today, traffic seemed particularly aggressive. Mantas was keen to get his frustration out and just stood in front of the first lane with his hand in the air and acted like a crossing guard for Tanja and two old ladies who were also trying to cross. He repeated the process for the second, third and fourth lane until they got to the river side.

He took a deep breath as he leaned on that railing. "I apologize for the other day; you caught me off-guard; of course, you have the right to raise your child. You're good at it. I just wanted to have some type of role in the baby's life. You mentioned that we could still be friends; I'd like that. I was just wondering how it might work."

Tanja seemed more relaxed now; she had won; they would never be together. It was a reality he would have to learn to accept.

"I'm glad about it, Mantas. Of course, we can be friends; when the baby is born, we can find some time for you to come over – I know you'll be busy with your master's programme. We could start with once a week and work from there? If you're still tutoring Vlad, you'll have additional opportunities as well."

Mantas nodded his head; it was a pittance of a concession and she could end Vlad's tutoring at any time or simply not be there when he came to give a lesson.

"Ok; that sounds good, but I can do more babysitting than that; if you need it."

"Well, you can't really babysit a newborn, Mantas, but when the baby gets a bit older, that might work, we can talk about things as time progresses."

"Is there any chance I could be there for the birth?"

"Actually, I'll have Luce with me; I prefer a woman; Tadas is going to watch Vlad and the girls."

"Ok."

"What about the surname? Would the baby have my surname?"

"I'm sorry Mantas; I know that's a difficult question, but the baby will have my last name – we don't know where the child will end up and Smith is much easier and simpler than Jancauskas; particularly in the West – and it's the same name as his sisters' and mine."

"Ok, could we discuss given names together? I mean we could just discuss it and talk about some ideas together."

"Ok, I tell you what; we can do that - for girl's names. I already have a name if it's a boy."

"Ok... just curious would you be willing to share the boy's name with me?"

"Ata."

Mantas didn't know how to respond at first; it was something weird; not a name for a child. "Oh, that's unusual, where did that come from? It doesn't sound European."

"It's a long story."

"Ok, what about a middle name for a boy? If it's a boy, could I help with that?"

"No need; I've made a decision on that as well, but we can talk about girls' names."

"Ok, could I ask what you've chosen for a middle name – if it's a boy?"

"George."

At that moment, a sense of rage came over Mantas. He was more than angry now. This was supposed to be a peace-making meeting; he had to calm down; he could risk everything. He started breathing exercises to try to calm down, he couldn't, he tried to think pleasant thoughts, he couldn't, he wanted to shout at her what he really thought, that he could do. He started to shake before he spoke and was so angry, he could see the spit coming from his mouth as he began the monologue.

"Are you kidding me? You're going to name my son after your dead husband? What are my parents going to say? You can't do that; it's half mine. It's nothing to do with your dead husband – that's just weird."

Tanja was horrified by the disrespect and her blood began to boil even hotter than Mantas'. This was supposed to be a conciliatory meeting, but Tanja now suspected it was just another psychological trick, she had had enough and that last statement was not going to stand. She'd offered him a part in his son's life and he'd just spat at that offer.

"You know something Mantas, I think you're the one who's weird; my dead husband is the reason that I'm standing here having this conversation with you. He took care of us and made sure we had what we needed. You're just a little weird boy who is able to pull off a few psychology tricks. I told you that you were a donor; that's what you're going to stay. I don't know if you noticed but you are shouting at a pregnant woman; that's the kind of guy you are – you're a boy who shouts at a pregnant woman. You know something, I don't need a self-centred little boy in my life; I not only don't want you in my baby's life, I don't want you in Vlad's life anymore either; he deserves better. So, don't come round again and don't talk to me - ever."

Tanja then grabbed her wallet out of her bag and counted out some banknotes. "There - that should cover any money we owe you." She threw the money at Mantas. It bounced off his jacket and fell to the ground.

Tanja marched off toward the crosswalk. Mantas looked down at the money; he had now completely blown it. He looked up; he had never seen Tanja so angry; it must be the hormones; she was now almost running toward the crosswalk as if to create as much distance from him as possible in as short a period of time as possible.

He watched as she took the final powerful strides toward that crosswalk; the traffic would have to stop for her now, she wasn't going to stop for them. Except that wasn't quite correct. Mantas looked in horror as Tanja seemed almost to trip in front of the moving car. The car's brakes screeched and the horn blared as the car swerved off the road and stopped on the walkway beside the river. Tanja's limp body travelled those last few metres with the car and now lay on the front bonnet of a Mercedes Benz as smoke emanated from its tires, blocking the footpath overlooking the Danė River.

CHAPTER 8

Beginnings

George leafed through the glossy brochure. He was relieved that the place existed and slightly surprised that it did.

"See," said Lamia, "it is a real university."

George smiled and looked back at the brochure. The cover said 'Trent University' and there was a picture of a bridge over a beautiful river. It was the river that he studied; it was supposed to be an optimistic and beautiful scene, but George looked at the river on that leaflet and began to think about his own life quietly slipping away in that little cell in the basement.

"I apologize, Lamia. I was just surprised that I'd never heard of it. You know how protective I am of you – and maybe I'm also a little paranoid."

"I think you a lot paranoid and a little protective... Do you know that city where is the university?"

George smiled, "I've heard of Peterborough; I haven't been; it's not a big place. I think it will be good to be in a small city; better for you to be in a small place for your first experience abroad."

George handed back the brochure through the bars. He was eager to talk about something else. "Lamia – I've been thinking – why do you think that they only sent someone to interview me now?"

"It's not clear; I might be right – maybe they think you are Israeli helper."

"It just seems odd to me; my wife would have said something; others would have told them that I don't have any connection to Israel."

"They might not believe them."

"Well, the Israelis should have said something; they wouldn't negotiate my release; I have nothing to do with them."

Lamia looked thoughtful for a moment. "George – I don't know how this works, but I don't think we are sitting with Israelis everyday and talking about prisoners. They keep our people for years; I think we may not hurry."

George took a moment to contemplate. That did make sense. Maybe, the Israelis hadn't set the record straight yet; maybe now if his captors had become suspicious; maybe now they could accelerate negotiations with alternate parties.

"Lamia – I'm worried what my wife thinks. You know I wouldn't ask this question, but if I were to compose a letter and told her to keep it secret; do you think you could send it for me? I mean not now; maybe if nothing happens before you go to university; you could post it from Canada; no that would be a bad idea; someone might work that out. Your flight wouldn't go directly to Canada, would it? You must change in Europe I suspect."

Lamia looked worried about the request. "Forget it," added George, "I was just thinking out loud."

"No, we can talk about it, but I can't see how she wouldn't give it to the British and it would all come back to my father; we can talk about it. We have three months to talk about it. My father's friend is buying ticket for me; I don't know how I go to Canada yet."

George thought about it and now regretted having raised it; it was time to change the subject.

"Lamia – when you said you talked to someone important about me? How important?"

"Very important. But I'm not going to let your paranom take over our talk. So, I will stop you there; I'm not telling you the name."

"But... did you take a risk talking to that person?"

"A small one, that's why I don't talk to you about it; also, I don't think it works, but now I am happy that I did it."

"Ok, so please don't do that again; we talked about it; I don't want you to do anything to put yourself at risk. I couldn't have survived this ordeal without you... I'm sorry; I don't want to get on your nerves, but is this person that you talked to... is it someone; I mean is this someone important or important and dangerous?"

Lamia didn't answer right away; she just looked at George and seemed to be thinking how to phrase her answer, then she continued.

"You know when I came back from grandmother's farm and I talked about watching BBC news and you used a word about when you said something and I said we had a different view of things."

"Perspective?" asked George.

Tanja couldn't quite figure it out. Sometimes, at first, it seemed like she was in a long dream about her life. It seemed to cover her entire life, then she would dream about seeing Luce in a white room, then Mantas in a white room, then Tadas in a white room. Sometimes, she could hear strangers talking about things that weren't part of the dream and then they began to be part of the dream. Each time, she'd return to a white room, but different people would be there. Tanja began to realize that she wasn't quite there anymore; she wasn't alive anymore; she must have entered purgatory.

Sometimes, she could control the dream. When she could gain any control over the dream, she would try to think about Maria and Edita. She would try to focus on them and try to let them know that she was ok, but her control over the dream often gave way. Edita's face would grow older and she would become an adult; sometimes Maria would be playing but she'd be playing at the same river as Tanja had played at as a girl, which wasn't possible. Sometimes, she would return to the white room and a man would be holding her hand, but she didn't know who that man was. She tried to refocus on what was really happening; the white room must be purgatory and the strangers talking and the man who held her hand and Mantas and Luce and Tadas; they must be helping her to cross over. Something must be happening as the white room appeared more in her dreams, or maybe that wasn't right, time was difficult to understand.

She also tried to think about how she got here. She went to talk to someone by a river; maybe it was something to do with the river that she played at when she was a girl; but how did she go from playing by a river to being in the white room? She had her own children; maybe something had happened to Maria by that river and she had tried to save her. Maybe, Maria was here somewhere; she would try to focus on Maria; maybe she had already crossed over or maybe she needed her help. Others were trying to help Tanja; she needed to focus on Maria's face so she could help her daughter.

"Tanja, Tanja, can you hear me?" It was a man's voice speaking Lithuanian, her adopted language; Tanja began to realize that she was being called. It must be time, time to cross.

"It's ok, sweetheart. If you can hear me, you're ok; things are ok." Tanja looked at the white room; she wasn't sure where she should go to get to the man. She looked at the white ceiling; it was a little clearer than it had been before.

"That's better; can you hear me?"

Tanja tried to speak but no words emanated; she tried to nod her head, but she didn't seem to be in full control of it.

"Nurse, nurse! Come quickly; I think she's responding." Tanja thought there was something interfering with the instructions he was giving her; he was now shouting for others to help her. She started thinking again about Maria; she didn't want to leave without Maria; if she were there as well.

A bright line suddenly shone into her eyes. They had done it; they had managed to guide her to the light, it was a very bright light.

She now heard a woman's voice. "Can you hear me, Tanja? I'm holding your hand; can you feel it?" Tanja couldn't feel it, but could hear her. She tried to nod again.

She heard the voice continue. "Ok, she's slowly coming out. Are you able to stay here? If not, we'll assign someone to stay with her or if you need breaks. It could take up to a full day for her to fully revive."

Tanja was confused with the interference and the light had gone; she went back to thinking about Maria.

"Tanja, it's Mantas, you're in hospital; don't try to talk. Just blink your eyes; if you can. That's good. You're going to be ok; you were in an accident. You're fine, Edita and Maria are fine – and they miss you. You were really lucky; a visiting German doctor took care of you; they also had good equipment in that room. You had some minor surgery to release some pressure on your brain, but it's ok now."

Tanja wasn't quite sure if she was completely out of the dream, but it was the first words that seemed to make sense and it was the first time she could really feel anything. Unfortunately, it was a headache that she was feeling.

"So, a car hit you and your head collided with the windscreen. You had some pressure buildup in your brain as a result, but they got to it quickly. They wanted to keep you sedated for a few days. So, you're waking up now. You're going to feel a bit groggy; that's ok. The doctor will come by later to explain everything to you."

Tanja tried to move her head; she was able to do it a little, but it hurt. She decided that she would try to say something. She opened her mouth, but couldn't really get any words out. She realized that she had a mask over her mouth and nose; probably for oxygen. She practised opening and closing her eyes. It felt good to be out of the dream state, but she was now experiencing pain. She could feel something in her spine; the rest of her body seemed numb.

Mantas kept talking. It was good that he did; it was good to listen to something that made sense. After a while, the German doctor came into the room. Tanja was able to move her head a little to look at him. He spoke in English to her and moved very close to her face when talking.

"Hello, Tanja. My name is Dr Bohner. Your husband tells me that you speak English, so I wanted to update you personally. I'm a visiting surgeon from Germany. I was here to train local neurosurgeons on advanced brain trauma techniques. As your accident required this type of skillset, I was able to assist.

You experienced blunt cranial trauma and a resultant traumatic brain injury. I performed a craniectomy. That's a fairly serious operation to reduce pressure on the brain and control haemorrhaging. It is serious but I was able to get in there quickly, which is important, and I was able to do it with a fairly small removal of skull matter. You'll have to wear a neck brace and helmet for a while. You were lucky in that the car looks like it hit you at a peculiar angle or you fell into it. Normally, we would see fractures in this type of accident. The main trauma was to your head. We only found bruising on the remainder of your body. The baby still appears to be ok, but we'll get to that in a minute.

So, here's what you should expect. Right now, your brain is still regaining its stability; as a result, it will take time to regain some of your cognitive abilities and there is a chance that you may not regain some of them or it could take an elongated period. You may experience headaches, slurring, nausea, trouble walking or gripping things, bladder control.

As for the baby, the fetus itself was unharmed and ultrasounds appear positive. However, any severe impact to the brain can impact the fetus. We were careful about your drug treatment and treated the fetus in tandem. A nurse comes and moves your torso regularly and massages the fetal area; the idea is to keep the fetus stimulated. Right now, signs are still positive, but we won't understand the impact until the baby is born."

It was hard to decipher, but it made sense. The good news is that she was alive; the bad news is that it sounded like a difficult life to live.

"It's good news, Imad. The web account was dormant, but we were able to restore it and reset the password to the original. So, do you want us to send the initiation request?"

Imad pulled at his beard and seemed to go into deep thought.

"If they responded, what would we say?" asked Imad.

"Well, we could start by just fishing a little. We still have their package and wondering how to proceed."

"Hmm… that makes sense, but let's think how they could respond."

"Well," Bashar continued, "I think the most likely scenario is that we hear nothing; that's what we've talked about. And then, I think we need to finish the situation and cut our losses. If they respond and want him back, then we need a position on what we want. Again, there are risks, they may want him back for free and that could stir up trouble."

"I don't think Bin Laden would play a game like that; I think we've made a polite overture by offering his package back. If we don't contact him and destroy his package and he finds out about it, that could be worse."

"True, very true."

"Ok, request the contact; you're right, just fish around a little."

It was hard to get over the sense of guilt. Mantas had always prided himself on being able to detach himself emotionally. It was true that Tanja was once an obsession, then he was focused on getting access to his unborn child, but now he regretted it all – he had accidentally really hurt her – and she didn't deserve it. The pregnancy scheme seemed so juvenile now, unworthy of someone like him, the argument seemed so stupid; over a name; he should have just given in. Over a name, he had almost killed the woman that he had professed to love. He still loved her, but it was a different kind of love now. It was almost a month since the accident; Tanja still needed help eating, couldn't control her bowels and still couldn't walk. He was trying to make it up to her. The university term had ended just before that fateful day. He was originally planning to spend the summer conducting tutorials to make some money, but he had a new mission now.

Each day was the same, he would co-ordinate schedules with Luce and Tadas in advance. His shift was always the longest by far. He would arrive at the hospital at 7 am and be there when she woke; he would sit and help her with breakfast, alert the nurse if she needed changing, help move her around to get her comfortable, take her for walks in a wheelchair, help with lunch. If Tadas or Luce could relieve him, he usually took a break in the afternoon. Then, he'd be back again to help with dinner; sometimes he'd stay till she nodded off for the night.

When Tanja would nap during the daytime, Mantas would frequently think about the words that she had said to him just before the accident – she'd called him self-centred, weird; implied that he was unworthy to be in her child's life or in Vlad's life. The words were delivered in the height of anger, but were also very true. He knew that now; he didn't deserve to be part of her life; he didn't deserve to be part of her family. The only way that he was allowed to be with her now was that he had almost killed her – and almost killed his own child – and there was still a chance that either of them could die as a result. And, if she only knew what he had done, then she would surely know that her riverside rant had been filled with so much truth.

But, now she just lay there. At first, she didn't show much emotion when he would come, but as the days passed, she would smile when she woke up and saw him or smile when he would take her for walks in the wheelchair or tell a funny story. It should have made Mantas feel happy when he saw that smile, but he was just ashamed.

Tanja counted herself as lucky to have someone like that who was so devoted. She'd been really cruel to Mantas and yet, here he was, every day and long days helping an invalid. He probably felt guilty for the argument, but it wasn't his fault, it was even hard to remember now; she could have given in a little; it was dumb. And here she was, her whole life depended on him. He cared for her, made sure the girls and Vlad always had Tadas or Luce with them. He was a good guy; she'd misjudged. With the exception of seeing her girls again, there wasn't much to look forward to in life, but she did look forward to seeing him each morning; it was good to have someone who cared for her like that.

And what a woman to be devoted to. Tanja often looked at herself with a pocket mirror. Her beautiful hair had been shaved and replaced by a helmet. Her face was badly brutalized as if she'd been attacked with a bat. She'd lost control of her bowels – that was the most humiliating thing and couldn't walk – and it was unclear whether she'd regain either of those capacities again. Only a few weeks ago, she had felt so happy on that park bench with Luce. She'd also been so smug – dismissing Mantas as irrelevant. It wasn't Mantas who was irrelevant – it was herself that had become so irrelevant and a burden to everyone around her.

It was early June when one of the doctors suggested that she might be able to go home and receive outpatient care. However, she would need 24-hour support; she was not to be left alone, was not to lift things. Tanja's head hurt from the suggestion; she desperately wanted out of there; wanted to see her girls; Vlad had come to see her a couple of times and she wanted to spend more time with him as well. However, in order to leave hospital, she was going to need time to hire nurses to stay at the apartment; she couldn't ask Tadas or Luce for that type of help.

After listening to the doctor's suggestion, it was Mantas who spoke first.

"Tanja, would you like to go home today?"

Tanja still had trouble speaking; she spoke slowly and slurred a little, "I would love it, but I need time to find help."

Mantas replied. "How about I take you home and stay with you while we work out the details."

"Thanks Mantas, but I can't ask that of you. I can't even use the toilet."

Mantas leaned forward and held her hand, "Tanja, I love you." When he said it, he realized that it was the first time that he'd really meant it and that he'd never really been in love before. He continued, "and the girls love you and they miss you. I think you should go home. I'll take care of you while we find some nurses to help."

1999 was turning into a frustrating year for Sayed. Bin Laden was becoming obsessed and it was causing issues. The man was absolutely focused on the destruction of the United States; Sayed was no fan either. However, since he didn't seem capable of doing much to the Americans, Bin Laden seemed to be devoting all his efforts to turning his beloved Afghanistan into a kind of Islamic Disneyland. As the leader's rhetoric became more and more bizarre and extreme, Afghans seemed to become increasingly accepting of that vision. When the Taliban group had started, Sayed had hoped that they would just fizzle out. They didn't; they just got stronger, then weird Arabs started appearing from all over the middle east. They were not just weird – they all seemed obsessed with turning his country back several hundred years on the pretext of some type of Islamic purity. In their world, Islam meant painting house windows black so people couldn't see the women inside, stopping girls from going to school and teaching the boys only the Koran and military training. It was increasingly difficult to have any kind of normal life in this environment. Villages had no running water, the electricity supply could be sporadic, hospitals were poorly equipped, because the focus was supposed to be on Allah. And it all seemed counter-productive, the West had shut them off completely; even close allies didn't want to have anything to do with them. Sayed no longer could use an Afghan passport; he used a fake Pakistani one and it was almost as useless as his Afghan one. And Bin Laden and his tribe would talk about waging a war on the infidels – for what and - with what? No one would sell them a bullet and he had attracted such negative attention that no one could travel anywhere to wage any type of war on anyone anyway.

In the end, even Sayed had had to align himself with the Taliban or risk suspicion that he wasn't pure enough. Sayed yearned for the days of

Afghanistan without foreigners. After all, that's what he'd fought for. They had defeated the Russians, but these current foreigners were going to be much harder to unseat.

It was a June evening when Sayed saw an email in his inbox. He was used to getting email from people he didn't know; most people would delete that type of spam, but Sayed had special connections. He needed to check each of them carefully for any coded references. He almost deleted that particular email. Then he looked again; 'it has turned sunny in cairo' was the first sentence. He remembered that meant something. It was a code, but couldn't remember where it came from. He would need to think about it. He wouldn't delete it; it would come to him and it could wait till morning.

When the first call to prayer occurred just before sunrise, it came to him. It was the Lebanese; that's who cairo was. When he returned from prayers, he scurried to find where he'd written the protocol. It was difficult not only because it had been a couple of years, but because he always 'masked' his notes. He was using a different way of masking back then and he had to carefully read each page; he found one page that was definitely a protocol; only to decipher it and find it wasn't the correct one. Eventually, he deciphered one which contained reference to a webmail portal. He logged in, and the password still worked, and drafted a note.

"Greetings, I have received. Best wishes. I am here."

Then he waited. He logged back in after about 15 minutes and saw a new draft, then began the process of reading the new drafts and deleting them, then creating new ones. At first, the Lebanese noted that they wondered what they should do with the package. Sayed was beginning to believe that they were possibly the worst communicators in the middle east, if they hadn't discarded the package by now, what were they waiting for? The corpse would be rotten. Then, he became curious, maybe they were talking about something different or maybe they thought they were communicating with someone else. It was the latter thought that was interesting; Sayed believed that there could be no one on his side who could be talking with them; he was curious to find out if that was the case.

"Is package the same as 97?"

"Yes."

"Please remind of origin?"

"Britain."

So, it wasn't anyone else; they were still on about the Briton from two years ago. Sayed thought the whole thing rather odd and then a peculiar thought came to him.

"Has packaged been damaged or still working?"

"Working."

Sayed stared at the word 'Working;' he wasn't really sure if that meant his corpse was still in reasonable condition or whether the man was still alive. He began to wonder if this might be a trap. There was no longer a way to contact Zurab; the Taliban may have created a 9th-century caliphate, but they were more modern when it came to software; there was too much tracking of communication now; it had become too risky.

"Please provide photo of package in working order."

"We can, but need time. Please confirm that package has value; if not, we will discard."

"Yes, it has value. Please confirm. I await your contact. Over for now."

Sayed stared at his keyboard and began to think. The scenario had become interesting, but it wasn't so much the hostage that interested Sayed. No one was talking to the Lebanese; it might be even worth discussing his strategy with Bin Laden's inner circle. Sayed started going through all the possibilities in his mind; they were great ideas, great ideas. If he could play his cards correctly, there could be substantial personal and political gain. He just needed to be careful; he needed to know he was talking to the right people.

It was good to be back in her own bed. It had been wise to leave that hospital. In the few days she'd been home, she had been able to alert Mantas a couple of times that she needed the toilet, which was substantial progress. If someone put her in the bath and stayed with her, she could now manage to clean herself. It felt good to be clean; she wasn't allowed to clean her face or head area, but Mantas would gently do it for her; ensuring that no water got under the helmet. Tanja now regretted her choice of buying an apartment on the third floor; that was the hardest part. It would take both Mantas and Tadas to carefully guide that wheelchair up and down the steps. She yearned to walk. They had started some exercises before leaving the hospital, but the movement made her feel nauseous. As she was pregnant, they suggested that she take it very slowly.

For the first two nights in the apartment, Mantas made a little bed for himself on the floor on the other side of the bed. He didn't want to disrupt the household by sleeping in the sitting room. On the third night, he'd asked Tanja if she would be ok with him sleeping on the floor directly beside her side of the bed, then he'd be able to hear her more clearly if she needed help or if she had trouble breathing. Tanja was glad of it. After he made his bed that first night and lay beside her, she reached her hand down so that she could hold his hand. It felt nice to lay there in the dark and hold his hand. It was better than the hospital room; she was beginning to feel like a human again.

It was difficult with the girls. At first, the reception wasn't what Tanja had hoped. The girls seemed scared of the woman in the helmet. Then, they wanted to climb all over her but Mantas was there trying to explain. He would have to explain each day, the very same thing - that they weren't allowed to climb on her. They could only give her gentle hugs. If they wanted to roughhouse, he would volunteer to play castle and roll around with them; Tanja would sit and watch from her wheelchair.

In the end, Tanja decided to hire a nurse only for four hours in the mornings. The nurse would come and help her get to the toilet and wash and get her dressed and help with some exercises – Tanja would sit on the bed and the nurse would push her legs and Tanja would need to resist. She didn't really like having the nurse there, that's why she kept the schedule to just the mornings, it was an admission of what she had become. She preferred to get her physical support from Mantas or Luce – or Tadas if either of the first two weren't there.

It took several days for Sayed to receive another cairo protocol request, which seemed suspicious. He wondered why they were taking their time. He logged in immediately and created a draft indicating that he was ready to receive. He logged out, waited a few minutes and logged back in again – his draft had been deleted and replaced by an attachment - the photo had arrived. Sayed saved the attachment to his laptop, then quickly deleted the draft.

It was a difficult thing to work out. He'd destroyed the original photos almost two years ago. This one looks like it was taken through some bars; it was definitely a European man with longer hair now. However, the face looked so much older. Sayed recalled that the man was only 28; he remembered that because it had just been his birthday. He would be less than 30 now. The man had almost a ghost look about him; he held a newspaper in front of him. Sayed enlarged the photo on his screen; he could make out the date – June 15, 1999.

Sayed spent the next 15 minutes just studying the photo; it could be the same man; it didn't make sense why they would hold him for two years without saying anything, it could be a trap; on the other hand, it didn't really appear to be and, if he played those cards correctly, and it was a trap, he should be able to figure it out in advance.

He then went into the web portal and composed a draft.

"Very interested in retrieving package. Would like to meet to discuss; can come to you."

It was perfect, he thought. If it were a trap, he wouldn't involve anyone else. And, if it wasn't a trap, if nothing else, he could get out of there for a while and they'd be able to arrange a visa. He loved his time in Lebanon and loved the prospect of going back. It would be an added bonus to the plan that he hoped to deploy. He logged back in again to see his draft deleted and the message.

"Will confer. Over."

It only took a day to get a response, but it was a negative one. The Lebanese clearly didn't want to meet on their own soil, but Sayed was surprised by the suggestion "Gulf Hotel, Ghandi. Confirm location."

Sayed was shocked that they would know that hotel. In fact, he was more than shocked. He became increasingly suspicious of the situation. 'How would they know we use that hotel? Why would they want to meet there?' Sayed knew he could get there – if he could get permission to go; others had done the journey recently; it sounded like they used fishing boats from Oman to get there. Sayed decided to ask for 10 days to arrange; he would confirm.

He closed the web portal and thought – now he would need to ask permission and help to get to the city of Al Ghaydah in Yemen.

Bashar had been reluctant about sending the photo, but understood it was likely the only way to broker any type of deal. Besides, there was no evidence of where the photo came from. If it were intercepted, there was still plausible deniability. He smiled to himself when he tried to envision the reaction to the suggestion of the Gulf Hotel on Ghandi Street. The Lebanese had stumbled on that Al Qaeda nest by accident. Bashar thought 'they must be thinking we take the hostage business seriously.' The reality was quite different; they had their own reasons for being in Yemen.

Sayed left early the next morning for the long drive to Kandahar. He drove alone and, as he drove, he went through his scheme and any objections that his proposal might raise. It was a simple plan really – he would give Bin Laden his dream and, in exchange, Sayed's influence would grow. And while the Al Qaeda crew channelled their energies toward their primary goal; Sayed might gain abilities to channel his own vision for a new Afghanistan. It would leave Sayed a much more powerful man and the Americans would pay the price for all their antics in the middle east. It could be the best plan that he'd ever envisioned – Bin Laden and his crew were cash-rich and arms poor; they were also restricted in their ability to move around. The Lebanese had armaments and those armaments would all be sitting close to the Mediterranean Sea – a sea that also served the ports of Europe.

Sayed found the Saudis at the meeting to be particularly frustrating. Their objection was predictable, but also seemed immature. Variations on 'we don't want anything to do with those Shia pigs' were common as the meeting progressed. It was obvious to Sayed that he was losing the argument. He wasn't deterred; the meeting went on for four hours while he was derided, informed that the idea was unworkable, told that the Lebanese couldn't be trusted. It was particularly frustrating as Bin Laden's right-hand man, Yusuf Ali, just sat amongst the naysayers and said nothing.

Then it all seemed to turn a different way. Sayed thought the meeting was about to come to an end when Yusuf Ali raised his hand. "Let's see what they say; you can go; we'll arrange a boat for you." He then turned to the group that had just spent the last four hours criticizing Sayed and said "who cares what colour the cat is, as long as he catches the mice."

By the end of June, Tanja's recuperation was progressing nicely. She had regained control over much of her body. She could control her bowels completely now with no accidents and, with some assistance, could make her way to the toilet. She could walk a little. It had started with some exercises on parallel bars at the outpatient's clinic. Now, if two people would stand on either side of her, she could walk at home. Mantas and Tadas or Mantas and Luce were often called upon to help her move around. It was hard to pull the extra weight around. The doctor had told her that she needed to be extra cautious. She should try to do daily walking exercises, but to keep the duration short and to rest at the first sign of nausea or fatigue. The stress would be hard on the baby.

It was ok; the nurse's bed exercises got her legs feeling limber at the start of the day and she tried to do most of her walking exercises in the morning or early afternoon. By late afternoon, she could feel tired and would mostly sit in a chair.

The other positive development was that the helmet had been newly removed at the outpatient's clinic. She could just cover the area with a cotton headscarf. Tanja thought she looked like a babushka with it, but it was much better than wearing the helmet.

From a neurological perspective, Tanja thought that her memory was ok. She could remember most things now; she even remembered walking to that crosswalk; she could also remember her wedding day, Maria's birth in Seattle and Edita's in London. But, there was something wrong and she just couldn't put her finger on it. When she tried to remember things, her emotions about the situation weren't quite the same. When she looked at her daughters, she didn't feel that sense of adoration that she'd once felt. When she woke and the sun shone, she didn't feel that sense of optimism. She just didn't feel herself; she felt odd. She also seemed to have lost a filter; she asked the young assistant at the outpatient clinic why she had dyed her hair pink, she asked Luce how it felt to be old, she'd asked Tadas why he stayed with her mother when she was ill. It wasn't that the questions were particularly rude, but when she asked them, she could tell that her interlocutors became uncomfortable. The old Tanja would have been embarrassed to have asked a question that made someone feel uncomfortable, she was surprised that the new Tanja didn't seem to care as much. Maybe, the accident had been a wake-up call, maybe she shouldn't worry about this kind of stuff.

Mantas was always trying to test her memory functions and would get her to talk about things that had happened in the past. She would report them like a reporter would report the news – with dispassion. Each day, she would sit in the sitting room after lunch and he would bring her the wedding photo from the mantle. He must have seen her looking at it when she'd first returned from the hospital and now it was part of a daily routine. Tanja would look at the photo and often take her finger and outline the shape of her face with that finger; then she would do the same to her husband. She would think about who those people once were; they looked so young and happy; she wondered if she'd ever feel that intensity of emotion again.

One afternoon, while looking at the photo, Mantas was busy dusting the sitting room while Luce and the girls played around the castle. Luce would try to get them to play quietly when Tanja was deep in thought; it was a fairly fruitless exercise. Tanja sat there and stared at the two in the photo and began outlining their heads with her finger, then she became curious.

"Mantas – why didn't I have a funeral for my husband?"

"I don't know why you do things, sweetheart. I think it was a stressful time in your life."

Tanja nodded her head, "I guess we never had a body either; I just had a photograph." She continued to finger her wedding photo and then another thought came to her.

"Mantas – would you ever get married?" Mantas paused his dusting for a moment.

"Yes – I think so."

"Would you marry me?"

Mantas laughed, "I'm not sure if that's a hypothetical question or a proposal?"

"Well, if you spend all your time with me and we have a baby together; won't it be difficult to find a wife?"

"I guess so, Tanja, sometimes you say funny things."

Tanja went back to circling the couple on her wedding photo.

It had all been worked out in advance through the process of deleting and adding drafts on that web portal. Now, Sayed found himself sitting in the lobby of the Gulf Hotel with a red pocket square firmly planted in the upper chest pocket of his western business suit. He smoked while he sat there; it helped to relax him. He could be walking into a trap and he knew it. However, he also knew that he should look confident; he was there to negotiate and needed to look like he was doing that from a position of strength. He tried to relax himself by thinking about that cat reference that had been made during the meeting. It had quickly silenced the group. When he returned to Kabul, Sayed had mentioned that reference to a close friend, who laughed. "It's ironic that Yusuf Ali would quote an old communist – that is a quote from Deng Xiaoping; a dead Chinese communist." Sayed smiled to himself; they are a foolish bunch.

Almost at the stroke of the proposed meeting time, a woman appeared. She was completely covered in black from head to toe with a burka to cover her face and eyes. She said nothing; she just bowed slightly toward him. He got up and followed her out of the lobby of the Gulf Hotel. They walked for a few minutes; Sayed kept about 5 or 6 paces behind; he knew this routine; they used this method too. At one point, the woman turned into a back alley; she approached a white van then turned around and scanned the area before knocking a sequence of knocks on the backdoor. The door was opened; Sayed knew to get in. The woman did not get in. She just closed the door once he was inside. Sayed looked at his three guards; they were also completely covered and wore balaclavas. He was surprised at their choice of machine guns; each carried a Kalashnikov, the Russian rifle struck Sayed as slightly odd.

The van shuddered into gear, causing Sayed to brace as he painfully noted the lack of shocks. He sat staring at his guards. They drove for about 10 minutes before the van seemed to pull over and stop. The engine was turned off. One of the guards pointed to his clothes; Sayed knew what was being requested. He began to undress. As each piece of clothing was removed, he would hand it to the guard who had made the request. The guard would pull at each piece of clothing and ran a metal detector over the garments. Sayed hadn't brought a wallet or any identification; however, the man even carefully checked the banknotes and coins that were in his pocket.

Once all his clothes had been confiscated, save his underwear, Sayed began to dread what might come next. The man signalled that he should remove them. Sayed obeyed and now was nervous about the next procedure. However, the guard seemed satisfied only to run his metal detector across his orifices; he was spared the probe.

Sayed's underwear was returned to him and he was given a robe and sandals to wear and was signalled to put them on. It appeared that he was to wear this local garb to the meeting instead of the western clothes and shoes. Once dressed, the guard banged on the side of the van and the driver started it again and their voyage continued.

When the van finally stopped, Sayed was blindfolded and walked up a series of stairs until he was placed in a chair. He could hear that there was at least one guard still with him when he heard the voice.

"It's nice to meet you," said the voice.

"The pleasure is mine. I'm Sayed." It was peculiar to talk while blindfolded.

"It is my pleasure," said the voice, but he didn't provide a name.

The voice continued after a brief pause. "Anyway, why don't we come right to the business at hand? It sounds like you're interested in the Briton. You'll understand, brother, our cause against the Israelis is expensive, we're hoping he might have some value to you."

Sayed couldn't have asked for a better segue; money was the one thing that the foolish Al Qaeda bunch certainly did have.

"Oh, we would be pleased to contribute to the cause. In fact, I was hoping you might be willing to hear out some additional thoughts; since we're here."

Sayed was then told to proceed. It was a monologue he had rehearsed thoroughly. In exchange for access to some of their munitions in Lebanon or Syria, they would be willing to pay a very generous price. Sayed went on to emphasize that there was little that they needed to do. They would just have to provide some of their existing arsenal and safe passage for one of their agents to get to Syria or Lebanon.

Sayed was impressed with his monologue; it was perfect and they'd already admitted that they needed money. He must have spoken for close to 10 minutes before he finally stopped and waited for affirmation before he continued. It wasn't what he'd hoped.

"Impossible," said the voice, "No way, we have already upset too many Europeans, I know where those weapons would end up, no way."

Sayed went quiet; it was to be a useless trip. He thought it a perfect idea and yet, it wasn't. The Lebanese considered it flawed; they didn't want to risk inflaming the Europeans. Sayed was anxious to think, maybe there was something else, maybe they could use the hostage as a means for further negotiation, maybe there was some compromise that could be made. He decided that he would just keep talking; he would feel them out, maybe there was something they could do.

Sayed continued. "What if, in exchange for a generous contribution, we were to take delivery somewhere else and promise that nothing would be used in Europe. America is our real enemy anyway. Maybe, if you just brought them to us here; you seem to have figured out how to get here – to Yemen."

There was more silence and Sayed sat there with his blindfold; he was thinking that he would have to come up with a third idea, when he was surprised by the voice's reply.

"You know, brother, that might be worth a conversation; I guess it would depend on the size of that generous contribution."

It took a couple of days of negotiation. The Afghan had to be driven back and forth between the Gulf Hotel several times so he could consult, but, in the end, Bashar couldn't have dreamed of a better outcome. He had attended the meeting in the hopes of maybe a million dollars for the return of a hostage, but this deal had grown much bigger. The final sum was close to $16 million. They seemed desperate; Bashar had even secured a promise that no one would come to Lebanon for the prisoner; he would be handed over in Yemen.

It almost seemed a crime to take their money. The Korean munitions would be part of a bigger shipment and the share that they'd sell was only worth approximately $5 million. The only added service they would have to supply would be delivery, but that was going to be easy. The Afghan would have been shocked to understand that the only transport they'd need to provide would be to haul the arsenal from the drop site near Socotra Island to the Yemen mainland. It would take several boats over several days to do it, but they'd done it before and the stuff would have to be brought to the mainland in any event.

For Sayed, the deal represented something very very significant. He had just facilitated the procurement of close to $16 million in munitions and he'd managed to get the Lebanese to ship them directly to Yemen; one of the few countries they could move in and out of easily. It would establish himself as a major player; it would hurt the Americans; it would refocus the foreigners and might encourage them to return where they could be more useful. It was all working according to plan. He might even be able to deliver that favour to Zurab. There was one minor issue on that front - the Lebanese wanted to deliver the hostage to Yemen; Sayed couldn't risk that; if they wouldn't just let him go, he would have to be treated as collateral damage; this deal was too big to risk.

Lamia was proud of her new plan and George sat on the bed and listened intently. Now that the flight had been booked to Canada, she knew that she would have a layover in Frankfurt and that layover was almost six hours. She would procure some Euros in advance and could call George's wife. That would work fine. She would also disguise her voice. She still had almost 7 weeks to practice; she knew that she could do it.

George wasn't sure if it would work. How would Tanja know that it was legitimate?

Lamia had already thought it out, "You need to tell me something that only you and her would know; then you will write exactly what you want me to say; and when I say it, I will hang up. So, you need to think carefully and, when I come back, I will give you pen and paper, but I want to get it back from you at the same meeting. Ok? You still remember the phone number?"

"I'll give you two numbers; what happens if you get voicemail?"

"I'm sorry George, I can try two numbers, but then I have to leave a voicemail."

"Ok, ok, it will work."

When Lamia left, he stared at the fluorescent light; what was something that only he and Tanja would know and that no one else would know, then the joke came to him "Next Christmas, I'm getting socks."

Tanja looked at the window and thought to herself, then decided it would be prudent to ask Luce about it.

"Luce – Why is it that Mantas doesn't want to marry me?"

Luce laughed, "I'm pretty sure he's obsessed with you, Tanja. It was you who made it very clear that you didn't particularly want him in your life."

"But that was before the accident, now I think I need him. I can't keep up with a baby; I can't even cope with the girls. You do all the work. I asked him about marriage and he didn't answer me."

"I was there for that discussion. I wasn't sure if that was a proposal or a hypothetical question either. Your communication is sometimes a bit funny these days, Tanja."

"What do you think of Mantas? You weren't a fan before."

"True. I think tragedy can sometimes bring out the best and worst in people. I guess I'm in the same boat as you – I was mistaken about him. Over these last couple of months, he has been absolutely devoted to getting you better. He always came across as self-centred; that was a very unfair assessment, I know that now."

Tanja tried to digest that statement; it made a lot of sense; Luce usually made sense.

"Do you think George would approve of Mantas?" asked Tanja.

"Well, I never met him, but from what you've told me about him, he always wanted the best for you. So, I would say 'yes,' he would probably approve."

Tanja decided that her earlier proposal hadn't been taken seriously because of all the things that were going on in the sitting room at the time. She felt that sometimes her thoughts skipped around these days and people might have trouble following them. She settled on a different plan; she would wait until she had his undivided attention. She also felt like she needed to move things along. Their baby would be born in less than three months. She needed him to make a firm commitment that he would stay; that she wouldn't be left alone.

She waited until bedtime. Mantas tucked her in first then made his little bed on the floor; she then reached down and held his hand.

"Mantas – would you marry me?"

"Are we back to that? Then I say 'yes'." He laughed and used his other hand to stroke her hand that he was clasping.

"No, I'm serious; will you marry me?"

He still laughed, "Absolutely; if you come to me in six months or a year and you've completely recovered and you ask me that question, I would say yes. Right now, if I said yes, I would be taking advantage of a woman that is dependent on me to tuck her in and help her walk."

"Mantas – you're a different person than I thought. I thought you were self-centred, but I was wrong. I'm sorry."

"You weren't wrong, Tanja, I was that person, but I hope that I'm changing."

She now used her fingers to caress his hand that held it.

"I don't want to wait six months or a year, I want my child to have a father."

"It looks like that accident may have changed both of us. I don't want you to worry; I will take care of our child – the same way that I take care of Edita and Maria. I love you, but I won't force you to make a commitment to me."

"It's you that isn't making a commitment."

George was particularly enjoying this week's book. It shouldn't have been an uplifting book, but somehow, he enjoyed it. The book was about Stalingrad. He could empathize with the Germans; he was locked down with no way out. However, at least he had food and drink. Maybe, that's why it made him feel better – he had food, drinks, books, cigarettes, Lamia and English lessons to teach.

He couldn't help feeling just a little bit optimistic these days. It wasn't because he thought his release would happen anytime soon. He had been interrogated three months ago and then nothing had happened. Maybe, they made a point of interrogating their hostages every 20 months! That would mean, it would be well into the new millennium before he'd see an interrogator again. The thing that really excited him these days was Lamia's offer to call Tanja.

He had carefully scripted a message that Lamia was to read to her from the payphone at Frankfurt Airport. It read "your husband is alive and well. So, you know this message comes from him, he wants you to know that he will be happy with socks next Christmas. He will be home soon. He loves you and Maria very much and looks forward to meeting the new one." It was simple but to the point; he'd also told Lamia to see if she could buy a phone card to use for the phone calls so they wouldn't be interrupted if the coins ran out.

He tried to envision Tanja's face; she probably felt as lonely and desperate as he did. It would give her renewed hope; even if George wasn't really sure that he would be home 'soon.' It was all taking so long to figure out. He was beginning to think that Lamia's 'important friend' may have just conceded a symbolic gesture – interviewed the inmate in the basement to give her the illusion of progress. It had been such a polite thing – he'd imagined something rougher from a hostage interrogator; especially from what little he understood about Hezbollah.

He was also happy about Lamia; it was going to be lonely without her; in fact, he would have no one to talk to at all. However, something inside him now believed he could survive without her. It was a new feeling because, not so long ago, he'd felt that he could not carry on without her. Part of his happiness about Lamia was her enthusiasm for beginning her new life. She tried to hide it a little when she was around him, but George had assured her that she should be happy; in fact, seeing her so happy made him feel happy. In only a month, she would be on a plane and destined for a new life. George's only regret was that he wouldn't be on that plane with her.

By the end of July, Tanja felt like she was back to her old self – more or less. The physiotherapy and walking practice had paid dividends. Even with all the extra weight, she could walk quite reasonably now. She walked with a slight limp and got tired quickly, but the main thing was that she could walk again. Her mind was also much clearer; she still sometimes asked 'straightforward' questions, but she rationalized that having almost lost her life, she didn't have time to beat around the bush anymore. She was also told that she could remove her headscarf; the scalp no longer needed that protection from germs. She loved to look at her blonde hair again; it wasn't as long and beautiful as it had been, but it was slowly returning to normal. She loved to take showers and wash it; before, she'd needed help to keep things away from the scar on her head, but now, she could do what she wanted and she liked it.

It wasn't just her physical health that had changed. Mantas had been right; her worldview had changed. When she was recovering, Mantas would bring her wedding photo to her every afternoon. While she looked at it and traced the figures with her finger, she would think. Looking at that photo of her past gave her plenty of time to think about her future. She was so happy in that photo and she wanted to be happy again. As she circled, she thought and then began to plan how she would achieve that goal. She would spend more time with her girls and Vlad. Luce, Mantas and Tadas had been devoted to them and she had largely ignored them – especially Vlad who didn't seem to demand her time as much as the girls. She was going to be a mother again and that would be something to look forward to – and Luce said she would help and Tadas said he would help. She was surrounded by people who loved her, she just needed to find a way to get over this current slump and she might be as happy as she was in that photograph. And then there was Mantas.

One evening in mid-July, as he began making his little bed on the floor beside her, Tanja concluded that he had really become her manservant. It wasn't fair and it wasn't just. She invited him to lie beside her in the master bed. At first, he refused and said it wasn't appropriate. Tanja reminded him that she was pregnant with his child and would appreciate it if he would lie beside her and rub her tummy and stroke her hair like he used to. He conceded and now spent every night in the bed beside her; more befitting someone she loved rather than a manservant.

And she did love him. Luce had been quite correct – sometimes tragedy could bring out the best in people. He had given up everything to care for her, even after she had rejected him. He was a real man, she thought, and regretted having called him a boy. One night, as he lay there beside her, Tanja again asked whether there was a future for them. Mantas kissed her on the forehead and said, "Of course, my love," but didn't seem to want to be more specific. She decided that she was pushing things too much; she would have to wait for him to bring it up again.

As Mantas, Vlad and the girls returned to the apartment that following afternoon and she heard the key in the lock, Tanja was excited. She really did have a lot to be happy about and soon, she would be as happy as the girl in that photo.

The excitement was heightened by the invasion of Princess Maria, who ran first through the door. Maria now spoke hundreds of words and loved to impress everyone with them.

"We got present," Maria exclaimed.

Then, Edita ran over and jumped on Tanja's lap. Finally, Vlad came bounding over and gave her a hug, which seemed very unusual.

Tanja just laughed while Edita sat on her lap, Maria ran around the sitting room and Vlad stared at her, when he normally would be staring at his video games.

"To what do I owe all this excitement? It must have been a great outing. And where's my present?" Tanja looked toward Mantas, who just smiled.

"We can't say nothing," said Maria.

Mantas came toward her and said "This is a little unorthodox but we decided, as a group, to get you this."

He held out a small crushed velour box, it was similar to the necklace box that he'd given her, but it was a ring box. Tanja opened it; it was a simple gold ring with an amber stone.

"So, I know it's not much, but I will replace it when the time comes. You asked me about getting married and I said you should wait six months or a year until you are fully healthy before asking me that question, and I will keep you to that. But, this ring represents my betrothal to you. When that day comes, this ring represents a standing offer of my answer. I know that I would be marrying all of you, so I also got Vlad and the girls' permission to buy it and they helped choose it."

Tanja looked down at the ring. It was the most beautiful thing she'd ever owned; accompanied by the most beautiful speech she'd ever heard. She stood up and gently kissed Mantas on the lips. "I can't wait; believe me, the offer will be made and this ring will never be replaced." Tanja placed it on her right-hand ring finger; her wedding ring remained on her left hand; it was an English custom that pleased George; she'd have to consider what to do about it; in the meantime, the amber ring looked perfect on her right hand, where an engagement ring should rightly be placed in this part of Europe.

Mantas smiled then looked a bit sullen, "There is only one thing; we need to talk. I need to tell you all about me – the old me. If you still feel I'm worthy, then I will wait for that question."

CHAPTER 9

Changes

Mantas lay there that night with Tanja's head on his chest. It was a particularly hot summer night; they lay there together without any sheets; it was too hot for Mantas to wear a t-shirt, so Tanja lay on his bare chest. He wondered if he should discuss it tonight or whether she was even awake. She had had such a happy day. Lately, the old Tanja was definitely coming back. She was happy, optimistic, loving. His patient was very much on the mend; almost completely her old self. That's why Mantas lay there and thought – should he really threaten her progress and their special day with his confessions? Could it slow her recovery? On the other hand, how could he live with this guilt? He had betrayed the woman he loved.

He wasn't sure how she would react to the confession. He knew she was a believer in fate; perhaps she would let it all go – perhaps she would say that it was all water on the bridge. Her life had been a tough one; he knew she'd had to become accustomed to inconvenient truths. Her father had left her when she was 12, her mother had died of cancer, her husband had died violently, she gave birth alone to Edita, she'd become a single mother and widow by the time she was 23. He sat and thought and wondered how she would react and wondered some more about whether he should tell her tonight. There would be other nights and this was such a special night; she'd been so pleased with her ring. He was finally winning his great conquest, yet the victory felt hollow. He would just see if she was still awake. He would just whisper quietly.

"Tanja, you sleeping?"

The reply came quickly. "I'm 7 months pregnant and it feels like 30 degrees in here; I can safely say that I'm not sleeping. Little Ata seems to be particularly keen to keep me from that tonight."

Mantas allowed himself a nervous laugh, "Feel up to a chat?"

"Sure, about the speech when you gave me the ring?" She raised her finger to her lips and kissed the ring.

"Yeah, if that's ok or we could talk tomorrow."

"I think you have a very captive audience tonight. We're both listening." She took Mantas' hand which was draped around her waist and moved it to her tummy so he could feel the baby. The gesture made Mantas feel uncomfortable. It was not conducive to the message he was about to deliver.

"Tanja – I'm worried that I'm not the man that you think I am. I'm more like the person that you thought I was before you walked toward that crosswalk."

"Not true," she leaned toward him and gently kissed him on his lips.

"Well, let me tell you a few things first – and then you decide... you remember our second kiss?... I was using a psychology tactic to get you to believe that you wanted to kiss me. It's used with obstinate children. At the time, I thought you were having 'buyer's remorse,' but now I know I manipulated you. Do you think you could find it in your heart to forgive me?"

Tanja giggled, "I figured that out a long time ago. You may have tried to manipulate me, but I allowed myself to be manipulated. I wouldn't have kissed you unless you'd unearthed something in me. Fate played a role, Mantas. So, I would say that yes, you are forgiven. And I don't think you should feel guilty about it." He was relieved to hear her mention fate; it might make the next segment easier, so he resumed.

"So, back in December, I was hoping to seduce you. I bought that protection in the hopes I would use it with you. I didn't think it would happen on that French restaurant night, but I was hoping it would happen sometime and I prepared for it. I also worked on trying to charm Vlad and the girls so you'd like me more – that's why I bought all the elaborate presents."

Tanja giggled again and reached up and kissed him again. "You know, men always think they are somehow different, but they're pretty much the same. All men try tactics like that. And, if you remember, I was the one who seduced you. If anything, you should be commended for being prepared; I wasn't."

"So, do you forgive me for that?" asked Mantas.

"Of course, silly."

"Ok, I have one more."

Tanja interjected, "Before you start, since we are having confessions heard tonight; I need to confess something and you can decide whether you can forgive me. Ok?" She started gently tugging at his chest hairs and rubbing his chest as she continued, "When we talked about names and I said you could help with a girl's name, I already knew it was a boy. I had an ultrasound and asked for the sex. I wanted to call him Ata because I had a dream that a little boy ran to me and said that was his name. As the boy lay in my arms, his face turned to my husband's face. It felt like he was sending me a sign. When I woke, I found a book which had the origins of names; it means 'gift' in Arabic. I promised my dead husband that I would call him Ata. And I still want to call him Ata; but I'm ok to come up with a different middle name and he will have your surname. At the time, I'm sorry, I just didn't want you in our lives. Is that ok and can you forgive *me*?"

He reached down and kissed her forehead. He felt he had never been more in love than at that moment. Here was a woman willing to bare her soul to him and forgive him for his obsessive behaviour. He caressed her stomach that possessed his unborn son.

"Of course, it's a great name and there is nothing to forgive… now, can I do my last one?"

"Of course. I like this process, Mantas, it's good to clear the air. Keep going so I can grant you clemency. I feel like Princess Maria."

Mantas smiled; he had an overwhelming sense of contentment. He continued to stroke her hair and she continued to stroke his chest before he carried on…

"So, on the night before New Year's Eve, when you came over, I was hoping we would be intimate again." Tanja let out a giggle as she stroked. "So, I prepared the place and the protection, but then I was hoping the protection would fail."

Tanja chuckled, "You're funny; a school boy's fantasy on catching his dream girl."

"Yeah, well, I might have taken it one step further than fantasy. It was more than just a hope." He paused for a minute; she continued to stroke his chest.

"I'm sorry Tanja; I sabotaged that condom. Just before you got there, I stuck a pin in the package. I didn't think it would actually work. I'm so sorry; I know how wrong it was, I'm ashamed, but we can't base a relationship on a lie. Do you think you could ever forgive me? I don't deserve it."

Tanja stopped rubbing his chest, her body froze; she didn't say anything, there was nothing to say. She had just learned that she had been betrayed by someone she loved; by someone who professed to love her, who had cared and nursed her for the last three months. She just lay there – with nothing to say.

"Tanja, what are you thinking. Can you forgive me?"

She extracted herself from his chest and rolled over to her side of the bed with her back facing him. "I need to think about that one."

The next morning was awkward for Mantas. She wouldn't talk to him; she wouldn't look at him. It wasn't that she wouldn't say anything; she did say "morning" when he had said "good morning" and there were a few words exchanged regarding Vlad and the girls, but nothing else. He was finally getting what he deserved.

It was supposed to be a happy day; Luce arrived about 9 and Maria immediately went to tell her the news. Mantas smiled at Luce when she congratulated him; Luce then went over to hug Tanja; Tanja accepted the hug, but not the congratulations. She told Luce that the proposal was a standing offer of acceptance if they ever got to that point in the relationship. Luce smiled awkwardly; she'd obviously never come across a proposal like that.

Mantas thought that things would likely improve as the day progressed; she may not be able to forgive him for a long time but she would have to stop with the cold shoulder at some point. He was wrong. After lunch, Tanja disappeared to the master bedroom for a few minutes.

Mantas was suspicious and looked at her hand when she returned to the sitting room – she had removed the ring. She seemed to be pondering something; he didn't like it. He wondered – maybe he should prepare his usual spot on the floor tonight; she clearly needed time to think.

At late afternoon, he was in the kitchen preparing dinner. He looked up from cutting vegetables and she was standing there. She had obviously been waiting for a time where he would be alone – away from the girls and Luce.

"Mantas – thanks again for everything. I think I can handle it tonight. After dinner, why don't you take the evening off and spend the night at your place?"

He just looked down. He was so ashamed. It wasn't a question; he knew that, it was a command. He wanted to ask if he should come back tomorrow or if she needed some time, but the words just didn't seem to fit the moment.

"Ok." Tanja began to walk out of the kitchen. "Tanja – one more thing?" She turned around. "I love you." She said nothing and turned around and left the kitchen.

This was a special meeting; it was their last secret meeting. It had been two years of secret meetings and this was the last one that Lamia and George would spend together – or so they both hoped. They were both hoping he would be out of that basement by the time she returned from school in May.

Lamia started the meeting the way that she had started their first real clandestine meeting. She removed her burka. Then, she put her hand through the bar and George clasped it. He held it with both his hands; he held it extra firmly and for an extra long period of time. He needed to etch that moment into his mind – it would have to last him.

She looked at him with her deep brown eyes, "So, I give you one more present; the old one is looking bad." She gave him another heart; it was similar to the one that she'd given him for Valentine's Day. It said "I love you" on it. George smiled as he took it; he had cherished the previous one and now, he would have two to cherish.

"Sorry, George, I want write 'I miss you', but if some person find that, they might be suspicious."

"I understand; this is perfect; my other one is quite worn. I use it to save my page in the books and I look at it several times a day. Now, I can read two books at the same time."

"You funny, George." She smiled and gently pulled her hand back.

"Are you excited? Is everything in order?" asked George.

"Oh yes, a Lebanese man in Toronto will take me from airport and drive me to residence at the university. He's doing a favour. I worry I will be too tired to talk; it will be almost 20 hours to get there."

"Yes, you might have jetlag, but I think you'll be wide awake. The adrenaline will be pumping."

"And I am also praying I will speak to Tanja. She is a very lucky woman; you love her so much."

"If you met her, you'd love her as well. One day, I hope we can all meet. Lamia?" George stopped talking for a minute, he wanted to make the pause dramatic, "thank you... thank you for keeping me sane, thank you for talking to me and making sure I was ok and bringing me hearts. I think I would have died here without you. You are a very special person. Use that kindness to bring love to this world. Ok?"

"You dramatic, George. I come here because I want that; I love you. Don't worry, everything going to be ok."

It was hard to say goodbye that morning. She wanted to leave, but it didn't seem right. He had been her teacher and mentor and supporter; now, she was leaving him behind – locked in her parents' basement.

It was hard to say goodbye. He had fallen in love with the Lebanese teenager; it was a love that he hoped he would have for Maria and his other child one day. She had risked her life to save him; she was brave and strong; smart and resourceful. He knew that she was anxious to go and start that new life without him. It was he who decided to finish the conversation that morning. He put his hand out the bars, "Goodbye, my dear; I will always love you. Be brave; there is nothing you can't do."

She held his hand with both her hands and then a tear began to run down her cheek. She kissed his hand and then put her forehead over the clasped hands. She sobbed as she held it for those last few precious seconds. She then looked at him and made one last comment, "I love you." She turned her back and began walking toward the stairs; then she began the ascent away from her teacher and away from a life she was about to leave.

At Frankfurt Airport, Lamia was able to find a convenience shop that sold phone cards. She was happy to see instructions on the phone card in English; she could have a shot at understanding how to use it. George had made it easy by including all the digits that she would need to dial when calling from Europe. She first placed her card in the slot and dialled George's home number; the phone rang and rang and then went to voicemail. She hung up. Then, she dialled the mobile phone number, but there was a message saying something about it couldn't be called as dialled. The latter call didn't seem to cost her any of her phonecard credits, Lamia tried again – and got the same message.

So, now she would have to dial the home number again, she was rehearsed and ready to leave the message on the machine. She dialled it and it began to ring, but then someone picked it up. Lamia hadn't been prepared for that. It was a woman who answered, but she sounded quite old. Lamia decided to ask before beginning the message.

"Tanja, is you Tanja?"

"No dear; you have a wrong number."

"Sure? You know Tanja?"

"Sorry dear, it may have been one of the previous tenants, but there is no Tanja here. Did you just call?"

"Yes. Just now."

"Ok, sorry, dear. Bye. Bye."

Lamia put down the phone. She had always prided herself on thinking through things, but she'd never thought about this scenario. She'd always imagined that she'd speak to Tanja or that she would leave a message. Now, she had failed at both. She thought for a minute about what she could do next. She looked up at the big board with all the names of the cities and the departure times. As she stared, she began to realize that there was nothing that she could do. She would have to accept failure. She picked up the phone and tried to dial the mobile number again; it failed again. She still had credit on her phone card; she picked up the phone and called her parents' number. Her mother picked up; it was some consolation; she was out in the world by herself for the first time. She would have preferred to have used that money to talk to Tanja, but it was nice to hear her own language from her own mother in that very busy German airport.

The first half of August was particularly difficult for Mantas. His routine was now very different. He would go to Tanja's apartment every morning around 10 to ask how he could help. Tanja would say that she didn't need help and would thank him for coming. She would let him in and sometimes he would play with the girls for a few minutes or talk to Vlad or Luce or sometimes Tadas. Tanja didn't seem interested in talking with him. If he asked her a question, she would answer. However, any conversation would be distant and aloof. It seemed apparent – the love of his life was slipping to an end.

There were times when he wondered if he should have told her about the deception, then he remembered that he couldn't go on with a lie. He had touched beauty and been able to possess it for a few short weeks and he would always see her beauty in his son's eyes. He no longer wanted to possess her; loving her meant letting her go. He was still hoping she would let him see that son; whatever her decision on the subject, he would abide by it.

The only positive aspect of the August situation was that he could throw himself into his work. Parents were pleased that he was working again and seemed more than frustrated about having their kids at home all the time for the summer break. His calendar was filling up with appointments. It was good to be busy, but it was also good to have some income again. The ring had added to the debt of a very expensive Christmas with a fancy dinner and luxurious gifts for the kids.

It was those luxurious gifts that got him thinking that evening. He had put his own present away and hadn't really touched it much. He went to the cabinet and found the Highland Park scotch. He looked at the bottle, "It was you that got me into this mess." Then, he smiled at the bottle; that wasn't really true; it was he who had gotten himself in that mess.

He sat on his sofa and drank the scotch that evening and thought about the world that he had lost over those last few weeks. Then, there was a knock at the flat door. It must be one of the parents; he was now so heavily booked that they were wooing him to open additional timeslots. He stood up and walked to the door.

"Tanja?" there she was; one cheek still slightly bruised; Mantas thought she also now looked huge and she looked exhausted and was sweating, but Mantas thought she still looked beautiful.

"Come in, sit down, did you walk here?"

Tanja sat on the sofa. It was difficult for her to sit down with all the weight, finally, she just seemed to collapse into the chair.

"I did; I needed to think. I'll take a taxi back."

"Can I get you something?"

"Water, water would be nice please." Mantas ran to the little kitchen area and retrieved a glass. It wouldn't be good enough to serve her just water. He rummaged through the freezer and found an ice cube tray. He put four ice cubes in a pint glass and filled it with water. He then returned to the sitting room and put the glass on the coffee table in front of her.

"Mantas – I wanted to return something to you." From her handbag, she pulled out the velour ring box. He took it from her.

"Thank you," he said and looked down at the box.

"Also, I want to give you some money. You spent your whole summer helping me and you weren't able to take any students." Tanja began to take out her wallet.

"I won't take money from you, Tanja. Please don't ask me. I will take the ring back, but I won't take the money."

"Mantas – this isn't like the last time I gave you money; I'm not throwing it at you. You did a good deed and I don't want you to lose your flat over it; please take it."

"It wasn't a good deed; it was my duty. You know how ashamed I am; I did this to you; I shouted at a pregnant woman and that caused you to get hurt. I will keep the ring; Maria loved that ring. If it's ok, when the baby is born, I'll give it to her as a memento of the birth of her brother. Is that ok?"

"That's ok, Mantas. It's kind of you to think of her. She will love it." Tanja stopped a second. She looked at him, then looked down, then looked back toward him. "Mantas – I loved you... how could you do that to me?"

"I don't know; you didn't deserve it. I guess I thought a guy like me could never be with someone like you. I'm humiliated; I can't make it up to you. I only hope Ata will have beautiful blue eyes so that you are not reminded of me each time you look at him."

Tanja smiled sheepishly. "It's not like that… I'm sorry Mantas, I know you experienced some type of epiphany when I had the accident. I know things are very different with you now. And I admire you for telling me the truth. I'm not sure what you expected. You did the right thing, but, right now, I feel betrayed. I need more time to think things through. I still want you in our lives; you'll be a great father to Ata. I'm just not sure where you fit in my life. What you did to me was actually assault. Do you understand that?"

"I do. I also don't deserve the kind way that you are treating me now. If it were a different person, they would cut me off completely and maybe call the police. I want to be a part of your family's life; I will take whatever you will give me and I'll be any type of father you want me to be."

Tanja smiled again; it was an awkward smile. She stood up. "Ok, Mantas. Will you come round tomorrow to see the girls? And can you talk to Vlad about some tutorials? That way, you can at least earn a bit of money in your free time."

Mantas returned the awkward smile. "I will find some time for Vlad, but I still won't take money for Vlad. He will be my son's uncle."

Tanja smiled again and gently kissed him on the cheek. She made her way to the door and closed it behind her.

George was surprised at how lonely he got and how quickly. She'd only been gone a fortnight; he knew he was going to feel lonely, but didn't realize that he'd feel this lonely this quickly. Without the English lessons and the secret visits, it meant the only human contact he had was with Lamia's father. The man in black would bring the tray three times a day and come down once after dinner to light his cigarette. He would also bring him a razor, shaving cream and mirror twice a week and observe him while he shaved. George had trouble believing it could become so monotonous so quickly. Even the books didn't give him quite the escape that he'd once experienced. He found that his mind wandered; he would often end up looking at the two hearts that Lamia had given him. He would hold them up beside each other and compare the minute variations in handwriting and the size and shape of the hearts. He loved looking at the hearts; one reminded him of Valentine's Day and the other reminded him of the day that she left for her new life.

The other thing on George's mind on those late August days was Tanja's reaction to Lamia's telephone call. He wondered if she believed that the message really came from him. Maybe, it gave her comfort or maybe it scared her; he hoped it wouldn't be the latter. He also thought about Maria; she would have turned 3 in May; she was probably talking now; he had missed all the rituals surrounding his toddler growing into a girl. He then thought about his other child; in his mind, he thought it would be a boy and that boy would be turning 2 next month. He'd missed his first laugh, his first walk, his first words; they'd all been missed while he waited in that cell; and perhaps, he would never leave it.

Mantas had become accustomed to the new regime. He would drop by once each day to check on the family. Twice per week, he would give Vlad a tutorial. The tutorials were harder now; Mantas was no longer a 'teacher' to Vlad but more like a family member, so Vlad could be difficult. Mantas was considering 'creating some distance' by being harder on him; he would have to think about it as the sessions could get derailed.

Tanja seemed to be warming up to him. She would always greet him with a kiss to the cheek. He treasured that ceremony. They could have conversations now about things – they had become like two close friends. In the back of his mind, he was hoping to win her back, but he wouldn't try now; it would have to wait.

He wasn't strategizing about putting together a plan to achieve an objective. He would never approach her like that again. It wasn't her that stopped him from either trying to win her back or leaving the idea completely. The problem was with him.

Mantas was overwhelmed with a sense of guilt that he couldn't have imagined just a few months ago. When he looked at the mirror, he would see a person whom he loathed, whom he despised. When he conducted his tutorials and a child couldn't get a concept, he would first be angry at the student, then feel ashamed that he was angry – it wasn't them, it was him. He was a useless human being that didn't deserve to teach them.

By mid-August, the sense of shame and guilt became so intense that he began to worry about it. How could he be a father to his son when he was emotionally unstable? He needed to talk to someone about it, but the only person he could think to talk about it with was Tanja. He called her and asked if there was a time when she could find a few minutes to take a walk with him, so he could ask for some advice on a problem. Tanja said that, if he came over the following day, she could ask Luce to watch Vlad and the girls and they could take a walk.

It was a very warm August morning when he arrived at the apartment; it was late morning and it felt particularly hot outside. Once Tanja opened the door, the girls were excited to see him. And that's when it happened, as Edita ran to hug him, she called out 'daddy.' This seemed to catch Maria off-guard; she pushed Edita to the side and hugged him and then she called him 'daddy.' He smiled at the girls; maybe this would be a better day.

"I'm not sure where that came from," remarked Tanja. "Maria was asking lots of questions last night and I told them that you will be their brother's father. That started a whole long conversation about George being their father and why their brother would have a different one. I guess Edita determined that she wasn't going to let that happen." Tanja smiled as if it were just a funny thing for the girls to have said. It meant so much more to Mantas.

"Shall we go?" asked Tanja as she waved goodbye to Luce who stood near the kitchen. "We won't be long, half-hour tops."

They walked down the stairs, but Tanja already seemed out of breath. They walked out of the old town and crossed the crosswalk; it was the same crosswalk that had almost ended her life. They made their way toward the river.

"Mantas, I'm sorry; I know you wanted a walk, I'm not sure I'm up for it today. The baby is just too heavy in this heat. Would it be ok if we found a bench in the shade?"

Mantas scanned the river pathway. There were benches but they all seemed to be taken; there was one that was free, but it was in the sun. He eyed one elderly couple and wondered if their rest was coming to an end. He motioned Tanja to follow him as he walked toward that bench. It had been the correct calculation. As they got closer, the couple stood up. Mantas ran the last 50 metres toward the bench to sit on it and reserve it for their private conversation. It was a beautiful bench. It was close enough to the Baltic Sea to feel a light breeze from it. A giant tree afforded shade.

Mantas had to stand and help Tanja sit on the bench. She seemed to be really struggling these days. Tanja sat and looked at him and smiled and then she seemed to have an unusual thought.

"I wonder what people think. This is a small town really; I'm sure everyone knows our story. Here you are on the bench, but we're not really together, but sometimes you live with me and I'm pregnant with your child. I'm sure the grannies have lots to gossip about. I'll give you a kiss when I leave to give them something to talk about."

Tanja laughed at her own joke; Mantas felt compelled to smile.

"So, what's on your mind, Mantas? It sounded important."

Mantas looked at the river. He watched it for a second before starting. "Tanja, we talked about forgiveness; you're not ready to forgive me, I understand that. However, I'm finding that I can't forgive me either; I feel a kind of self-loathing. And it's not just about the pregnancy and the way I treated you; I'm a very calculating person; I use people and now I can't get past it. I just don't feel emotion the way others do; I think I'm some sort of a psychopath."

Tanja smiled and then she did something unusual; she put her hand over his hand. "I'm pretty sure that psychopaths don't worry about being psychopaths, Mantas. The fact that you are worried about your emotions likely means that you have emotions."

Mantas thought about that for a second; it made sense, he was the one interested in psychology, yet she had just dismissed a diagnosis with a great deal of common sense.

"I guess that's right." Mantas now kept staring at the river while she had her hand on his.

"Mantas – you can't control the past; it's over. You can only control the present and the future. Luce once told me that tragedy brings out the best and worst in people. In you, it brought something beautiful out. You helped me recover from my accident, you found the courage to confront the truth and now you're starting the process of trying to find it in yourself to forgive yourself."

Mantas nodded his head and the two sat in silence for a minute, before Mantas spoke.

"Do you think you could ever find it in yourself to forgive me? I mean – I don't expect us to be together again; I just want to know if you could forgive me?"

Tanja squeezed his hand, "I think so and maybe we will be together again. I just need a little more time to think things through. It's possible that you will also want to move on, Mantas, you have so much to offer; and now, you have a clean slate; you're becoming a new man – a very kind and precious man."

Mantas smiled awkwardly, "Not exactly a clean slate" and he looked at Tanja's tummy.

Tanja smirked and then continued, "You know, you've always been an analytical guy. There's nothing wrong with that; it doesn't mean you're evil because you are less emotional than others or because you've done a few bad things. And, by the way, I don't know everything about your past, but I have a sneaking suspicion that the 'using people' that you mentioned was amplified by that one deception with me. I don't think you're a bad guy, you did something bad, but it doesn't make you a bad guy. And look at all the good you've brought to the world – all the children that you've helped, my girls love you; they even called you 'daddy', Vlad loves you; Luce used to despise you, but now she likes you."

Tanja paused for a second and took a breath, "Because you're an analytical guy; I'll try to explain it in numbers for you. Imagine, at the end of your life, that you're able to tally all the bad things you've done in your life and subtract them from all the good deeds you've done in your life. If the number is well into the positive, you've had a good life. If it's negative, you haven't added anything. You're a young man; whatever you've done, you've got plenty of time to get yourself well back onto the positive side… I'm sorry, Mantas, that all sounds a little silly, but I hope it makes sense."

Mantas looked at the river and thought to himself, 'it's not silly and it does make sense.'

Sayed was pleased with himself; everyone was pleased with him. The people that seemed most pleased with him were Yusuf Ali and his inner circle. That circle had doubted him and cast derision at his plan, but not anymore. It looked like the most effective feline was an Afghan cat; he smiled as he thought about it; if only they knew the original connection was via British military intelligence. He smirked again when he thought about it.

The arms were now stored away in Al Qaeda safe houses throughout Yemen. Sayed wasn't sure what they were going to do with them now. He didn't care that much; it was now up to them; he had delivered the goods; they would have to figure it out from there.

He'd also enjoyed working with the Lebanese; Sayed wasn't concerned about the Shia and Sunni business. He thought Muslims should stand together; that's how they could defeat American influence in their countries and liberate the Palestinians from the Israelis. Yes, the Lebanese had acted in good faith and delivered the goods. Sayed thought he'd played his cards wisely – he offered to let them continue to hold the hostage until the money was transacted and they were satisfied with the payment.

And they were satisfied; they seemed very happy at that final meeting at Al Ghaydah. They seemed even more pleased when Sayed told them that they did not need to deliver the hostage to Yemen. If they were willing to let him go, that would suffice. The Lebanese warned that the Briton thought he was being held by Al Qaeda and might blab to the world. Sayed tried to think how Yusuf Ali and Bin Laden would interpret that. Then, he thought, their issues were with the Americans; he would have to position it with them in advance – it was an opportunity to show 'good faith'; they'd received nothing but bad press; they could demonstrate that the organization was capable of showing compassion toward innocents. Besides, the Briton appeared to have no strategic value. Sayed told the Lebanese to let him go.

Tanja was enjoying the slightly cooler weather that September had brought. She also enjoyed spending more time with Mantas. He was busy with his Master's studies and tutoring, so he would come by in the evenings to see the girls, then the two of them would walk down to their bench. Tanja now called it 'our' bench because that was the tradition. They would make their way down to the same bench that they'd first found the previous month. Sometimes, if the weather was cool and Luce was around, Tanja would walk herself down to that bench. She liked being beside the river; it gave her a chance to think about things. She also enjoyed the slightly quieter atmosphere. She was about to start another very busy time in her life, she needed to relax herself and get away from Vlad and the girls for a few minutes.

She liked spending time with Mantas but she wasn't quite ready to forgive him. As the weeks had progressed, she'd decided that she probably would forgive him one day and they would be together again, but she needed some space and he needed to know how angry she was. When her daughters grew up, she would never have a problem telling Maria and Edita how they were conceived. The first was something she'd obsessed about and planned; the second was a wonderful Christmas present – both were conceived in love, but she could never share a conception story with Ata; he was born out of deception. It was a very difficult thing to let go of.

However, it was also hard to stay really angry at Mantas. He demonstrated genuine contrition; he had fessed up to his deed; she wouldn't have known otherwise. When they'd first been together, he was more of a boy, now he seemed more like a man. He took good care of the girls, who clearly loved him; he could take accountability for his actions; he could demonstrate compassion. Tanja decided that she genuinely loved the new Mantas; after the baby was born, she would have to find a way to let go of the past.

That evening, Mantas and Tanja strolled from the apartment, across the fateful crosswalk and walked toward the river, only to find an elderly couple sitting on their bench. Mantas looked at them and smiled; he was hoping that they'd see Tanja with her huge belly and let them sit. They just smiled back; there was another vacant bench only 20 meters away; why would they offer?

Tanja and Mantas made their way to the vacant bench and sat.

"Do you think that will be us one day, Mantas?" Tanja asked.

It was a funny thing to say. Mantas looked at her to see if she was serious. She wasn't smiling; only staring at the river and seemed to be daydreaming. He wondered if his long wait for forgiveness might be nearing its end. He needed to figure out why she said that.

"Why would you ask that?"

"I don't know, baby brain; my mind wanders when I get close to delivery – it gets worse after birth."

Mantas now stared at the river. He tried not to think so much psychology with Tanja anymore, but that was clearly a Freudian slip. She must be thinking about forgiving him. He was wondering how to respond when she changed subjects.

"Are you getting excited? For me, this is baby number 3, but you're going to be a first-time father."

"I am, sweetheart, I am excited. I think my mother is more excited, but I'm very excited."

"Well, tell her I am looking forward to meeting her; I need a couple of weeks to recover, but if she wants to meet the baby, anytime after the end of next month would work."

"If I describe that timeline proposal to her, she will be at your doorstep before Halloween."

Tanja laughed, then seemed serious. She contemplated for a second. "Mantas, I was thinking about something... for Ata... I've decided not to give him a middle name."

Mantas nodded his head; he didn't think he should say anything. It was the name argument that had preceded the accident.

Tanja continued, "I'm also thinking... If it's ok with you... about the last name. I haven't decided yet. I know I said I would before the confession - and a child should really have his father's surname. Would it still be ok with you if he were a Jancauskas?"

Mantas thought a minute then smiled. "It would be ok with me; I think it would be more than ok with my mother. She'd likely adopt both of you."

Tanja smiled again, "That's funny, I'll think about it; maybe a good omen. You know, Edita's middle name, Barbara, I named her after my mother-in-law. It helped to build bridges; we went from enemies to close friends. Who knows?"

Mantas pondered; the current conversation seemed to hint at it. He decided he would raise the issue again.

"Tanja, I don't deserve it, but have you been thinking about forgiving me?"

She didn't look at him; she just looked at the river. "Maybe, I'm thinking about it; maybe after the baby is born. Who knows?"

George listened carefully as the landing door was opened slowly. It didn't sound like Lamia's father. It sounded much more like Lamia. And the timing was one of her traditional slots – mid-morning. George began to get excited. He went and sat on the bed; this was part of their revised routine; he couldn't believe it could be her; maybe something happened. He couldn't wait to touch her soft hand again and see those beautiful brown eyes. He just couldn't believe it could be her.

It wasn't Lamia. The person who accompanied Lamia's father toward the cell that morning seemed the opposite of Lamia; it was obviously a man, but covered head to toe in black, he wore a funny bandana at the top of his burka with some Arabic writing, he looked intimidating. Even more intimidatingly, he was carrying a small case with him; a case that looked like a large drill case to hold a drill and the accompanying drill bits.

The two men just stood at the cell door; George just sat on his bed. It wasn't clear what was about to happen. Besides Lamia and her father, the only person who had stood outside that cell door for the last two years had been the interrogator. George's mind started to move and move quickly; the interrogator never brought anything with him; this man had a drill kit. He began to think, Lamia may have been giving him more help than he knew; now that she was gone, maybe, for the first time since entering that cell, they were going to hurt him.

George's worst fears seemed confirmed when Lamia's father took out his keys. George wondered what was about to come through that trap door, but it was worse than that. Lamia's father didn't use the keys to open the trap door; he used the keys to open the main lock on that cell door. It was a lock that had never been opened during over two years of incarceration.

George just sat on the bed. He sat on the bed and began to sweat. Lamia's father let the man into the cell with George; he then closed the cell door again and locked it. George was now alone in the cell with the torturer and his weapons of torture. Lamia's father just stood there – on the other side of the door -and watched them.

The man in black with the bandana positioned the chair so that it was directly beside George's dining table, but several feet from the wall. He then directed George to sit in that chair.

George complied; he moved quickly to the chair; whatever was about to happen, he wanted over with it. If he co-operated, maybe the man would show some mercy.

The man took his case and placed it on the other side of the table. He put it on the other side of the table at a distance from George; George knew why he did it; he didn't want to risk George grabbing one of those instruments in self defence.

The man opened the box and extracted a long razor. It was like one of the old straight razors that men used to shave. He then extracted a leather strap and sharpened that razor.

George was now pouring with sweat; he looked at Lamia's father. In an instant, a sense of betrayal came over George. He'd always co-operated with him; in fact, he thought they had some sort of relationship. George had succumbed to the Stockholm Effect; he had tried to obey his rules; the man even gave him concessions; he had tried to be the ideal prisoner; he'd even given English lessons to his daughter. Then, George finally got it – that was it; what was he thinking? He was never getting out of that cell alive; Lamia's father thought George would blab to the world about the English lessons; Lamia's father would be in trouble. The only way for that secret to be kept was for George not to be able to blab. He felt a sense of anger toward the man now; George had been used.

The man put down the razor on the other side of the case, so George couldn't see it. He then extracted a long pair of scissors and began sharpening them as well; he was using both sides of the leather in a way that George had never seen before. George couldn't figure out how the scissors were going to be deployed against him, but it wasn't going to be good.

The man then did something odd. He extracted a small bowl from the case and squeezed something into it. He then removed a large cup. Were they going to drug him?

George watched the man walk over to the metal sink and add water to the concoction in the bowl and fill the large cup with water. He then returned to the case and extracted a shaving brush and began mixing the contents of that bowl.

It was now getting confusing. Were they going to give him a haircut? After over 2 years, he was now going to have a haircut by a barber?

The man brought the bowl, brush and scissors over toward George and placed the razor in the case and closed it. He then stood behind George and began trimming his hair while George looked at Lamia's father. It was a surreal moment, George thought, and it wasn't clear why they were doing it. He tried to think about why they would do it now. He thought that they were either getting ready to let him go or they were getting ready to execute him. George preferred the former option.

After his trim, the scissors were returned to the case and the man went about lathering the back of his neck with the contents of the bowl and used the straight razor to shave his neck hair. He periodically paused to shake that razor into the cup of water. He then lathered George's face and began shaving it. George had a funny story go through his head as the man shaved his face. He remembered the story of the barber who shaved his enemy's face and let him live; he was a professional barber, that's why he didn't kill his customer in the story. And as the man shaved George's throat, George knew that he was now living that story. Here was his enemy – shaving him; he hoped he would be as professional as the barber from the story.

When the man was finished with the shave, he directed George to sit back on the bed. George looked at the hair clippings on the floor and wondered if the man would sweep them. He didn't; after cleaning and packing up his tools, Lamia's father opened the cell door to let him out. The door was then shut and locked and the two climbed the stairs.

George went about trying to tidy up the mess. He would have to ask Lamia's father about borrowing some cleaning supplies. In the meantime, he used a book and his hands to push the clippings in a neat little pile near the cell door. That would do for now. He had already had a shower that morning, but decided to take another one to clean off the residuals of shaving cream from his face and neck. He decided to do a full wash – with shampoo. He loved the way that his new hair felt; the barber had done a good job; he couldn't see the finished product, but the feel of it was special. He wondered that, in addition to the cleaning supplies, whether he could make the hand gestures to request a mirror.

When the shower was completed, he sat on the bed and just rubbed his face. The man had done a good job on it; much better than the shaves he'd completed with the disposal razors that Lamia's father let him use twice a week. George had never had a straight razor shave before and was surprised at the difference; his face was completely smooth.

At lunchtime, George heard Lamia's father open the landing door. George sat on his bed and waited for his tray. He was surprised when he heard a voice – it was a voice he recognized.

"Good Afternoon, George." It was the interrogator accompanied by Lamia's father who held his lunch tray, but the interrogator also carried something – a garment bag and a pair of shoes.

George noted that, in addition to the traditional black cover head to toe, the interrogator also sported a bandana with the same Arabic writing as the barber.

George sat on the bed and spoke to the interrogator, "It's nice to see you again."

"And you, my friend, we brought you lunch; an extra-large portion today. We're taking a trip, so we don't want you to be hungry."

George just thought for a minute; was the two-year ordeal coming to an end with a haircut, shave and an extra-large lunch? It seemed like a strange climax to the two years in that cell.

Lamia's father opened the trap door and the tray was put through it. George waited for the door to close before retrieving it and moving it to the table.

The interrogator continued, "I hope it's alright; I thought we could have a chat over lunch." George nodded his head and began to eat the chickpea salad.

"So, it's a big day for you. I understand that you've been a model prisoner. On compassionate grounds, we are going to set you free."

George closed his eyes and put down his plastic fork. He wasn't sure what he should say or whether they were toying with him, but, at that moment, he believed the man. They were going to set him free.

"Please continue your lunch. I want to tell you that our plan is to let you free, but only if you co-operate with us – as you've done in the past." George nodded his head and picked up the fork. "So, firstly, do you think you've been well treated here in this basement?"

George swallowed quickly. "I do; this man has been very compassionate, brings food every day and even lets me read books." He pointed to Lamia's father as he spoke.

"Good, please let the world know that – we are not thugs. So, when we met last time, you said you thought we were Al Qaeda. So, I will share with you that you are correct – and we want you to tell the world that we are capable of compassion. Do you understand?"

"I do." George then thought about the bandanas on the barber and interrogator; they must be trying to convince him that they were Al Qaeda; it must be some sort of writing about Al Qaeda on the bandanas.

"Good – so, you have a journey tonight. You are currently in Israeli occupied territory; we will take you to Beirut where we will release you." George nodded again and began munching on the falafel. He thought that a rather creative lie; he could still be in Lebanon and be in Israeli occupied territory. "We will release you at a petrol station; it's about a kilometre from the British Embassy. You are to go there. If you need it, there will be some local money in your pocket when we release you. Do you understand?"

"I do."

The interrogator continued, "You can ask people for directions when you get there... You once told me that you were also an American. We could find no evidence of that; only a copy of your British passport. I don't know why you told me that lie. However, under the circumstances, I guess you felt that might help you. It doesn't."

George nodded his head; he understood the direction; they wanted to portray themselves as being oblivious to his real nationality. That was fine; whatever it took to get out of there. It was a strange thing to say though; if he'd really seen a copy of his passport, he should have noticed his place of birth in Milwaukee.

"So, when you've finished eating, I want you to put on this suit and these shoes. Ok?"

"Yes." George started to eat faster; he was going to get out of there. He had finished drinking a soft drink and now opened a bottle of water.

"And save about half that bottle of water."

"I will." It was an odd request, but George was determined; he would absolutely comply with whatever directive was given him.

After a few minutes, the lunch was consumed. George placed the tray at its traditional place near the trap door and sat on his bed with his half-full bottle of water.

Lamia's father unlocked the trap door and took away the tray with its dirty dishes and soft drink can. The interrogator then unzipped the garment bag and started pushing the contents gently through the trap. The first garment pushed through was a western business suit, then a business shirt, then a pair of black socks and finally the dress shoes. George was waiting to see if a tie would come through the trap, it didn't.

"Please get dressed."

While the two men watched him, George collected the clothes and put them on his bed. He took a few seconds to finger the business suit; he had missed wearing a suit and this was a decent one; it was obviously not new, but it looked to have been only gently used.

He removed his robe, then he ceremoniously folded it. It represented a life he was about to leave behind. He gently placed it near the trap door. He then removed his sandals and took a moment to look at them before gently placing them beside the robe at the trap door.

George put the white shirt on first; it itched him; he thought it must not be all cotton. He then put on the trousers, then the socks and then the shoes and finally, he put on the suit jacket.

He looked at the men who were staring back at him and smiled at them. "I wish I had a mirror."

"There'll be time for that later. Now, there's one more thing we require from you. We could have hidden this, but we trust you and trust that you will comply with our requests."

George nodded his head although he couldn't figure out what the interrogator was asking.

"Please come over to the bars and bring your water." George moved toward the cell door.

"Now, I want you to take these tablets with the water." The man reached through the bars and, in his hand, were two pink tablets. George put them in his mouth and took a swig of water.

"Now, open your mouth and show me both sides of your tongue." George opened his mouth and showed him his tongue, then lifted his tongue so the interrogator could see underneath.

"Good."

George returned and sat on his bed. He looked at the two men, who just stood there like ghosts outside his cell door staring back; the interrogator said nothing; he was finished talking. George knew what would happen over the next few minutes; he'd been drugged before. He started to feel tired; he looked out the bars and the men began to look fuzzy. He lay down on the bed with his head on the pillow and fell into a deep sleep.

Tanja stood in front of the sitting room window and looked out at the river. It was a very rainy late afternoon and, as the rain hit the window, it dripped down the pane. It all got her thinking. She looked over at the mantle and looked at her wedding photo; she studied it. Then, she looked back at the river and watched the rain pound the surface of it. She then came closer to the window to look at the traffic below. She watched the windscreen wipers go back and forth on the passing cars. She looked back at the photo and then toward Maria who was sitting watching a television programme, while Vlad played with one of his hand-held video games. Luce and Edita were busy reading in the master bedroom. She looked back toward the storm.

It wasn't long before Luce emerged from the master bedroom with Edita. Edita had overheard the television programme and wanted to watch it as well. It was a rare moment of peace in the busy household.

Luce wandered over to the window and looked at Tanja, "What are you thinking about?"

"Not sure," replied Tanja. "Just have a weird feeling this afternoon; like something is about to happen."

"Is it the baby?" asked Luce.

"I don't think so; just a weird feeling. I was looking at the river and somehow it reminded me of when I looked at the Thames River when we lived in London. With the rain, I guess it just reminded me of a former life."

Luce now looked out at the rain; the two were mesmerized by it as the storm seemed to be intensifying.

"Luce – speaking of former lives. I guess you're wondering about the Mantas situation." Luce didn't say anything in reply; she just nodded her head then looked back out the window. "So, we had an argument; that's when he started staying at his place."

Luce sighed, "I thought as much. It's a pity; things seemed to be going so well for you two. It must have been something, took you a long time to talk about it."

"Well, it was kind of a serious argument about something he didn't tell me about and I still haven't quite forgiven him for it."

Luce nodded again and turned round to check on the children.

"Luce – I want to move on, but I still feel betrayed; I was thinking of waiting till the baby was born to forgive him."

Luce didn't reply, which annoyed Tanja. She wanted Luce to say something, to provide some advice, to say something insightful, she didn't say anything. She just kept looking out the window.

"So, what do you think?" asked Tanja. Luce looked out at the storm and seemed to study it before answering.

"I think only you know what is right, dear. Let me ask you something… this thing that started the argument is it still ongoing?"

"No."

"Did he apologize for it?"

"Yes."

"Do you think it will happen again?"

"Absolutely not."

Luce paused for a minute and looked at the rain, "Do you still love him?"

Tanja watched as the rain got even harder and pounded the surface of the river. "Yes, I think so."

Luce took a deep breath, "So, Tanja, none of us can control the past, we only control the future."

Tanja was waiting for Luce to continue the advice, but she just went quiet. Tanja thought it an odd afternoon – there was the late summer storm, she had that weird sense of déjà vu about the river and then Luce had repeated almost the same words that she herself had uttered to Mantas only a few days prior.

George tried to move after the long sleep. As soon as he did, he heard someone bang on the side of something metal. Then, the engine started. He must be in some sort of van or lorry; he could feel the metal underneath him. He couldn't see anything; they had blindfolded him and, as he tried to move his hands which were around his back, he realized that he'd been handcuffed as well. He had been handcuffed to something at the side of that vehicle.

The vehicle was moving now. It moved slowly at first, then after about 15 minutes, it moved faster and then it moved very fast. George concluded that he must be in a van. A lorry wouldn't be capable of that type of quick acceleration. In his early days as a hostage, he would have studied everything occurring around him in an attempt to glean information. He would not do that today. He started thinking that, even if he saw the faces of the people transporting him, he wouldn't tell anyone. He would keep quiet; he would keep everything quiet and he would repeat all the lies that the interrogator had told him. He couldn't risk hurting Lamia's family; he would keep the Hezbollah secret to himself.

The van seemed to travel over an hour before it finally came to a stop. Then, it reversed back. George had a slight headache, but it wouldn't interfere with him now. His adrenaline was beginning to pump. The van was still running when he could feel someone gently push his body close to the side of the van and remove one of the handcuffs. The handcuff was then quickly replaced on that hand and George heard it click locked. They must have removed him from whatever he had been handcuffed against in that van. A man then manoeuvred him to a sitting position. At that point, he felt some sort of sack being placed over his head; there must have been a string on that sack as he could feel it being gently pulled near his neck.

The next minute seemed like a dream. With the van still running, George heard a door open. Someone jumped out and then there was a short delay, then someone grabbed George and then handed him to the man outside the van. That man then frog marched him for maybe 50 meters or so. There seemed to be another man with him now and then George was pushed into a chair. Someone uncuffed one hand and then seemed to lock it to something. George could feel one of the men put something in his jacket pocket. There was then a scurrying of feet and a slam of a door and then, George heard the van pull into gear.

George sat there for a moment. He wasn't sure if he should attempt to get loose or wait. So, he waited for a few seconds. He tried to raise the hand that had been uncuffed; yes, he was able to move it freely. He tugged at the string at the bottom of the sack. It took a few tries, but it soon came loose. He used that free hand to pull the sack off and let it fall to the ground. He then pulled at his blindfold. He tried to push it up over his head, but it was on too tightly, he pulled it down instead and it dangled around his neck.

He looked at the darkness. It was night and he had been abandoned in an alley and handcuffed to a chair. They had been so deliberate about having put something in his pocket. George used his free hand to check that pocket; there was something that felt like banknotes and coins, but more importantly, there was something that felt like a key. George extracted it and looked at it. An odd thought went through his head; 'I must not drop this key'. He held it tightly and looked at his handcuffed hand. He took the key and inserted it into the lock and turned it. The handcuff sprung open.

For the first time in 2 years and 1 and a half months, he was free. He stood up and gazed down at the chair and the handcuffs; they were final symbols of his imprisonment. He was now free in a back alley, which he hoped was in the city of Beirut.

CHAPTER 10

Developments

On that warm September night, George emerged from that dark alley and found himself in close proximity to the promised petrol station. He decided to try there first to see if he could get directions. He walked toward the lights; the whole petrol station was illuminated with bright lights. He found it ironic that he was breathing the first breaths of fresh air in over two years and he was confronted by strong fluorescent lights that reminded him of his cell. He approached the kiosk window; only to find that no one was there. The station was closed. George considered that a difficult sign; maybe he wasn't in Beirut; surely a petrol station in a city that size would be open through the night.

He decided to keep moving. It was a strange journey; he was surrounded by expensive-looking apartment buildings with expensive cars parked on the street, but there was one thing missing – people. George thought it was like a movie as he walked those deserted streets; as if the aliens had taken all the humans away and he was the only one left. He walked and walked, then got nervous that he had walked so far. If he were walking in the wrong direction, he would have to get back somehow. He decided to just pace a little; he needed to think.

It was then that he spotted movement. Someone was coming out of one of the apartment blocks. George ran toward the movement; it was a man in a business suit who looked terrified when he approached. George realized that he was running toward someone in the middle of the night, but niceties would now have to be dispensed.

"Do you speak English?"

The man shook his head, but George continued, "British Embassy. Where is the British Embassy?"

The man didn't look quite as terrified now. He replied, "British Embassy?"

"Yes, please can you tell me where is the British embassy?"

In quite perfect English, with only the slightest accent, the man replied. "Yes, just continue straight down this road;" he pointed the way as he spoke, "It's about a kilometre or so. It'll be on your left."

"Thank you," said George and then as a consolation for scaring him, George offered him a handshake; the man smiled and shook his hand.

George now wandered the empty streets of central Beirut. He was a free man now; free to breathe the night air, free to walk past the apartment buildings, which gave way to shops. It was a sense of exhilaration that was unimaginable; the night air smelled sweet; he kept breathing heavily, he wanted to taste it in his lungs; he moved his head frequently; he wanted to see as many of the lights and apartment buildings and shops. Others would likely have passed by without noticing those apartments and shops, but not George, not tonight. During those first few minutes, George wanted to notice everything. As he moved into the shopping area, there were occasional people around. George kept asking for directions. He not only wanted to ensure he was moving in the right direction, he also wanted human conversation again; his first human conversations as a free man.

The guard at the gate of the British embassy was helpful. George wouldn't have to wait for opening hours; the guard could call out an emergency consul. George waited about 45 minutes wandering in front of the gate waiting for someone to arrive. He heard the phone ring in the gatehouse; another guard then asked him to follow him onto the compound. As he walked toward the main embassy building, a dishevelled young woman appeared at the top of the steps. She tried to smile, but she had obviously been dragged out of bed for the occasion.

"Good morning," said George.

"Good morning, sir." George was now near enough to her to shake her hand; it was a limp handshake; she was clearly not pleased by the interruption.

"I understand you've been attacked? You require emergency repatriation?"

"Well, I guess that's right. I was held hostage for the last two years and, yes, I would like to go back to my family in London."

"Hostage? What do you mean?"

"I've been held hostage somewhere in Israel for the last two years and now I've been left here."

The woman looked confused. "Oook, well let's get you inside."

George and the woman entered the building and both emptied their pockets before proceeding through security and a metal detector. She then led him to a small office with a desk, chair, small fridge, tiny window and a large portrait of the queen on the wall behind the desk. George sat down and stared at the queen. She looked particularly regal in that portrait, he thought. He turned round briefly to look out the window into the Beirut night.

The woman sat in front of the computer on the desk and asked for his particulars. George told her his full name and date of birth and that he'd been taken hostage by Al Qaeda and was held in a basement, but then he couldn't stop talking; his adrenaline was pumping. He talked about being born in Milwaukee but being a British citizen by descent and how he lived in Canary Wharf with his Lithuanian wife and had two children, well, he knew he had one child because the other one wasn't due to be born till after he'd been taken hostage, so he'd never met that child.

The woman was busy typing away on her computer and seemed more than surprised by the story. She just seemed to keep typing while George kept talking. So, George stopped talking but the woman kept typing. He let her type for another minute before posing the question.

"So, did you find me in the system?"

"I think so. You were born in the US. Is that correct? Milwaukee?"

"Yes."

"Would you like some water?"

"Yes, please."

The woman opened the bar fridge beside her and retrieved two bottles of water.

"Mr Smith – for your new travel document, we'll need to take a photograph of you. Would you like to bring your water and follow me?"

George nodded and the woman walked in front of him down the hallway and led him to another small room. This one had no windows, which made him feel slightly nervous as it served as a brief reminder of the world he'd just left. All the walls were white and a cream colour photographer's background had been hung on one wall. A large camera sat in the middle of the room. There was a desk with some computer equipment on it.

George posed for the photograph; it was rather odd, the woman made him not only do a portrait pose but also a profile pose of both sides of his face. When the photo session was complete, she asked him to move over to the desk and place his fingertips individually on a scanner. Then, she asked him to stare into a box while she photographed his eyes. In normal circumstance, George would have enquired about the profile shot and the strange scanner and the eyeball exam, but he wasn't in the mood today. He just wanted to get it over with. However, he spared a moment to consider Lamia's comment about people with computers in their pockets. He wondered if the world had really changed that much in 2 years.

After the photo shoot, the woman led him back to her office and they both sat. George had finished his water and asked for another. The woman went back to her typing on the keyboard.

"Mr Smith – I know it's been a harrowing ordeal and I do apologize; I haven't dealt with a hostage situation before; would you mind waiting a bit? I think the ambassador should be involved. In the meantime, you are welcome to use the phone if you have people you'd like to call. International calls are fine."

George accepted the offer; it was exciting, he was going to talk with his Tanja. He was unaware that the woman wasn't really requesting time to consult with the ambassador because he'd been held as a hostage, she needed to consult because he was dead. She was in the process of sending his digital photos, fingerprint scan and iris scan to London for review – and she was curious whom he might phone.

George looked at the clock on the wall. It was 4:30 am; 2:30 am in London; he'd phone Tanja's mobile first. The woman handed him the phone across the desk and kept typing into her computer. George picked up the receiver, dialled the number and got a message saying that his call could not be completed. He put down the receiver and dialled his home number. A very tired old lady picked up the phone and told him he had a wrong number. George put down the receiver and picked it up again and called his parents in Milwaukee. He got a fast busy signal; it wouldn't connect.

"I'm having some bad luck. Maybe some numbers have changed while I was away."

"I see; anyone else you'd like to try?" said the woman as she typed and typed.

"Well, those are all the numbers I know by heart."

It was after 9 am when George finally got shuffled into the office of Mr MacLennan, UK Ambassador to Lebanon. It was a grand office with ornate wood furnishings and a giant gold flagpole with a huge Union Jack in the corner. George was ushered to a plush leather chair and across the desk from him was an even grander figure, Mr MacLennan. He was a tall elegant figure, George thought, or maybe he thought that because, in the last 24 hours, he'd been shaved, drugged, carted round in a van and then was awake most of the night wandering the streets of Beirut and sitting in the emergency consul's office.

As Mr MacLennan started speaking, George thought his original supposition was quite correct. He spoke with a hint of a Scottish accent, but was also a man that had clearly had a public-school education. He was an elegant fellow, very elegant.

"A grand good morning, Mr Smith. Brenda's been telling me your story. We are eager to assist." George then realized that he'd spent the last six hours with the woman and had never asked her name, nor did she actually introduce herself. It had been a strange night and he had accidentally dispensed with the usual social graces. George nodded his head and the ambassador continued.

"Hostage issues are fairly unusual for us, so Brenda suggested I might be able to assist." George now realized he was getting tired; the adrenaline was finally beginning to ebb. He was hoping Mr MacLennan would jump to the part about getting him home. "Our first step in assisting any traveller in distress is to verify the traveller's identity. We received verification of your identity just a few minutes ago." George wondered how they had done that; he'd only spoken to Brenda; how could they verify his identity? She must have typed his whole speech into that computer and sent it somewhere.

"There's also something that makes your case slightly more complex… our documentation shows that you are no longer with us."

George was confused by the comment, "No longer a citizen?"

"A tad more complex, I'm afraid, we show you as deceased."

George sat upright in the chair; whatever fatigue he was encountering a moment prior had just disappeared.

"Deceased? Does my family think I'm deceased?"

"I'm not certain, Mr Smith; we'll find that out for you. Brenda tells me you had trouble getting through to your family on the phone? If so, we'll track them down for you." Mr MacLennan then leaned forward, "I apologize, Mr Smith, we'll get this situation rectified and we'll get you home. We have a studio apartment within the complex for emergencies; we'd like to offer it to you for the next couple of hours. You can lie down there and we'll get you something from the kitchen." Mr MacLennan then attempted a comforting smile, "Any special requests from the kitchen? Something you've missed?"

George thought a minute, "A pint of bitter?"

"I'm sure we can manage that."

The studio apartment was a comfy place with a beautiful view of an English type garden contained within the compound's courtyard. It had a double bed that faced a wardrobe with a large flat screen tv and George had never actually watched one before; they were only coming onto the market when he'd left. There was a nightstand with a phone. There was even a small en-suite bathroom, which was fully equipped with shower, toilet, mirror and sink.

Shortly after his arrival in that room, a breakfast tray was brought by a Lebanese lady. She set it up for him at the foot of the bed on a collapsible television tray. The food was a celebration of all things British – eggs, sausage, bacon, toast, fried bread, baked beans and a can of Webster's Yorkshire Bitter; along with a cup of tea and a small glass of orange juice.

While he ate his breakfast, George sat on the bed and watched the BBC television news. He took a moment to space out and watch it. There was a report of Chechen guerrillas bombing Moscow flat blocks. The devastation was significant and George wondered how the rebels got their hands on that quantity of explosives.

It was hard to think now. George kept replaying the ambassador's pronouncement from the meeting. George was hoping it was a bureaucratic mix-up, but as he sat on that bed, he began to wonder if the world thought he was dead; if Tanja thought he was dead. He hated it but the scenarios started to run through his mind – maybe that's why no one came to see him for 20 months, but that couldn't be right, why would Hezbollah hold a hostage that everyone thought was dead? It didn't make sense. George hated when his mind wandered to scenarios; he'd spent the last two years playing various scenarios through his head. His analysis was often incorrect and his head always hurt afterward – as if his head didn't hurt enough already from the drugs and the long night. He wanted to close his eyes and sleep, but it wouldn't be worthwhile; he knew he wouldn't be able to sleep.

He decided to try his home number again. He looked at the phone on the bedside table. Maybe, he had misdialled the number; it was the middle of the night, he may have pressed an incorrect digit. A flow of optimism came upon him, that's it, that is very likely what happened.

He picked up the receiver and dialled the number again; again, it was answered by an elderly lady.

"I'm terribly sorry to bother you, madam, I'm calling from the middle east; I think I may have spoken to you last night?"

"Yes," said the woman; it was obvious that she wasn't impressed by the follow-up call.

"It's just – I was wondering if you might have any knowledge of a woman called Tanja Smith."

The woman sighed, "Well, ok, but first, may I please ask you not to call in the middle of the night."

"I apologize again, madam, I am sorry."

"So, you're not the first person calling for Tanja; a young lady called last month. I think she was a previous tenant, but I'm not certain."

"By any chance, are you on the 19th floor at South Quay 1 at Canary Wharf?"

The old lady hesitated a moment and then confessed, "I am."

"Thank you, madam, I'm grateful." George put down the receiver, Tanja must have moved. He began to play that scenario in his mind while he also thought about how long he might be in the studio apartment, but his daydreaming was cut short by a knock on the door. George beckoned, "Come in."

It was Brenda. George smiled at her; he realized that he'd treated her poorly during the night; she just seemed to keep typing and didn't seem to know what to do with him. He now realized that she had to follow a protocol; he had just shown up in the middle of the night insisting he was a dead man who wanted to be repatriated to Britain.

"Hello, Brenda, please come in; thank you again for all your help."

"Well, actually, Mr Smith, I haven't done much for you till now. I'll ask you to follow me. You're going home."

George stood at attention. "Really? Now? Are we going to the airport now?"

"Actually, you're going to receive our VIP treatment, we won't risk a freed hostage using civilian facilities; there's a helicopter on the grounds for you."

"Really, I'm taking a helicopter to England?"

"Well, not exactly, the helicopter will take you to Cyprus. Then, you'll connect with an RAF flight to an airbase in Oxfordshire. I hope it's ok, we've arranged for temporary accommodation for you at the base. We'll do a physical and debrief there, but not to worry, we are tracking down your relations. I hope by the time you land in England, we'll have made contact for you. I have a couple of questions before you go; personal things so, when we reach your family, we can verify their identities."

Brenda had a large black book and she began writing and peppering George with questions as he talked about growing up in Milwaukee and how he used to spend time with his cousin, Gary, and he told Brenda about his parents' middle names and their birthdates and about the dog they had when he was a child. Then, he talked about Tanja and Maria and where they'd lived and where Maria was born and that they should have another child by now and about Tadas and Vlad and his Down Syndrome and about Vlad's passion for video games and his favourite cartoons. The conversation lasted almost 20 minutes; Brenda kept writing in the book and trying to extract information that only his parents or Tanja would know.

"I sorry; I not understand, my English; I forget." Tanja was having trouble understanding what the woman was saying; she used her English infrequently these days.

"Sorry, madam, my name is Brenda Harkness. I'll try to speak slowly. I'm calling from the British Embassy in Beirut. I'm wondering if you are Tanja Smith, the spouse of George Smith?"

Tanja thought the call very suspicious; she thought about putting the receiver down; it was some sort of spam call. She would be careful not to say anything that the caller didn't already seem to know. "I am Tanja."

Brenda detected the air of suspicion in the Lithuanian woman's voice. "And did you ever live at South Quay 1 at Canary Wharf on the 19th floor?"

Tanja reluctantly divulged, "Yes."

"I apologize madam, this call must be coming out of the blue. I have some news about your husband, but I must be certain about your identity; I can tell you are suspicious. I'd like to ask you some verification questions; would that be ok?"

Tanja decided that it would not be ok, this was a scam. "How you know this number?"

"Gary Smith in the United States."

Tanja thought that very odd; how did she know about Gary? "Ok?"

"Ok, so your daughter Maria was born on May 27, 1996. At what hospital?"

Tanja thought for a second; this information hardly mattered, she would co-operate for a minute "Seattle Children's."

"Your mother had a boyfriend just before she died. Can you tell me his name?"

Tanja suddenly was confused. How did she know all this stuff? It might be a real call after all. "Tadas."

"When you lived in Seattle and Tadas brought Vlad to stay with you, Vlad had a favourite television programme. Would you remember it?"

"Well, he watch Flinstone everyday."

"Thank you, Mrs Smith; I apologize, this is sensitive information and I needed to ensure it was you. I have some very very good news for you."

"Yes?"

"I met with your husband, George, this morning; he is alive and very well and is on his way to England."

Tanja looked out the window to the river; she couldn't quite understand it. She interjected, "I not understand; I sorry; my George is dead."

"We were under that impression as well; it appears he may have been held captive. I can't say too much about the details; I'm afraid he'll be asked to stay on in Oxfordshire for a few days to help us commence our investigations and debriefing. You are welcome to join him there for a visit."

Tanja looked down at her belly, "I...I... not understanding. He is not dead?"

"He is not dead; he is alive. He is very excited about seeing you. May I forward your number to him? He can call you when he gets to England."

"Ok."

"So, next step will be for him to call you directly. He should be there in a couple of hours. Any questions?"

Tanja had one million questions that she wanted to ask, but none she could translate to English at that moment. This just couldn't be true; he was a dead man; how could he be alive; it must be a mistake.

"No; I, I, no, thank you."

"Thank you and congratulations, Mrs Smith. Goodbye for now."

"Bye."

Tanja put down the phone and just thought about the word 'congratulations'; what did it all mean? She needed to sit down. She moved to the sitting room and sat beside Tadas who was watching the news. Edita tried to climb onto her lap; it was hard but Tanja managed to find a place for her beside the giant belly. Tanja felt numb and sat dazed for a moment before turning to Tadas.

"Tadas – that was a strange phone call. A woman said she was calling from Beirut; she said that George was alive. Could it be some kind of black humour?"

Tadas didn't reply right away; it was a shocking piece of news and he needed to think about it. Then he changed the channel from his Lithuanian newscast to BBC. He couldn't understand English, but he had a hunch about something.

"It doesn't sound right, sweetheart... they never found a body... no, I'm sorry, I think you're right. It might be a prank."

"Yes, but that lady knew all about you and Vlad and Maria." Tanja contemplated while watching the BBC news report about the bombing in Moscow; Tadas kept talking but Tanja faded out for a second; she didn't want to talk or listen at that moment, she just wanted to think about it. She watched the aftermath of the Moscow explosion and just thought and thought. Then the report on the bombing ended and the commentator in London began his introduction to the next story.

"And breaking news from Lebanon this morning. A British businessman, missing and presumed dead for the last 2 years, has allegedly identified himself to British embassy personnel in the capital city of Beirut. Officials currently suspect he may have been held captive by a militant group in the area. His name has not yet been released pending notification of family members; we'll continue to follow this story for you on BBC World and provide updates as they become available. Turning our attention to sport..."

Tanja's jaw dropped; could this really be true? She sat in the sitting room; she wouldn't leave the apartment; she wouldn't leave the apartment until that phone rang. A hundred thoughts were going through her brain – they'd likely identified the wrong person, that was the logical thing. It was Luce's day off which was a pity. She wanted to talk to her about it. Yesterday, Tanja had mentioned her eery feeling and now, this was going on. She thought about calling her and decided against it; she would wait until she could confirm it. Tadas was already worked up because of the news report, which Tanja had interpreted for him; Tanja tried to explain that it was likely someone else but they'd identified George; she tried to calm him down, she didn't want to talk about it with him right at the moment.

The phone rang. It had only been an hour since the woman had called.

He must be early. Tanja picked up the phone and said 'allo.' It was Mantas; he wanted to know if she wanted to sit on the bench later. Tanja decided that she wouldn't tell him about the news yet. She said that she would take a rain check for tonight; she wasn't up to it. She felt guilty when she hung up the phone. Mantas had been her confidant since the accident, but she just didn't know what to tell him; she also didn't know how he'd react; she also didn't know how she herself should react or how she should react with him.

She began to pace around the sitting room and was quickly joined by Maria, who thought it was a great game and paced back and forth with her. She bent down and looked at Maria who gave her a big smile in return. For a moment, Tanja studied Maria's hair and cheeks; those were the features that most reminded her of George. Would Maria get to have her father back? He was a man whom she hardly knew; she didn't remember him. She paced holding Maria's hand and then she paused at the photo on the mantle. It didn't make sense; it just couldn't be true.

Another hour passed and the phone rang again.

"Allo," said Tanja.

"Hello?"

"Allo," said Tanja again.

The man continued in English, "Oh my God, my princess, my Klaipėda princess, you went home - I've waited 25 months to hear that voice. It's me – can you hear me?"

"Is it real you?"

"It is real me. My love – oh my God, I thought I'd never hear that beautiful voice again."

Tanja continued in Lithuanian, "George – can you speak Lithuanian? It's easier for me."

George complied with the request, "I will, but I forget to speak it. How is Maria and Vlad? How about other baby?"

Tanja suddenly felt a surge of excitement; she had felt slightly numb at first, now she felt a surge of energy; she was talking with the father of her children, he was really alive. "Maria is very well; she's really grown, she looks like you, she will be so happy. And Vlad is fine; he's a fine teenager, very handsome and has learned a lot. And your newest princess, Edita

Barbara, was born on September 20, 1997; maybe you can be here for her birthday. And..." Tanja suddenly stopped herself, she wasn't going to share that news; she would have to think about how to share that news.

"Oh, my love, I want see you now. Edita Barbara – that is beautiful, like my mother."

Tanja felt a sense of dread come over her, "Do you know about your parents?"

"Yes, they told me. Someone's talked to Gary; I call him, but talk about that a different time. Did you miss me?"

"I did. I thought you were dead. Were you a hostage?"

"I'm sorry and yes. Sometime, I also felt like I was dead in that cell, but talk about that a different time. They want to keep me in England for some days. Can you come to England?"

Tanja looked down at her stomach and bit her lower lip, "It will be hard with the girls, can you come to us? We will wait!"

"I have waited 25 months; I can wait some more time to see my loves. I can't wait to see your beauty again."

Tanja giggled; when she did, she realized that she hadn't giggled like that for a long time, it was a giddy giggle. "I'm not really beautiful anymore; I had a bad accident in May."

"I no care if you are the most ugly girl in Lithuania; you are my beauty and I love you. You ok now?"

"Oh, much better now; I can't believe it, George, I have so much to tell you about. About Maria; she loves to talk; about Edita – she loves to walk, about..." George cut her off.

"I will take my girls together and I will cover them in kisses."

The conversation continued for several more minutes. It was strange to hear his voice again and wonderful all at the same time. Tanja provided full reports on Maria, Edita, Vlad and Tadas and talked about Luce, whom he would soon meet. Tanja thought maybe she should ask more about George and his time as a hostage, then she decided that he probably didn't want to talk about it. It was hard to put the phone down, George promised that he would call back later and that he would call every day, several times a day until he could see her. It felt good to be loved so much, to be missed so much.

Tanja put down the receiver. She hadn't noticed but Tadas had been standing only a few metres away; he'd been listening. She ran to him and put her arms around him, "He's alive, it is true, he's really alive." Tadas squeezed her then looked at her in the eyes, then kissed her cheek, then continued hugging her. Tanja began to cry and kept hugging him. She squeezed him so tightly as if her very life depended on how tightly she could hug Tadas.

Then, from the corner of her eye, she glimpsed her wedding photo on the mantle in the sitting room. She held onto Tadas while she thought. She was in love with one man and was also in love with the memory of that man in the photograph. She was carrying the first man's baby, while being married to the second man. She had betrayed her husband and didn't know how to tell him. However, was it real betrayal? She had thought he was dead, but she had been betrayed and tricked by the man she now loved. Her husband had never done that. She suddenly felt overwhelmed with guilt. She had always been loyal – loyal to her mother, to Vlad, to George, to Tadas, to her children, even to Mantas, but now she was filled with a sense of having been disloyal. It was hard to figure out the villains or how this story would end, but there was one innocent character in this play – and that was George.

It was meant to be a quieter evening for Mantas. After Tanja declined the walk to the bench, he thought he'd just stay at home. Between the start of his master's degree and the tutoring and Tanja, he was starting to get tired. Tonight, he decided he would stay at home, make an assortment of smoked meat sandwiches and cheese and open a cold beer. He'd watch a little television, which he hardly ever found time for and then do some reading before bedtime.

After the sandwiches were prepared and the beer opened and placed on the coffee table, he turned on the television and sat down on the sofa. It was news time and he watched about the Moscow explosions. He watched and was torn by the report. Innocents had been killed and that wasn't right, but his own country had been occupied; he felt some sympathy for the Chechens and wondered how they managed to get their hands on that quantity of explosives. He munched on the sandwiches and drank his beer.

Although he loved spending time with Tanja, it was nice to have a night off. He had been disappointed when she'd declined his offer, but now he was glad it hadn't pan out. And it was kind of nice to catch up on what was going on in the world.

The Lithuanian news anchor continued, "Our next story comes from Great Britain where businessman, George Smith, who was presumed dead for the last two years has resurfaced in Beirut. Mr Smith went missing in Beirut in July 1997 and was pronounced dead shortly thereafter. Initial reports indicate that he may have been held hostage by an Al Qaeda cell, possibly operating on Israeli occupied territory. Mr Smith is now back in Britain…"

Mantas jumped from the coffee table and made his way over to the phone near his desk. He dialled the digits quickly.

"Tanja? Put the news on; turn on channel 3 quickly."

Tanja paused for a minute. "Is it about George?"

"Yes, he's resurfaced; they're saying he's alive."

"Yes, I just spoke to him."

There was a long pause on the line as neither seemed to know what to say, so Mantas decided to lead.

"What did he say?"

"He says he's fine; he wants to see us; he's coming in a few days."

"Did you tell him; I mean, did you tell him about the baby?"

"I didn't. He's been through an ordeal; I will; the timing wasn't right."

"Ok, well, you must be happy." Mantas paused for a second, he was hoping she would validate or not validate that comment, she certainly didn't sound very happy, it was as if she were in shock. She didn't say anything.

"Tanja – where does; I mean, how do… actually, it must be a difficult time; can we talk tomorrow?"

"Yes, Mantas, thanks for calling; let's talk tomorrow. Ok?"

Mantas put down the phone. He could feel a pit in his stomach now. He tried to digest how his life had just been altered in the last five minutes; what did it mean? Was she going back to him? And then a terrible thought returned to him, he didn't want to think it – 'if only I hadn't said anything, maybe everything would be ok now.'

George kept his promise. He phoned that evening and the next morning and then again in the afternoon. By the afternoon call, he had an ETA for Klaipėda. He would be held for another 3 days, then he could fly to be with his family. Tanja was conflicted with the plan; it would be nice to see him again, but she would need to tell him that she was pregnant and she would also need to figure out the Mantas situation.

However, even though she was deceiving him, she didn't want to spoil those precious phone calls. George would talk about how much he loved her, how much he missed her, they would talk about all the wonderful memories that they'd shared – when Maria was born, living in Seattle, funny things that Vlad had done, wonderful holidays, her attempts to learn English. During the conversations, George's Lithuanian was also rapidly improving; it was almost perfect, like it was before. On the afternoon call, George even talked about having another baby; he wanted to be less involved with work and more focused on his family. It was difficult to hear George talk about growing the family; she was already doing that without him.

She had spent most of the day on calls with him, but was looking forward to sitting on the bench with Mantas that evening. She'd arranged a meeting earlier that day but was watching the weather – it was slightly iffy; she was hoping the rain would hold off. She wanted to see him, there was just one complication – she didn't know what she would actually say to him.

She had suggested they meet at the bench that evening; she just wanted to get away from the family without waiting for him to collect her.

It was nice to sit by that river on her bench. At times of stress, she loved to watch the river, it calmed her and let her think. She had arrived fifteen minutes early, she just wanted to sit there and think. She was surprised when he arrived shortly thereafter – about 10 minutes early; he must have been anxious to see her.

He gently kissed her on the cheek before sitting beside her.

"I missed you the last couple days," Mantas said, "I'm glad the rain held off."

"Me too."

There was then an awkward silence; it was awkward because they were sitting on a bench, about to have a baby together with Tanja's dead husband returning from the grave and appearing just before the arrival of that baby.

Mantas sighed, "Congratulations, Tanja, I'm really excited for you." He took her hand, but then she began to cry. She really cried and she moved toward him and embraced him and put her head on his shoulder.

"I don't know what to do, Mantas." Mantas didn't say anything; he just pet her hair; it smelled so good, she always smelled good. She kept sobbing. "I love you," she leaned up from his shoulder and gently kissed him on his lips before returning to his shoulder. "But... I think I love my husband; I just feel ashamed."

Mantas continued stroking her hair. "Why? Because you love two people?"

Tanja was still sobbing, but she was trying to get control of that sobbing, she took two big sobs and gasped for air, "No, look at me; I betrayed him."

"You never betrayed him; the only person that was betrayed was you - by me. You didn't do anything wrong. You mustn't feel that way. You did not know he was alive – in fact, you used to tell me that you weren't ready because it was too soon after he was gone and after we finally got together, you came back and told me again that you weren't ready – you were loyal even after death."

Tanja now gently touched his shoulder and caressed it with one hand. The gesture gave him that sense of undeniable love that he had sometimes felt toward her since the accident. It wasn't the love of a lover, it was something different – almost like a paternal love. He decided he would probably regret what he was about to say, but he had to say it, he could not allow himself to make her so sad. It was going to hurt, but he was going to have to set her free...

"Tanja – I never want you to be conflicted. You have given me such love and respect – you opened your heart to me; you opened your family to me – and I did not deserve it. I know the type of person you are; I think, or maybe I want to believe, that you were about to forgive me – and I still hope you can find it in your heart to forgive me. But I will not allow you to experience any more pain. If you're worried about loving two men, I'll make it simple - you have an obligation only to one. George is your husband; you always compared me to him; I always knew I was a distant second. The pregnancy may have confused things, but it shouldn't, especially the way it happened. You need to move on with your life – and that means returning to your old one, which doesn't include me."

Tanja now began sobbing again and then reached up and kissed him again. She just kept her arms around him for a minute or so before continuing.

"Thank you. I, I didn't know what I was going to say to you tonight; thank you; I needed someone to help me; you always help me; you should never be second; I'm sorry for the way I treated you."

He lifted her head and looked into her blue eyes; they were as beautiful as the first time that he'd seen them when she came to his flat to lobby for Vlad. "It's all going to be ok; I'll find someone someday, but they'll always be second to you." He then gently kissed Tanja's lips.

The phone conversations were wonderful, but Tanja grappled with a difficult fact; she would talk to her husband but not say anything about Mantas or being pregnant. There were lots of reasons she didn't talk about it – she didn't want to upset him, she didn't quite know how he'd take it, but the biggest problem is that she didn't quite know how she felt about anything anymore. Mantas had pushed her a little toward her former husband; she'd accepted that because she needed someone to guide her somehow. She knew that Luce and Tadas weren't going to give her any advice; she was almost nine months pregnant and it was hard to think; it was the worst possible time to reconcile with an ex-boyfriend or welcome a dead husband. She had intentionally wanted to put off reconciling with Mantas until after Ata was born, but now, here she was – only a day from welcoming George back into her life and she had not even told him about her pregnancy. It would have to be today; it was her final chance.

George was very animated on their final call. He had obviously been thinking about things - they would start with a family vacation – to someplace warm – to a beach somewhere and Vlad and Tadas would also come and then the conversation became slightly odd.

"Or Canada," George proposed, "we could go to Milwaukee to see my cousin and then go to Ontario."

"I'm pretty sure it gets cold in Ontario about now, besides I don't think I'm up to a trip at the moment."

"That's ok; forget it, we'll go somewhere warm, the girls will love it, I've got to spend some time with Edita because we've never met. I hope she's excited. I am so excited; I think it might have been worth those whole two years to appreciate you again and be with those beautiful girls. I am blessed; you bless me. I love you."

Tanja thought he was about to get all sappy again; a part of her wondered if she shouldn't tell him, maybe she would just see him tomorrow and explain it. No, that wasn't right.

"Anyway, my sweet, I should go. We'll save the taxpayer some money. I will be there tomorrow and we can talk live; we'll work it out."

"George – can I have one more minute?"

"Sure; if you have a different plan, we can talk about it, I know you talked about Mexico when we lived in Seattle. The solicitor here thinks we'll be able to keep the insurance money; he says that it's really compensation for lost income, so we should have money."

Tanja could tell he was excited. She'd known him intimately for four years before his disappearance. When he was excited, he would ramble. It was one of the things that spouses get to know about each other – their eccentricities. In addition to the rambling when excited, there was one other eccentricity that she recognized about her husband which was going to make the next few minutes of that conversation so difficult. He was possessive. Oh, George could be calculating and pragmatic when it came to business and knew how to walk away when he got the worse part of a deal, but, when it came to Tanja, there appeared to be no losing. He didn't like when men looked at her; he could be controlling and would occasionally ask her not to wear certain clothes when she went out without him. He hated when business colleagues would feign flirting. To Tanja, it had seemed cute at the time, but she also knew that sense of possession was very real and didn't know how he would react to the words she was about to tell him – that she had another man's baby in her womb.

"It's not that, my sweet, can I talk for a minute?"

"Of course, but do you want to do it in person tomorrow?"

"No, I want to tell you now." He finally went quiet so Tanja began. "I'm pregnant."

"I know you were pregnant."

"No, I'm pregnant now."

"I don't understand."

"I'm having a baby – in about two weeks."

George paused a minute… "How?"

"I'm sorry George, I was lonely, I thought you were dead." There was now a very long silence. Tanja recognized the significance of that silence. Her whole future might depend on the words that he uttered now.

"So, where is the father?"

"He lives in Klaipėda."

"Are you, I mean, are you married?"

"No."

"Do you live together?"

"No."

"Are you together? A couple?"

"No."

"Do you love him?"

"George – I am sorry; I was lonely; I was with him twice and something went wrong, I was going to name the baby Ata, because I had a dream about a little boy running to me and saying 'my name is Ata', it means gift in Arabic, and then his face changed to your face and then, when I woke up, I promised you that I would keep our baby and call him that."

There was another long silence and Tanja held her breath.

"Good," said George, "That'll save a bunch of time, we don't need to try for a third baby, because you've already arranged for one. You always think of everything. I love you, baby."

"I love you too. See you tomorrow."

George put down the receiver. It was very odd news. Tanja wasn't like that; she wouldn't even allow him to be intimate with her until they were engaged and she told him that he was her first. Maybe she'd changed? Then, he thought about his time in the cell. He'd felt so desperate and alone without her, maybe that's how she felt without him?

Tanja put down the receiver. She thought that she'd handled it well. When she'd planned what to say before the call, she hadn't thought about talking about the dream, but it had actually worked perfectly. She had avoided the question and given an answer that seemed to please him. She had played to that possessive ego and it had worked.

Tanja made one more phone call that night and that was to Mantas. She knew he would likely do it anyway, but she needed to reconfirm that he should keep a low profile for a couple of weeks. She had promised that he could be part of the baby's life and she would stick to that promise, but right now, she needed to be careful. Mantas was agreeable to the appeal which included a request not to be there at the birth. Tanja would slowly work on George and bring him round to the concept of having someone else involved in Ata's life, but she had to be careful and slow. She explained to Mantas that it was a male ego thing; he seemed to get it.

When she rose the next morning, Tanja was excited. She'd be welcoming home an old friend, with whom she'd shared so many secrets; someone with whom she'd lived – someone whom she had loved. Tadas was to collect George at the airport that afternoon. Tanja busily tidied the flat and recruited Luce to help her. Tanja thought to herself that it almost felt like nesting; almost like she was preparing for a new child to come home. It took about 3 hours to clean the apartment that day; it would have taken less, but Maria insisted on 'helping' with the vacuum and then Edita wanted to help. It wasn't much help, but it was kind of cute to watch Edita try to push around the vacuum. The toddler had to reach right up well over her head to grab the handle.

While Tadas and Vlad went to collect George, all the ladies had lunch together. Tanja thought that it felt strange; it would be the last time the chemistry would all revolve around this group; there would now be a new member of the household. There would now be a new member of the household who was likely to want to stake his claim as the head of that household; it would no longer be Tanja; she would have to cede that authority; she knew he wouldn't accept it any other way.

She had tried to explain the George situation to Maria and Edita. Maria was confused at first, but then seemed rather excited about it. She kept referring to George as her second daddy; Tanja didn't say anything to Maria about that expression, because if she did say anything, Maria was very likely to keep repeating it. Edita seemed too young to really get it; Tanja tried to explain it in simple terms. She told Edita that her daddy had gone away, but now he had come back and wanted to see her and play with her. Edita would just nod her head and go on with what she was doing. It didn't seem to bother her either way.

After lunch, Tanja did the dishes while Luce occupied the children in the sitting room. It was annoying that it was taking them so long to get back. She wanted to commence the homecoming ceremony; she wanted to see what it would be like. The one-time love of her life was returning.

Finally, Vlad turned the handle and made his way into the apartment, but then no one followed.

"Where are they, Vlad?"

"They're coming; George looks old." Tanja thought Vlad had a wonderful way of getting to the point and it reminded her that she was older and the accident had even made her look older than that. She had tried to look nice for him that day, but it had been a difficult chore; she only had one maternity dress; she'd tried to use other clothing for most of her pregnancy, but now that single frock was the only thing that would fit her and it was beginning to look worn.

Then, Tadas entered with a suitcase, which seemed odd, did George have luggage?

Then, he entered. Vlad was right, he did look old; he seemed to have gone from young man to middle-aged man somehow – and he was only 30.

When he entered the door, he just looked at her – then he smiled. Then, he glimpsed Maria. He started running toward her, but the sudden action spooked Maria, who ran to Luce who was standing nearby and Maria then tried to hide behind Luce's legs. George stopped and looked a little disappointed, then he saw Edita. She was busy playing with a puzzle on the sitting room table. He went to her and put his arms around her; Edita didn't seem to be very bothered about it. She lifted one of the pieces of the puzzle and showed George then went about trying to construct the toddler's game.

Then, he stood up again and looked at Tanja. He walked slowly toward her as if he wasn't quite sure if he recognized her. He put his hand on her face. Tanja leaned her face into his hand so that it now rested between her cheek and shoulder; she kissed his palm. He then put his hands around her and tried to give her a kind of bear hug. This turned into a much more difficult manoeuvre than he'd probably expected as Tanja's gut protruded so far out. They stood in that awkward embrace for a minute, before George released it and gently kissed her on the lips. He then just stood there and stared at her.

Tanja thought the staring was a little uncomfortable. The whole incident wasn't what she'd expected; it seemed perplexing. She felt a sudden surge of regret and self-pity. She loved the memory of her husband; she'd cherished those memories. When he died, it was hard to get over him. She had to start a whole new life and she'd dragged her family across Europe to find it, but she'd achieved success and she'd been able to move on with those precious memories. The interloper in her sitting room had just invaded that paradigm of reality; those were no longer just memories; she would have to face a new reality with the stranger who had just hugged her.

"You look wonderful," he said. Tanja suspected it was a lie; she looked fat and her face was still scarred from the accident.

"You too, sorry about Maria; she was excited to see you; I think the moment was just a bit much for her." Then Tanja regretted those words; they were the first words she'd spoken to him face to face; she could have come up with something more befitting a man who'd been locked in a basement for two years.

"No worries, can we sit down a minute? I just want to look at you." Tanja started to walk toward the sofa and George put his hand in hers as they walked. When she sat, he sat beside her and held both her hands and just looked into her eyes. Tanja recognized the gravity of that moment for both of them, but somehow it seemed contrived or artificial. She sat and stared back at him. She waited for his next statement and predicted it would likely be something about her beauty – that was the most logical next act in the play that was unfolding.

"You're so beautiful; I missed looking at those eyes... and look at this place, you've done so well for yourself and the girls look great; you're the perfect mother, Tanja."

Tanja nodded her head. "We missed you, it was tough without you. Don't worry, the girls will warm up to you. It'll be nice to have their father back again."

Then, something rather horrifying happened, Maria who now peaked around Luce's legs shouted "Mantas!" Tanja felt suddenly nervous and looked at George for his reaction, but he didn't react, he didn't know that name and hadn't understood the significance of it.

George let go of her hands and outstretched them toward Maria and, this time, he very slowly crawled toward his toddler.

"I might have something in my bag for you." Maria looked curious about that. George retrieved his bag from near the front door and opened the suitcase on the floor near to her. He took out a colouring book and crayons. Tanja knew it wasn't one of Maria's favourite hobbies, but Edita would like it. Maria came close to collect her gift, close enough that he was able to steal a hug. Maria now giggled; she liked anything to do with rough housing and her 'new' daddy had just discovered that interest.

"I got something for you too, Edita." Edita had already put down her puzzle piece to watch the exchange with her sister. George extracted a doll; it was a princess doll. Tanja smiled to herself as she watched Edita accept her first present from her father, a man she had never met, who bore a gift that her sister would love.

After trying to embrace Edita, which involved her leaning her shoulder toward him so he could hug her from a side angle, George looked at Tanja, "That reminds me, I'll need to get access to our savings; I have to repay the emergency loan."

Tanja nodded her head; she was now expected to hand over her life savings; it had never really been hers anyway.

The next few days were mostly about getting to know the lost husband and father. Tanja didn't know what his expectations might be of her physically. She was relieved when he just wanted to cuddle her at night. She didn't want to be intimate at this stage in her pregnancy; it could cause premature labour; George must have known that. She also didn't know if she ever wanted to be intimate again ever; she still felt that her last intercourse had been an assault and didn't know how she would feel about it.

After the first few days of George's stay, Tanja began to make a series of observations. Firstly, George was drinking an enormous quantity of beer, which often started around lunchtime. Scotch was also being consumed in quantity, but this was only an evening thing. It didn't seem to much affect him though. Still, he wasn't like that before and he seemed to be ok to drink alone; if Tadas was there, he'd often join him, but only for a bottle or two of beer. George had also taken up smoking; each evening he would disappear to the street below to smoke; then he'd come home and smell of it. George also quickly took control of the finances and even reproached Tanja for putting all the money in a savings account. He said he'd invest it properly. Tanja thought interest rates were high and she had done rather well with the money.

They weren't all negative observations. He was still a great father. He said he'd wait a few weeks before returning to work. He wanted to spend time with the family. And he clearly loved those girls and Vlad. He would sometimes play video games with Vlad, but most of his time was spent with the girls – especially Edita. He loved to blow raspberries on her tummy and play puzzles. There was one odd thing – he seemed to be favouring Edita and seemed to spend more time with her than Maria. He'd mentioned that he wanted to spend more time with her, but it had gotten to the point that Maria would sometimes come over and push her sister out of the way. This would get George upset and then he'd spend even more time with Edita. Maybe, it was a small thing, but in the back of Tanja's mind, she worried about how he might treat Ata.

September 20th was Edita's second birthday and George had gotten up early and decorated the apartment with balloons and streamers and a giant sign that said 'Happy Birthday' in English. Tanja thought it was symbolic. Because Edita had limited language skills, George would only speak to her in English and Maria mostly in Lithuanian; this annoyed Maria as well as she felt that they were using a secret language.

When Edita woke up, she seemed impressed but was also confused as well. George had tried to explain about the birthday, but she seemed to have forgotten about it. Now, she was reminded!

George picked her up and then pulled her nightshirt up to give her the morning raspberry. "Edita – today is a very special day; you are a big girl now, you are 2. So, today, we'll have a very special day – just you, me, Vlad and Maria." Tanja knew about the plan in advance and had agreed to let Vlad take the day off school, she hoped it would be ok and that Maria would also get some daddy time.

"Today, we'll take a ferry to Smiltynė and visit the aquarium. You'll get to see dolphins and then we'll come home and have a big party with Grandpa Tadas and Auntie Luce."

Edita looked very impressed; even though she probably couldn't understand any of that English language. She knew it was going to be a big outing.

After breakfast, George got the girls ready for the outing and then the four of them left for the special day. Tanja was alone now; there was no Luce and no Tadas. Tanja suddenly realized that she was indeed alone in the apartment; she couldn't remember the last time she had been alone in the apartment. She thought she should tidy up a bit, but then decided that she might be only days away from giving birth, she'd just take advantage of the silence – and then she had another idea. She picked up the receiver.

"Mantas, good morning."

"Hello, sweetheart, how are things? Are you alone?"

"Yeah, it's Edita's birthday, George took everyone to the aquarium."

"Yes, I knew it was today; it's weird not being with her – give her a kiss for me. How's the homecoming?"

"It's good, he's a good father, but…" Tanja then gave an overview of the drinking, the control of the finances and the favouring of Edita and her worry about Ata. Mantas just listened as Tanja kept talking. It was good to talk to someone, she felt that she couldn't tell anyone else these concerns.

"It's ok; it takes time, you need to get to know each other again," Mantas replied.

Tanja thought for a second. That's exactly what it was – she was trying to get to know someone, it was peculiar. The conversation continued for a few more minutes. Mantas wished her luck if they weren't able to talk before the big event; that sounded so odd coming from a man who was so excited about being a first-time father.

After the call, Tanja thought it would be good to move around and she went about her domestic chores. She got out the feather duster and began dusting. She stopped at the wedding photo on the mantle, she dusted it at first, then put down the duster and picked up the photo. She studied George and started to think about the last few days – 'I'm sorry, my sweet, I think I liked you more back then.'

Vlad, Maria, Edita and George didn't return till late afternoon. Tadas and Luce were already there helping to set up the birthday dinner. The tribe seemed to be in a very jocular mood. Vlad talked incessantly about a seal that had tricked him. The seals played in an open-air pool area and there was a viewing area for the humans to watch them from above. The seals were taking turns jumping off a rock into the water. Everyone kept their distance from the viewing platform railing, but Vlad didn't see any harm in getting a better view and moved right up to the railing and leaned over. And that's when the seal did it to him, he climbed onto his jumping rock and jumped and, just as the seal was about to hit the water, he took his flippers and used them to propel a torrent of water toward Vlad. After the seal completed his dive, he jumped onto another rock and began barking and applauding at his prank. Vlad was giddy and had to tell the story several times, each time with more and more description.

Maria was also happy; she had a toy crown on her head. Tanja asked George where it came from; George said he bought it from the gift shop. It was supposed to be Poseidon's crown. Then George said something that pleased Tanja, "Yeah, I think Princess Maria has felt a bit neglected with me spending so much time with Edita; I tried to make it up to her today."

However, by far the happiest little girl at that party was Edita. Edita had gone into hyper mode; she reminded Tanja a little of Maria. She just kept running around the sitting room and shouting "happy birthday" in English. Tanja was worried that she was over-excited. Then, Edita did something a little out of the ordinary; she ran to Maria's castle and retrieved a sceptre. She then ran it over to her sister and handed it to her. Maria grabbed it – she now looked very much like Poseidon with her crown and sceptre.

All the adults laughed, but it had caught Tanja the most off-guard and she began to keel over with laughter – and that's when it happened.

"ooo," said Tanja as she bent down looking at the floor. Luce was the first to enquire.

"You ok?"

"Yeah, a contraction, it came from nowhere. It might just be a one-off."

All the adults who had been staring at the princess had now gone quiet and all the attention had moved to Tanja. She decided that she was becoming a damper on the party.

"Ok, everyone, let's get back to the party. Luce and I made a special dinner for the birthday girl."

Tanja had trouble getting through the dinner. The contractions were coming faster than she'd expected. She'd had two children previously and thought she knew what to expect, but these were coming fast. It wasn't that they were particularly painful yet, but they seemed to be coming every 10 minutes or so. She tried not to say anything about it, but when she got up to go to the kitchen at one point, George followed her.

"Do you think it's tonight?" he asked.

"I'm beginning to think so, tonight or tomorrow; I hope it's tomorrow, poor Edita deserves her own birthday." George moved toward her and gave Tanja a hug, "Or it'll be a great birthday present – who could say that they got a little brother for a birthday present?" Tanja smiled; she rather liked George at that moment, she kind of regretted her earlier soliloquy at dusting time.

Luce wanted to do the clearing up, but Tanja insisted that she wanted to do it herself. She wanted to keep moving and the cleaning felt like nesting, she was preparing. George confided the news to Luce and Tadas; Tadas offered to spend the night on the sofa and George accepted the offer. Luce was originally going to accompany Tanja to the hospital, but George had overridden that decision. After Luce went home, Tanja began to pace in the master bedroom, then she took a long hot shower. The contractions were now very painful and long and were coming quickly.

It was around 10:30 pm when Tanja made her decision that it was time. She asked George to call a taxi. They climbed down the stairs together and opened the main door to the waiting night. It felt like autumn; it was nippy. They only had to wait a couple of minutes for the taxi which whisked them to the hospital.

It was a little after 2 am on September 21, 1999, when Ata entered the world; a baby with two fathers and one very tired mother.

CHAPTER 11

Decisions

The next morning, Tanja woke around 8 am in her hospital bed. She was surprised that she'd managed to get close to 5 hours of sleep. George was there when she woke. He held her hand and then leaned up from his chair and kissed her on the forehead.

"Good morning. Your boys have been waiting for you for hours. Did you want to see our new son?"

Tanja smiled; she looked around, but couldn't see any crib. Then George moved toward the head of the bed and reached down; Ata had been sleeping in a little crib so close to the head of that bed that she hadn't seen him. George handed him to her.

Whatever confusion and self-pity that Tanja had experienced over those last few days seemed to slip away as she stared into the face of her newborn son. He had his eyes closed and just seemed to yawn a little after being moved. The yawn reminded her of how George yawned. She was about to say that 'he has your...' then caught herself.

Mother and son cuddled for about 15 minutes then Ata started to fuss a little. Tanja knew what it was all about. She fumbled to pull up her gown and offered her breast. He needed a bit of coaxing to latch, then she put the gown over his head and let him suckle.

"All men love that," George joked.

Tanja smiled.

"Tanja – there's one more thing. The nurse gave me some papers. You need to fill these out."

Tanja knew the timing was suspicious; she'd just given birth, and this was her first real chance to bond with her son, but George was obviously curious what she would write on those forms.

George placed the application for birth certificate and a pen on a table then wheeled it over for her to complete while she nursed Ata. George watched while Tanja took the pen in her right hand, while balancing Ata on the left. She started the section on details of the mother. Tanja wrote her name and place of birth and date of birth and address. He kept watching while Tanja entered the forename of baby as 'Ata', then left the middle name blank, then under surname wrote 'Smith'. Finally, she got to the section for father and for surname she wrote 'Smith' and then 'George' for forename and then completed information on George's birthdate and place of birth.

Tanja wasn't really sure about the legality of what she had just done. Technically, George *was* his father as she was married to him and Ata would be part of his family - and part of her also felt that if she wanted her son to be accepted by him, she should write that answer.

After a few days, mother and child were discharged and Tanja and Ata took residence at the Klaipėda apartment. Tanja thought she'd learned important lessons about completing registration documents. George quickly took to paternal duties. He helped with nappy changes, he carried Ata around when he had digestion problems; it had worked, she'd done the right thing.

Maria didn't take as well to Ata. She asked Tanja when they would take the baby back to the hospital. Tanja tried to explain that would never happen; that she was a big sister now with responsibilities, but Maria didn't seem impressed with that argument. Edita didn't seem to care either way, she was just happy to spend more time with her father. She seemed keen to please him all the time. She would point at the baby and say "baby" in English and George would hug her and say "smart girl," then Edita would repeat the phrase "smat gil" back to him. The one person that seemed particularly pleased with the new addition was Vlad; he was an uncle again and wanted to drag kids home from the children's centre to show Ata off. Tanja pleaded for more time; she'd be pleased to bring the baby to them, but she needed more time until he was at least a few weeks old.

The one thing Tanja was eager to find time for was a phone call. There hadn't been a telephone in her hospital room. On the day they returned from the hospital, it was hard to find private time to make the call. On the second day, Tanja suggested that George take all the children for a walk, but George said he was still tired from going back and forth between the hospital. Maybe tomorrow. Tanja was getting anxious; it had been six days since Ata had been born and Mantas wasn't even aware. And because the baby came a week early; he probably wouldn't even know to be suspicious. Finally, she decided to take a chance. George was in the master bedroom with Maria and Edita, Vlad had gone out with Tadas and she was alone in the sitting room with Ata. She quietly got up and listened; the rough housing in the bedroom seemed boisterous. She made her way to the phone in the kitchen.

She didn't know if he'd be home; it was almost mid-day; it didn't seem likely, but she would try. She was in luck!

"Hello," said the familiar voice.

"Hello, daddy," she whispered, "I'm looking at your new son, born on Tuesday."

"Really? Oh, my goodness. Is he healthy? Happy?"

"Yes, he has your nose. He's very handsome. Born at 2 am on September 21 – one day after Edita; just over 3 ½ kilos."

"Oh, my goodness, Tanja. I love you both."

"Tee hee."

"Any chance I could see him? I mean we could just meet on the bench."

Tanja had never thought of that before; it was an ingenious way to avoid any domestic issues and let Mantas see his son.

"That might work."

"I can come now; I could be there in a half-hour?"

"What about your school work?"

"It can wait, do you think you can get away?" Tanja listened; the girls were still rough housing.

"I think they can spare me. 30 minutes?"

"Ok – 30 minutes. Oh, Tanja, just one thing, I'm just curious, what did you decide? I mean about the name."

"I'm sorry, sweetheart, I used Smith. I hope you understand."

"Oh, I do. I was just curious. 30 minutes."

Tanja put down the receiver and heard a key turning in the lock a few moments later. George stopped the roughhousing to greet Luce. Tanja could hear them talking. Tanja went into the sitting room and gave Luce a kiss on the cheek.

Luce made her way over to inspect Ata, but he was fast asleep and didn't seem to care that he had a special visitor.

Tanja kept checking the time and, after 25 minutes, declared that she was just going to get some air; she'd take the baby and just get a breath of fresh air.

"I'd like to come," said George. "I need to buy some beer; I didn't realize we were low."

"Um, well shouldn't you watch the girls? I thought you didn't want to go for a walk. I'm not going to the shop, just to the river."

"I'd like the fresh air, then we can wander over to the shop. Luce – can you watch them for a little bit?" He looked toward Luce for a reply and Luce replied quickly "of course, that's why I am here. My job is to be the calming influence." George laughed.

Tanja didn't know quite how to object. George moved quickly to put Ata in his car seat. George had bought a special collapsible pram that they could keep near the entrance to the main door on the ground floor; the car seat fit inside it, so they would only need to lug the car seat down the stairs each time. While Tanja tried to think what to say, George was already gathering his things. Slip-on shoes were on; then a jacket. Then, he picked up Ata in the car seat.

"Ok, let's go."

Tanja thought about saying that she'd changed her mind, but that seemed like an odd thing to say now. She just complied, complied with her husband's wishes. She thought to herself 'that's what I always do.'

As they walked toward the river, Tanja began to get nervous. George was talking about returning to work; that Trans-ship said he could work from Klaipėda port, but he thought they should talk about London, but Tanja wasn't thinking about anything he said.

They crossed the crosswalk as George explored the advantages of living in England again. Tanja just nodded her head. As they got to the other side of the crosswalk, she craned her head to see if she could see the bench. They wandered another minute or so and then she could see the profile of Mantas' head; he looked toward the river and then toward them. While George pushed the pram, Tanja made a hand gesture at her side. She moved her hand back and forth while keeping it horizontal – the international symbol for not now or no.

"Why are you doing that with your hand?" George asked.

"Just trying to get the circulation going."

"So, anyway, it looks like they want to give me a more junior position; I need to discuss money with them…"

As he talked, they passed by the bench. Mantas just sat on the bench; he had understood the hand signal. He didn't get a chance to see his new son for the first time, but did get a chance to see her husband for the first time. Tanja felt like she had really let him down.

When they returned, Luce was busy preparing vegetables in the kitchen; she wanted the girls to eat healthier snacks and had introduced a healthy food regime. As Luce was alone, Tanja seized the opportunity to have a conversation with her. Tanja had been thinking about the bench and the emotions that she'd been feeling. She wanted to seek some advice while the rest of the family played in the sitting room.

"Luce?" Luce just nodded her head while she continued to scrub the carrots. "Could I ask you something?… When you said you didn't like Mantas, then you changed your mind - did you really think that or were you just saying that because that was my opinion?"

"No, no." Luce didn't seem too interested in the conversation; she just kept working.

"Can I ask you something in confidence?… what do you think of George? I mean honestly."

She now had peeler in hand to begin the next part of the carrot process, "Great fellow, very kind, I like him."

"It's just; I feel weird. When I look at our wedding photo, I realize I just don't feel the same anymore."

"Hmm," Luce was now well into the peeling.

"So, what should I do? I'm asking for your advice."

Luce continued to attend to her carrots, "My sweet, you are like a daughter to me and I must be like a mother to you because you keep asking me for advice, but, as a long-time mother, I make it a point to be very careful about dispensing advice especially on these types of issues. This is something you should work out yourself."

Tanja thought to herself that Luce was being difficult; she was usually more forthcoming.

"I mean, it's a weird situation – you know – it's a difficult situation to be in."

Luce then looked somewhat annoyed and she put down the peeler, then she looked at Tanja and then she picked up the peeler and continued her work, "I don't see anything difficult about it."

Tanja thought that Luce had an annoying habit of stopping mid-thought intentionally. "What does that mean?"

"You thought your husband was dead, you met a boyfriend and got pregnant, now your husband is back… and you were right to name the baby Smith; I was worried you were going to do something else. You did the right thing."

Tanja didn't like the reply which seemed delivered in a particularly testy way. She decided to protest, "It's just he's so controlling; he came and took over and started favouring Edita; he took over the savings, he just assumes he owns everything – even Ata."

Tanja could tell that she'd said the wrong thing; that she'd hit the wrong chord. Luce was now washing cucumbers, but not in a normal way, she was washing the cucumbers quickly and aggressively as if they were trying to jump out of her hands. She completed the washing and turned off the tap and then retrieved the peeler; she was obviously planning what to say next.

"Tanja – can I ask you something?" Tanja nodded, "Do you think George loves you and the girls and Vlad?"

"Yes."

"Did he ever cheat on you?"

"No, but I don't know where you are going with this. I never cheated on him."

"I never said you did. So, one more question - did he prefer his friends and drink the family savings away or did he spend time with you and your brother and Maria?"

"Well, lately he's knocking them back, but he didn't do it at the time."

The last response did not seem to impress Luce.

"So, you asked for advice and I didn't want to give it to you, then you seemed to press me for it, so I'm going to make an exception – only because I think this conversation deserves an exception. When you look at the photograph, you remember the passion you felt toward your husband. I was married for 37 years; I felt passion toward my husband for the first one – or maybe two – of those years. Oh, I loved my husband for the remaining 35 but it was different. And I loved him for different reasons – I loved him because he cared for my children, made sure we had enough money, spent time with us on holidays and evenings and weekends – passion was replaced by dependability. I can tell you are conflicted; you shouldn't be; you feel passion about the Mantas situation because he's the forbidden fruit."

Tanja had wanted Luce to be forthcoming, but she had never spoken to her like that and she was at a loss of words, but that didn't matter, Luce had plenty of words remaining.

"And that thing about Edita; I think he was trying to compensate; she'd never met her father. I don't think Edita cared much, but to George, it was important to make that up to her – and lately, I see him trying to be more attentive to Maria... As for the drinking – the man was held captive by terrorists for two years, he's self-medicating. He's trying to take the edge off those memories. He seems to be a man in control of himself. If it doesn't slow down or it becomes a problem, you should talk to him, he'll listen to you. I bet he spent every day in that cell thinking about you. I've seen two men obsess over you. One seemed to change his whole personality to suit you; George didn't move in and take control of your life. You control him; he's just trying to fulfil the role he thinks you want him to have. Look how he gravitated to the baby; it's not his baby technically, but it's a part of you and so he's trying to do what he thinks you want him to do – to be a father to him. You should feel happy about it; lesser men may not have done the same."

Tanja was more than shocked by the lecture. She just stood there with her mouth open. Luce had put down the peeler now; she didn't look at Tanja. She just looked forward at the wall. Tanja was glad that the lecture was over, but that hope was premature.

"Tanja – I'm from a small village. The old people there had funny beliefs. They were very superstitious. If a stork nested near a home, it was good luck; it would bring new life. If a crop didn't do well, you'd displeased God and you needed to make amends before planting another crop. Old folks would watch the cloud formations to see if the universe was trying to send any signals. It may sound daft, but there's also some truth in those strange beliefs. When you thought that your husband was dead, you got involved with a man and then you didn't really want him in your life, but you were pregnant. Then, you had an accident and you loved him because he cared for you. Then, something happened and you put him on a 'time out.' During that break, your dead husband arrives from the grave - at the very time that you had him on that 'time out.' If that is not a signal from the universe, I'm not sure what would be. Anyway, that's my advice; I didn't think you'd like it, but that's my advice.

Tanja thought to herself, 'Luce was absolutely right; I don't like that advice.'

Tanja thought about the predicament all evening and then she thought about it all night. There were risks in the way she was approaching things. It was during the wee hours, while she sat nursing Ata on a rocking chair in the sitting room, when Tanja decided that the previous day's plan was dangerous. If George figured out that there were clandestine meetings, he would become suspicious. She would just have to confront him with the request that Mantas be allowed to meet Ata. However, she had to do it in a way that it didn't impact that male ego. As she rocked, she thought about it.

After breakfast that morning, George seemed in a particularly jocular mood, so she decided that it was time to talk about it. She waited till Luce came and then she asked him if he'd like to take a walk – just the three of them – just down to the river. George agreed and, while they made that familiar walk, Tanja began to implement the plan.

"George – I was thinking; the baby's biological father; I know he'd want to meet Ata, but I feel I need your permission for something like that?"

"I'm not sure you need my permission, but the prospect doesn't thrill me; what if he decides that he wants him – and you as well?"

Tanja laughed nervously, "That's not going to happen; again, I don't even like to talk about it; I sometimes feel like I betrayed you."

George stopped pushing the pram and looked at her, "In our entire marriage, you never betrayed me, in the entire time I've know you, you were always loyal to everyone. You thought I was gone; I would have wanted you to move on and it all worked out – I got a great little guy out of it."

Tanja blushed; she knew she was blushing, so she just looked the other way. The comment was delivered with such sincerity – and it made her feel guilty about the plan she was deploying. They continued to walk along the river.

"Thanks, sweetheart, I was thinking, I could just go over there sometimes and take him along."

"I don't know if I'm comfortable with that, why can't he just come over to our place once in a while and maybe he'll lose interest?"

"I could try that. See what he says."

"Tanja – I'm just curious. I hope you don't mind me asking. You said you were together twice – you're just not a one-night stand type of girl. Did you have other lovers as well?"

"Of course not." Tanja tried to sound extra perturbed that he'd ask that.

"And I mean, you, I mean, you didn't use protection?"

"Of course, but something went wrong."

"And you never really saw him after?"

Tanja hadn't expected the question. She didn't know why she hadn't expected that question. Of course, he was going to find out about him staying at the apartment for almost three months and that he'd left a little over a month prior to the news of George being alive.

"Well, sort of, he stayed with us for a while after my accident; you know, he was worried about the baby."

"What? He stayed at our place? How come you never told me?"

"I didn't want to upset you; you had enough problems. I don't want you to be jealous; there's no need to be."

"How long did he say?"

"A little over two months."

"Where did he sleep? In the sitting room?"

"No, he made a bed on the floor for himself in the master bedroom."

Tanja realized that she'd just taken a carefully worded innocuous request and had just blown it. George just pushed the pram and said nothing. He didn't have a right to be angry and yet, she could tell he was processing it through his brain and it didn't make him happy.

"Tanja – can I ask you something? We've always tried to tell each other the whole truth. I have a feeling you're leaving out parts of this story. I'm not upset; even if you'd married someone else, I wouldn't be upset; you didn't know I was alive. I think you may think that you are sparing my feelings by keeping somethings secret, but it has the opposite effect – by not telling me things, it makes me suspicious, you shouldn't leave anything out. The past is the past; you didn't do anything wrong, but I am your soul mate, I don't want secrets between us."

George then stopped the pram completely as they walked by the river and he held both her hands and looked at her in the eyes. Tanja tried to look down, she didn't quite know how to respond. Mantas had told her just yesterday that he loved her.

"Can you look at me?" George asked. Tanja looked at his eyes, then she felt guilty and couldn't hold his stare.

"OK, I'll tell everything; I just didn't want to upset you." Tanja then downloaded the story about Mantas being Vlad's tutor and how it had originally started as a casual thing, then she broke it up, then she found out she was pregnant, then she had a fight with him and he witnessed the subsequent accident, then he stayed with her and she liked that and that she grew fond of him, but then he betrayed her and she asked him to leave. George just listened.

"Ok, sweetheart, I'm glad you told me; you shouldn't feel guilty; again, we could always tell each other anything; we shouldn't have secrets... I'm just curious, what was the betrayal? Did he have another woman?"

Tanja looked down again, there were secrets and then there was that secret. She weighed it quickly in her mind and realized that no good could come of telling George that particular secret, "Yes" she answered.

It was the first night of October now and George lay in the bed with Tanja on his chest. She was asleep now. George listened to the driving rain outside; the sound drowned all other noise out; it was pounding. It was strange to hear a noise like that one. When he was in the cell, he would have loved to have heard the sound of that pouring rain. He hated the never ending silence of those nights in the cell. But, now, while he lay there, it kept him awake and it kept him thinking. It made him think of things he didn't want to think about. There was work; he would have to go back to work, but he didn't know if he could do it. His mind wandered so much; he was afraid of the person he had become. He wasn't as confident as he once was; he was much more vulnerable. Indeed, he felt more like he did when he was a schoolboy; he was afraid, very afraid. As he lay there, he thought maybe he shouldn't go to work; the solicitor had been right, the insurance company wasn't going to try to recoup the insurance and Tanja had almost $3million in that savings account, maybe he didn't need to work, but that's what people would expect; maybe that's what he expected of himself.

Then, there was Tanja. She wasn't quite the same. She was clearly holding something back from him with that story. Maybe, she really loved that man. Maybe, she broke up with the man to be with him – and now she probably regretted it. The Tanja part of the story seemed so much easier in the cell. He would go back to her and they would live happily forever. Life was more complicated; he should have known that; it is always more complicated. Whatever transpired, he shouldn't feel jealous about it, but he did feel jealous about it. Tanja was his very symbol of pure light when he was in that dark basement; no one had the right to tamper with that glow. He needed some reassurance from her, but wasn't sure what that meant. He would start pushing her to be intimate again with him; he wanted to feel like a man again and that might help – if she gave herself to him; it might be reassuring. It all seemed so complicated.

It wasn't all bad complicated stuff. His relationship with Vlad had gone right back to where it had been – the two were like old chums again. And Vlad had grown and developed – when he was in that cell, he had never envisioned Vlad as a teenager; he'd never envisioned him as someone whom he'd be able to talk to. He realized now that his expectations of Vlad were low because of the disability, but Vlad had blossomed and he often liked spending time with Vlad. And the girls – he couldn't get over them. They were both precious. He realized now that he had never really thought about his second child much in that cell – when he did, he envisioned a boy, because he had wanted a boy. However, he would trade no boy for her now. Edita radiated goodness. George began to think that she was his kindred spirit – she loved to go places with him and she loved to please him by repeating English words. They always laughed together. It was a nasty thought to have while lying on that bed and listening to the storm, but he thought to himself, if he had to leave the family and could only take one person with him, it would probably be his second daughter. It wasn't that he didn't also love Maria, but Maria didn't need him quite as much and she was sometimes hard to calm down. She reminded him a little of Vlad when he was younger, except Vlad was harder to calm, but his hyperactivity also appeared less often than Maria's.

George lay there on that October night and also thought about the other love of his life. In his mind, he tried to calculate the time difference between Klaipėda and the eastern time zone of North America. It'd be early evening there. He wondered if Lamia was thinking of him now. George tried to figure out where she fit in his world. Was she like a daughter? She really wasn't; she was something different; after all, there was only a difference in age of a dozen years. And she wasn't like a daughter, she was something much stronger; she was stronger than him. He contemplated all the risks she had taken to visit him and her attempts to set him free. And he had learned from her; she had opened his eyes. He smiled as he lay there – he would always consider others' perspectives. He wanted to reach out to her – to call the university and see if they would give him a number or leave a message, but he knew that could put his angel at risk. Then, it struck him – that's what she was – an angel. And it was so poetic that his angel was a Muslim Lebanese girl – from the same tribe that held him in that cell.

The cell – in his early days of incarceration in that cell, he'd realized that he was not only a prisoner in a cell but that he had become a prisoner in his own mind. As he lay there, he began to think and realize that he was still a prisoner in that cell. He was no longer physically locked there but his mind had been impacted by that incarceration and it had changed him – and not for the better. The alcohol helped, but he thought that he couldn't keep doing that. He would need to face the reality of the person that he had become in that cell – filled with self-doubt, suspicion, jealousy and most impactfully – fear. He couldn't figure out where this life was going and it caused him fear. He lay there, he tilted his head down and kissed his wife's hair. He should be happy and yet he was so afraid.

It was the first night of October now and Tanja lay in her bed. She lay on George's chest; he needed so much reassurance now; he often pulled her onto his chest at night. During the days, he tried to hold her hand and kept kissing her and touching her. It was hard to sleep that night. The rain poured and drowned out all other noise; it was also hard to sleep because George kept moving. He must be still awake; she knew that nights could be hard for him. He sometimes bolted out of a deep sleep; one time, she had been nursing Ata and she returned to bed just as he bolted. There was a look of terror on his face. It seemed odd, he was free now and he was with his family – it seemed odd because she began to think that he still seemed like a prisoner in that cell. He had reproached her for keeping secrets, but he never talked about his time in that cell. She wondered if they had beaten him; since his return, he hadn't tried to be intimate with her; maybe they had done something to him.

She knew the feeling; it had been done to her. She thought about the conversation on that riverbank with George. She hadn't told him about the subterfuge, because she thought that he would never allow Mantas to get near them. But, now, while she lay there, she realized that she also didn't want to say anything because she was ashamed – she told Luce everything and she never told her that. She lay there and thought about that – maybe she didn't tell Luce because Luce would then say something that would be filled with common sense and that would make her afraid. Why did she feel ashamed to talk about it? She hadn't done anything; she was a victim. Maybe, instead of being ashamed of that, she should be ashamed that she has feelings for the perpetrator. Maybe, she was experiencing some type of Stockholm Syndrome. Mantas had taken her body hostage and now he had gained control over part of her soul. He had also confessed to the crime and begged forgiveness. As the rain poured down, she thought about what would have occurred had he never told her that secret. At the time of his confession, she was begging him to marry her. How would she have handled a husband and a returning dead husband? It was complicated; very complicated.

At that moment, while she lay on his chest, George reached down and kissed her. She wondered what he was thinking about and then, she felt even more guilt. She didn't really deserve him. Here she was lying on his chest and thinking of another man. Yet, she was with a dependable man who loved to be with her; maybe Luce had been right. Maybe that was more important now.

She would have to call Mantas tomorrow and relay the decision that had been made by the river – he'd be allowed access to meet Ata at the apartment. She thought it was going to be a strange meeting at that apartment. And, then, what would happen after that? Would it continue like that with formal meetings while they exchanged knowing glances? It didn't seem right; it didn't seem right to anyone. It was something to worry about; the future wasn't friendly; it was something to fear.

Mantas lay on his sofa bed and listened to the driving rain. He'd hoped that Tanja would have called him back after the bench incident. He wanted to see her and his new son. It was so odd to see her pass by him and make that hand gesture. It was as if he were a bit character now in her life; someone she could never admit to knowing in public. It reminded him of when they were first together and she had told him that they couldn't be affectionate in public. He lay there and thought – maybe I should have pushed her to forgive me; it just didn't seem right. I wanted to be a new man without secrets; yet, the telling of one secret meant I had to sit on a bench and pretend I did not know that my own son and the love of my life were passing by me. It was so complicated.

He then started thinking about George. He was so much older than he'd imagined; so much older than the photograph on the mantle. He looked like a powerful figure as he pushed his son's pram and talked with the love of his life. Tanja had been right – he was a boy and her husband was a man. And yet, she obviously still had feelings for him. He remembered the call 'hello daddy,' 'he has your nose; he's very handsome.' He also remembered the comment on the bench, just before George resurfaced, when she looked at the old people 'do you think that will be us one day?' It was an odd comment, but, at that moment, he wanted to stop thinking about it. He didn't want to think about any of those comments; they brought too much pain. If he loved her, he needed to leave her alone. He could never be with her; she had a real family that didn't include him; he had had to deceive her even to be considered worthy of spending time with him.

He lay there; he thought about what she might be doing now. She was probably lying there with her husband; he probably had his arm around her. He probably knew the value of the gem that he had in those arms. It was depressing; he would probably never touch that gem again; not the way that her husband touches her.

The rain continued to pound and Mantas wondered when he would hear from her again. Maybe, she would call tomorrow; maybe they could meet at the bench. He listened to the rain and then started to curse it; he wanted it to stop so she could visit him on that bench and bring along his son. If she came to the bench, for a brief moment, he would be able to indulge himself in a fantasy of a life with her – he hoped she would call.

Tanja thought about whether to follow George's request about Mantas coming to the apartment. She didn't really like the sound of it. It was going to be awkward. She really would have preferred to meet him somewhere else and without George. After some thought, she decided that it was best to have the first meeting with complete transparency. Once the men had met each other, maybe she could slowly start to do things her way. However, there were some precautions that she'd take in advance. The two loudmouths – Vlad and Maria – would have to be somewhere else. Vlad could show some restraint these days, but if Maria saw Mantas, she could say anything. She'd have to find a time when Vlad would be at school and then organize an activity outside the apartment for Maria and Edita – and Luce could take them. That might work.

As transparency was now the theme of the day, Tanja decided to wait till George was finished getting the girls ready for the day. It was Saturday, so Luce wouldn't be around. Tanja hung around the kitchen doing some dishes and cleaning the counters and cabinets. When George finally entered the kitchen, she reminded him that she was going to call Ata's biological father. While he stood there, she picked up the phone and called him.

"Hello."

Tanja spoke quickly so he wouldn't interrupt. "Hello, Mantas? It's Tanja, Ata's mother. I'm just here with my husband. You'd mentioned you'd be interested in meeting Ata. I was hoping we could find a time for you to come over and meet him and my husband."

Mantas got the hint and whispered, "Ok, I can come this afternoon or tomorrow?"

"How about Monday? 10 am? Noon?"

"I'll take the first available spot I can get – 10 am."

"Good; we'll see you then. Please call if you need to change. Bye for now."

Tanja put down the receiver.

"That was pretty official for someone you'd conceived a child with," commented George.

Tanja just nodded her head. That's exactly how she wanted that conversation to sound.

By 10 am on Monday morning, Tanja had cleared Vlad off to the Children's Centre and had convinced Luce to take the girls to a library; she'd also given Luce money to take them out for lunch. So, if either of them put up a fuss in the library, they wouldn't return home, they would go to a café and it would buy them enough time.

At a few minutes before 10, the buzzer at the main door sounded; George got up and pressed the entry button, then he went and opened the apartment door. Tanja could hear multiple people coming up the stairs and they were speaking loudly. There must have been some mistake. It wasn't Mantas. Now, she was going to have to figure out how to get rid of the interlopers. George stood at the door. Tanja remained in the sitting room with Ata in a little bassinette.

Then, she heard Mantas' voice as well. Maybe, he'd bumped into someone in the hallway and started talking to them. Then, in horror, he listened to the introductions just outside that door. George was very affable. He addressed Mantas and must have offered a handshake. Mantas then introduced his mother and father to George. George continued to be affable and said that was a pleasant surprise, they were only expecting Mantas.

George invited the three in; the old man and woman seemed very happy to be there and made pleasant comments to George about the apartment. Then, George began introducing Tanja. The father walked over to her and shook her hand; he seemed pleasant.

However, that was the extent of the pleasantries on that morning. The old woman approached Tanja in a much more reluctant fashion and with a look that did not try to hide her disgust. The woman looked down as she offered her hand and Tanja shook it. Tanja had never engraved a 'look' on her memory before but this one would be a first. The woman obviously loathed her – and she'd never met her. Tanja began to wonder what Mantas had told her – the woman clearly believed that she was some sort of Jezebel who had seduced her son then stolen the fruits of his loin.

"It's nice to meet you," said Tanja. Mantas' mother did not reply; she kept looking down and just nodded her head.

George must have felt tension in the air as he quickly interjected, "So, would you like to meet Ata?" The question seemed to be directed to all three, but it was Mantas' mother who strode right past Tanja and to the bassinette, shortly followed by Mantas' father and then Mantas, the father of Ata, came last. It was hardly a sight worthy of such a visit; Ata was fast asleep; he moved a little with the commotion, then took a deep sigh and returned to his deep sleep.

Mantas' father was the first to raise his head from the bassinette, so George decided to keep the conversation going as he addressed the old man, "I'm afraid Ata is a little tired. I'm sure if he knew who had come to visit, he'd be more alert. So, do you live locally?"

The old man explained that they came from a village in eastern Lithuania and had travelled 200km as a surprise to meet their grandson.

Mantas looked toward Tanja and continued that train of commentary, "Yes, I apologize that we didn't call in advance, I mentioned that I was going to be meeting Ata today and my parents arranged for a neighbour to drive them."

Tanja was about to say that it wasn't a problem, but George seemed to want to dominate the conversation.

"Oh, it's no worry, it's a pleasure. It sounds like you've had a long journey. Would you like juice or coffee or maybe a cold beer?"

The old man's eyes seemed to light up at that word beer and he accepted the offer. Mantas also said he'd have one. The old woman just wanted water.

When the drinks were served, Mantas went and sat on the sofa beside George and the old man sat in a chair immediately next to George. Tanja offered the rocking chair to Mantas' mother, but she said that she had been sitting for hours and she wanted to stand at the bassinette.

Tanja sat in the rocking chair; she had been right; this was more than awkward – and why on God's green earth would Mantas not have called; even if she had had 10 minutes notice, it would have given her time to psychologically prepare.

To top matters, George and Mantas' father seemed to hit it off. It wasn't even 10:30 by the time the second beer was offered and accepted, although Mantas declined. George and Mantas' father were discussing politics, then world events. The old man asked George about being taken hostage and George explained about Al Qaeda and how he was held in a basement – he didn't even discuss that with her and he was treating the old man like a long-lost friend. Tanja thought to herself that George was acting the typical American businessman that he was – he could talk to anyone on a superficial level and win over strangers quickly.

Mantas periodically interjected words into the conversation between the great old friends. Tanja just sat there. She decided that it was enough; the old woman was treating her like an outcast in her own home. It was time to break the ice. She looked over at Mantas' mother who still stood at the bassinette.

"Did you have a good trip?"

"Fine," said the old woman.

"That's a beautiful sweater, did you make it yourself?"

"I bought it."

"What do you think of Ata?"

"Well, he's a baby, he's beautiful."

The last comment had been delivered in such a flippant fashion as to make it very clear that she was in no mood to talk. Tanja decided not to try again; the situation was bad and awkward but it had the potential to get worse. If she just stayed quiet, maybe the meeting would end sooner.

Tanja's hopes were quickly dashed when George offered the third beer. Even Mantas agreed to have a second one. Tanja began to think about ways she could wrap this up. She thought that maybe she could excuse herself to make a call, then something urgent would come out of that call – or maybe she could say that she didn't feel well. No, no, she was getting ahead of herself. If she sat there in silence, that would prod them to go home. She tried to glare at Mantas, but he was busy interjecting into the conversation and peeling at the label from his bottle of beer.

As George was organizing the third beer, Mantas' father brought out an old camera that he'd been carrying in a plastic bag. Tanja looked on as Mantas' father took photos of Mantas, his wife and Ata and then the wife and Ata and then Mantas and Ata. Finally, he turned to Tanja and asked politely would she mind taking a photo of the three of them with Ata? It was humiliating – as if she had no role in that room, except as a photographer.

The commotion and photo-taking had a positive effect however. Ata began to stir and then cry. In normal circumstances, Tanja would have nursed him right there, but not today. She excused herself and took Ata to the master bedroom for his lunch.

She closed the door and sat on the bed while she listened to the party outside. Mantas' father was now talking about his farm, which seemed odd as she believed that George had probably never been to one. She continued listening and noted that she only heard the voices of Mantas, his father and George. The mother must be busy sulking, she thought.

Another half-hour passed and Tanja was getting nervous that Luce and the girls might come back. Ata was already asleep again, but she wouldn't go out; she now had an excuse to extract herself from the meeting. She was relieved when she finally heard Mantas' mother say "we should be moving along." Tanja decided she would wait till they started to move and then she would bring out the sleeping baby one last time for them to see.

She could hear them moving close to the door and then she took the infant out to the hallway. Mantas' father smiled and gently caressed Ata's sleeping face; Tanja detected that he seemed particularly jocular after all that beer. Mantas did the same and then the mother leaned toward the baby and smiled; then she looked right back to the floor again.

George shook hands with Mantas and then his mother but, when he got to Mantas' father, he gave him a manly bear hug and the man returned that hug and they both said what a pleasure it was to meet each other. Tanja was relieved when the door was closed and it was just the three of them again.

"Very nice man," said George.

"Very angry woman," said Tanja.

Tanja had trouble concentrating for the remainder of the day. She was hoping Mantas would call and apologize, but she wasn't surprised that he didn't. He had been asked to keep a low profile. In any event, the awkward meeting was behind her, but, when bedtime came, she had trouble sleeping; she kept thinking about the way that the old woman had treated her; if only she knew the real story.

The next morning, Tanja was up early with Ata, she thought about phoning Mantas. She could get away with a secret call at that time. Then, she thought that the parents likely stayed over – and that phone call would be even more fodder for her new enemy.

After breakfast, Tanja escaped to the kitchen and waited for the family to be occupied. She tried calling, but there was no response. Throughout that day, she found moments when the family was distracted or out and tried, but there was no response.

Finally, while doing the dinner dishes, she listened at the kitchen door. Vlad was watching television, Maria was playing castle with her dad and Edita seemed to be trying to figure out one of her puzzles. It wasn't the safest time to try, but she could always hang up if someone approached.

"Hello."

"It's me," whispered Tanja.

"Oh hi; hey, I'm sorry about yesterday."

"Yeah, Mantas, what did you tell your mother and why did you just show up that way?"

"I didn't tell her anything; she is just nuts; comes to her own conclusions; she watches a lot of that American programme, 'Santa Barbara,' each person is either a saint or a villain; most are villains and you're in that category for now. I'm sorry about everything. I told them on Saturday about our visit and I was shocked when I saw that Lada coming toward me with my father in the passenger seat. I'd already left for your place when they spotted me walking. I should have insisted that they not come, but it was such a big event for them. They spent Sunday trying to convince the neighbour to bring them; then got up in the middle of the night to get here before 10."

Tanja sighed, "Ok; well, it's done now."

"Can I come again; maybe just the three of us? I can meet you at the bench tomorrow."

Tanja paused to listen to the noise in the sitting room. "I think we should do one more apartment visit; otherwise, it'll make him suspicious. Let's wait till next week. Ok? I can call you to confirm. I should go. Bye for now."

Tanja put down the receiver and tried to contemplate the conversation that had just transpired. She wondered why she had said that "it'll make him suspicious." She was uncomfortable with trying to establish secret phone calls and meetings. Maybe, she should just find a way to tell George what she wanted and be assertive about it. The whole secret phone call process made her feel cheap; disloyal somehow. She hadn't really done anything disloyal to George and she wasn't planning to be disloyal. She wasn't going to give her body to another man; it was her heart that she was worried about.

That evening, Tanja was pulled onto George's chest. She knew the routine now. She was to lie there for a while until he fell asleep, then she could go back to her side of the bed and sleep, then the other little man who slept in a bassinette in that master bedroom would demand her attention. Nights were becoming one long shift of serving two men in her life.

She lay there and received her usual hair stroking. That was at least some concession; she liked having her hair stroked. Then, George's hands started stroking her back, then he lifted his head, Tanja looked up toward him and he kissed her once on the lips, then he kissed her rather passionately a second time. She wondered what he was thinking about.

"Tanja – I've been thinking. So, Trans-ship has suggested that I wait before returning to work; they think I could have been impacted by trauma; they're talking about January. They also offered two positions – a director role in London or a trader job here."

Tanja started rubbing his chest, she knew he liked that; she didn't reply.

"You know, Maria could start pre-school next year; she'll be 4. We could get her into a decent school; they don't even really have private school here. And Vlad could go back to his independent school. I just wanted to ask how you felt about it."

"I'm not sure; we have roots here now. I love this apartment; I bought it."

"I thought about that. You know, we love Tadas; he is also the stepfather of a millionaire – and he lives in a hovel of a Soviet flat. Maybe, he could live here. If you don't like London, we can move back and see about buying him another flat in the building. He deserves it."

Tanja lay in silence; she wanted to decline the thought outright; she had issues to deal with here. She had to confess that she'd never thought about Tadas and his living conditions. He was always someone who supported her and Vlad and the girls; he never asked for anything. George was right – she should buy him an apartment near to them – he did deserve it.

"Can we think about it?" replied Tanja. She wanted to give the impression of considering it before declining the idea of moving.

The next Monday visitation was similar to the first – but without Mantas' parents. With Vlad at school, Tanja evicted all the ladies of the household

– Edita, Maria and Luce – in favour of a formal meeting with three men – Ata, George and Mantas. It was good to see Mantas again; Tanja realized that she had butterflies in her tummy when he walked through the door that morning at 10 am. She was thinking that she'd made a terrible mistake – she'd just let circumstance push her into her current situation; she hadn't chosen her husband, he had been thrust upon her. She'd made her point with Mantas long before George had returned; she should have let it go.

Mantas held his son for the first time that morning. He had only looked at him during the previous visit. Tanja wanted to suggest that she take a photograph of him holding Ata, but decided that the suggestion might not play well with George. She always had to think about how George would perceive things.

While the visitation took place, George and Mantas mainly talked. Tanja didn't say much and the men mostly talked about Mantas' life as a tutor and school and his family and where he grew up. Tanja was surprised that Mantas didn't seem to ask any questions about George. He seemed nervous; Mantas kept adjusting his socks and scratching his head.

The meeting was much shorter this time; it was done in 45 minutes. When it was over and Mantas left, George made a curious observation.

"Well, I think we were right about keeping the meetings formal. He definitely has feelings for you." Tanja was shocked by the comment.

"What do you mean?"

"The sock touching; subliminal romantic interest... they taught us about non-verbal communication at the company; if we're face to face with someone, we can look for clues to tell if someone is telling the truth or if they're sincere or confident in their replies."

"And some of the traders had a subliminal romantic interest in you?"

George laughed. "I haven't had that kind of luck; there was a slide on interrelationship communication – if a male is interested in a female, he adjusts his clothes; you know, straightens his tie or checks his buttons – but socks are the main one, he touches his socks; it's a strange thing. And females groom males; if they are aroused by a male, they will remove a thread from his sweater or find another reason to touch and groom him."

Tanja watched George for another minute; he never expanded on the comment. He picked up Ata from the bassinette and made faces at him. He probably said that because he was clueing in; but it didn't seem that way, it sounded like it was an academic observation – like he was a scientist who happened to see a comet in the sky and thought he should mention it.

A few days passed before Tanja attempted to call again. There always seemed to be someone around. Either George would be near the kitchen or Vlad or Tadas or Luce or she would need to attend to Ata or Edita or Maria. She often thought about how her life would have been had she not had children or even how her life would have been had she not had her most recent child. Motherhood was a demanding role and it had sapped her energies as well as her self confidence; she didn't know if she could work again; it had been so long since she'd worked.

Finally, there was a free moment – George and Luce had taken the girls out; it was only her and Ata. She tried calling Mantas; there was no answer. After a few minutes, she tried again, then she waited 10 more minutes and tried and then, after an additional 20 minutes, she thought she would try one more time, then she'd have to give up. That final call was successful, but Tanja wanted to talk quickly. She was keen to set up an informal meeting with the three of them, but Mantas seemed overwhelmed; he'd obviously just returned to his flat and he was talking about tutorials and course schedules; it was easier before when she could just suggest a time and he would accommodate. He complained he was falling behind. Tanja decided to cut to the chase. "Very early Sunday morning?" she asked. He replied that he could make that happen. Tanja said that she'd be there by 7:30; she'd already rehearsed her backstory in her mind.

When Sunday morning rolled round, she was up at 6 pretending to care for Ata. She then went and had a long hot shower; she combed her hair; she looked at herself in the mirror; she thought she still looked somewhat beautiful – when she cleaned herself up. She looked round in one of the drawers and found a bottle of perfume; she never used it anymore, but today, she took a spray on both sides of her neck and one spray at her tummy. It made her feel better. She thought about what she could wear. She loved clothes and used to take such pride in her appearance. But now, she thought that she didn't really have many nice clothes; at least nothing suitable for the occasion; she hadn't really bought anything since she'd moved from England.

While George snored, Tanja dressed in her bathrobe and made her way through the closet. It was hard to see in the dark; the curtains were closed and she had to rely on the light that emanated from a small nightlight. In the end, she selected a blue dress, it was more of a summer thing, but it would do.

She lovingly and quietly placed it on a hook on the back of the bedroom door. She then attended to Ata; he was asleep, but she changed his nappy and put him in a clean bodysuit. Ata hardly reacted to the movement; he was in a deep sleep.

She then completed the usual ceremony of donning her undergarments and stockings; then putting on her dress and placing her wristwatch on her wrist. She went back to the bathroom and looked at herself one more time; yes, she thought that would do. She returned to the bedroom and removed Ata from the bassinette. She took him to the sitting room and put him in his overalls. She then placed him in his car seat. He still barely moved and just yawned at all the activity. She looked out the sitting room window – it was raining and pitch black; darn it, she thought, I don't need this today. She donned her long winter coat that morning; she would look silly, but she would have to wear her boots today; she could take them off when she got there. Before putting them on, she had one final task to complete.

She walked quietly back into the bedroom and gently woke George, "Sweetheart, I've had a rough night with Ata, I'm just going to take him out to calm him down."

"Is everything ok?" George rolled over; Tanja tried to keep her distance a little; she didn't want to explain the perfume. George was groggy, but continued, "I can take him if you've had a rough night."

"No, we both need it; we won't be long."

Tanja put on her boots and walked down the stairs with Ata and placed him in his pram and pulled a plastic tarpaulin over the pram and ventured into the predawn darkness. It was raining, but it was manageable. She looked at her watch; it was just after 6:30; she'd be early. She began pushing the pram, then the rain got harder, she tried to search the roads for a taxi, but it was too early on a Sunday morning. She walked faster. It seemed the faster that she walked, the harder that the rain poured. It was raining so strongly that she could feel the rain penetrating under the collar of her winter coat. She began almost a sprint to facilitate getting out of that rain. When she arrived, she was drenched and it wasn't even 7.

She pulled at the broken main door and was able to get it open. She dragged the pram up the concrete steps and through the door, closed the main door, then dragged the pram up another few steps to the first floor flat. She knocked. There was no answer. She rang the bell. She leaned her head against the door, she could hear water running – he was taking a shower. She rang again and knocked loudly. Then, she heard water being turned off; a few seconds later, she could see an eye look at her from the peep hole and then the door opened. Mantas stood in a towel.

"I'm sorry, sweetheart, you're early. Oh my God, look at you. Come in."

After she pushed the pram through the door, he leaned over and kissed her on the lips.

She removed her boots and then her coat. That seemed to send Mantas scurrying back to the bathroom. She looked down; her beautiful dress had not been spared the storm, it was wet and clinging to her. The winter coat was good for winter, the collar was cut too low for driving rain.

Mantas appeared from the bathroom with a robe and asked her to put it on. Tanja accepted it; the dressing up had been pointless, but she wasn't going to put a robe over her wet dress. She made her way to the bathroom, removed it and put on the robe. She stretched out the clothesline above the bath and placed her beautiful blue dress on it so that it could dry. She looked at herself in the mirror; her attempt to look beautiful had failed, she now looked like a drowned rat.

When she returned from the bathroom, Mantas was dressed in a t-shirt and pair of shorts and was admiring his son. He'd removed the tarpaulin and was busy making faces at Ata who seemed to be oscillating between sleep and confusion.

"He is very beautiful, just like his mother," he said.

Tanja sat on the sofa; she was exhausted. With the exhilaration of the morning and the run through the dark streets, she was tired.

"Can I get you anything? Coffee?"

"No, I can't stay long. I didn't think about the rain; that'll raise suspicion."

"You could tell him you were inside; in a café?"

"I'm not trying to make a habit of lying to my husband; I'm just making this exception."

Mantas thought he should be careful; she was obviously annoyed. "I appreciate it. We need to work out a different arrangement; maybe there's a way you could tell him the truth – that you just wanted to show the baby periodically to me and make it quick."

"I was planning to do that, but your sock pulling may have raised an issue. You kept pulling at your socks and then George told me that was a sign of romantic interest. I tell you; he's a funny character; that cell changed him."

Mantas didn't know how to respond; she was still annoyed. He tried to change the subject and talk about his parents. He talked about his studies and how he'd be going to Sweden for two weeks for a conference; another student who had been selected had to drop out and he'd go in his stead. Tanja seemed to just listen; he had said his part. At the last few meetings, Tanja hadn't had the chance to say anything, he would now try to prompt her.

"So, my love, what's new with you? How are the girls?"

"They're fine; everything is the same. The girls are becoming George's children; they're more interested in him; I'm Ata's parent. That's how it's working. Also, if you want, I think George is willing to adopt your father – let us know."

Mantas laughed, "I'm sorry to hear that, you don't deserve it. And I'll let my mother know, she'd likely take that offer."

Tanja didn't laugh but just continued, "I'm not complaining; it's fine; I guess I am happy about it. And George is busy plotting his next career move. They want him back in January; either in Klaipėda or London. I need to find a way to get London out of his head; I negotiate everything with him carefully these days."

"Well, I might be able to help if you need it. He'd need my permission to take Ata out of the country."

Tanja didn't say anything, then thought that her silence could imply something was wrong. She didn't want to talk about the birth certificate. "That's a point, but I don't know, on the other hand, Vlad was really doing well at that school and the education system is better there – I mean Maria could start preschool next year." Tanja was just thinking out loud, she was repeating the words that George had said, but it was nice to have an adult conversation again that didn't include her husband, stepfather or Luce.

"Well, again, you can't do that."

Tanja was confused by the statement, "What do you mean?"

"Well, like I say, he'd need my permission, so you'd have an excuse to stay."

"Sorry, Mantas, I mean, I might be willing to think about it; I promised him I'd think about it."

"Well, that's ok, my sweet, we'd work something out."

Tanja now moved quickly from confusion to suspicion, it was the phrase 'you can't do that' that had bugged her, "What does work something out mean?"

Mantas knew he had stepped into forbidden territory; he had only just woken up on a Sunday morning after having taken a shot at another whisky bottle the night before. "I mean, I mean, well, I mean to see Ata and you and stuff."

"Mantas, for the sake of this meeting and our relationship, I'm going to ignore the last minute of this conversation. I have one control freak to deal with, I don't need another."

"I'm sorry, sweetheart, let's change the subject. Of course, you do what is right for the children. That's why I love you; I'm sorry, I was just talking out loud."

The conversation in the tiny Soviet flat continued for a few minutes. Then, Tanja went back to the bathroom and donned her wet dress. She didn't care that it was wet, she just kept replaying those words in her head.

She prepared Ata, put on her coat and Mantas kissed her on the cheek. She made her way outside. She walked out of the Soviet block toward the river. The rain had stopped and the eastern sky showed a hint of what was about to occur – the sun was about to rise. It would be a new day, it would probably be similar to every other day, but as she looked toward the sky, she couldn't help feel a bit of optimism. The rain had stopped and she was welcoming a new day with her new son. It was a nice thought – and much nicer than the thought of that conversation she'd just had.

Tanja decided to wait several days before contacting Mantas again. The conversation on that Sunday morning was more reminiscent of the old Mantas; the one who manipulated and tricked. She preferred the new one who was more supportive. She would let him cool off a little; he seemed to do better when she made the boundaries clear. When she finally did call, she found that she was out of luck – he was heading to Stockholm for a fortnight. He wouldn't have time for a visit beforehand. And now she regretted having given him another 'time out'; now she wouldn't see him until well into November.

CHAPTER 12

Revelations

Revelation 22:1
Then the angel showed me the river of the water of life...

George was being annoying; he was up to something; one morning, she found him going through her dresses – looking at them. He was getting suspicious; the Sunday caper seemed stupid now; the rain was the problem. Who would believe that she went out in the pouring rain for a walk on a Sunday morning? George was also now disappearing for long periods. He had acquired a mobile phone and it seemed to ring constantly. He would often tell the caller that he had to call them back or he'd wander down the stairs and into the street to take a call. Tanja wondered what it was about; she couldn't believe it was a mistress; they sounded like business calls, but why would he take them in secret? When she confronted him, he told her that he was talking to Darius, which was clearly a lie. Why would he be talking to someone of that importance so often? She began to think he was planning the move to London without her; she'd just be dragged along like luggage.

Week one of the Stockholm conference passed and now she really regretted her decision to keep Mantas at a distance for those last few days before his departure. He'd made an innocuous comment; a throwaway remark; Mantas was just trying to be helpful. He was trying to stop her from being dragged like luggage away from him. She wished she'd responded differently.

He would be returning on Saturday; she would phone him at the weekend and confirm a time. She had also made another decision; it was time to have a serious conversation with him. She would start by forgiving him, then telling him that she had longed for him. It would set the stage for a future conversation, she needed to figure out what her future held and how she should live it; he would be able to help, she could trust him now; he would give her advice.

On the Friday prior to Mantas' return, George seemed to act particularly oddly. It was as if he knew something was up. He took Ata for a long walk that afternoon and left her with the girls, which was the opposite of how things usually worked. Then, when he came home, he brought Tadas with him. Tanja began to think that he was going to use Tadas as one of his pawns. George had won him over long ago and was not beyond using the old man to his advantage.

She became even more suspicious when she saw Tadas' little suitcase.

"Why did you bring that?" asked Tanja.

"George invited me for a sleepover with the children. I hope that's ok." Maria overheard the plan and immediately ran to her grandfather. She started trying to wrestle him, but Tadas was quick and turned the attempt into a kind of giant bear hug.

"It's ok; he just never discussed it with me." Tadas looked down and slightly nervous.

At that point, George came out of the bedroom and looked at her and said, "Can I have a word?"

Tanja nodded her head and complied; she always complied. She followed him to the bedroom.

She looked at him, but he didn't say anything and then he pointed to the bed.

Spread neatly across the bedspread was a dress, but it wasn't any dress, it was so stunning and familiar that she couldn't quite place it at first. It was black with a long tail at the back to expose the front of the legs, but not the back. The top of the garment was also low cut at the bust and high cut at the back. It was similar to a dress that she already owned, but it was the elegant cut of the legs that made it so striking.

George looked down at the garment on the bed, "It's for you. I don't know if you recognize it. Do you?"

Tanja felt the fabric; it was beautiful, then it came to her. "It looks like a dress I used to have years ago."

"It's the same dress that you wore on our first date. I found some old photos of you in it and I got someone to tailor a new one. Do you like it?"

Tanja absolutely did like it, "It's beautiful, George, I just wish I had somewhere to wear it."

"Ahh, that's why I employed Mr Tadas. He's covering tonight. You'll need to express some milk; he can handle it. I want to take you out."

Tanja was now busy holding the dress up to herself. She strode into the bathroom to see it in the mirror. She realized it had been a long time since she'd felt like a real woman; in that dress, she wouldn't be someone's mother, she would be a woman again.

She looked in the mirror and George continued talking, "There's only one thing, we may be a little overdressed; I have a reservation at a Georgian restaurant, where we had that first date."

Tanja giggled; sometimes, George made her giggle. He had wacky plans, she liked that.

After a hot shower, Tanja duly completed her duty of expressing milk with her pump, then put on makeup, stockings and that beautiful dress. She couldn't believe how she felt in it; she felt confident in that dress and she was about to get a night away from that apartment.

Before leaving, Tanja gave detailed instructions to Tadas on how to feed Ata, when to change him, when to put the girls to bed, Edita's favourite bedtime book, Maria's favourite bedtime book. Tadas just nodded his head, he was clearly just eager for her to leave.

Tanja put on her high heels, while George put on his overcoat.

"There's one more surprise. That dress doesn't really go with your old winter coat; I got you a new coat that's a little more stylish."

George presented the new coat from the closet and Tanja looked at it; it was also tasteful, not quite as beautiful as the dress but a far cry from her old winter coat. George placed it on her and she kissed his cheek to thank him.

The two made their way into the street and George held her hand. It was nice to be out of the apartment, to be free – even if it were for just a short while.

They made their way to the Georgian restaurant. Tanja couldn't believe it was still there. They climbed down the stairs into the basement. It was like it had been when she was 19 years old; it was dimly lit with candlelight. She remembered sitting at one of the tables – she looked at it now – she remembered sitting there with George on their first date and how she looked at him and how he looked at her. They had no real common language at that time; there had been a lot of looking and pointing and mixed phrases in three languages.

While they waited for the maître de, George whispered, "I know what you're looking at, I reserved our old table as well."

After the maître de removed their coats, they were shown to the old table, they sat down, and Tanja decided to ask the question that she'd been pondering since seeing that dress.

"George – what's this in aid of? I mean why tonight?"

"I know how much you used to love fashionable clothes; but you hardly buy anything for yourself, I thought you deserved a treat and a night out. I guess I've been back two months now and we've been busy with the baby and there's been no me and you time, but there's one more thing and that's why I chose tonight; let me order some wine first, I want to make a toast."

Tanja looked down at the menu; it'd been close to a year since she'd been to a restaurant; it felt nice to be there. "So, don't tease me, tell me what the other thing is."

"I won't; not yet." George summoned the waiter and requested a carafe of wine. Once the waiter left, George said "you expressed enough milk for tonight, you can have a glass or two; it'll work."

Tanja blushed. "You put a lot of planning into tonight."

The waiter was quick to bring the carafe and two glasses. George poured the wine into them.

"Ok, my sweet, so do you want a present?"

"I do," replied Tanja.

George put his right hand into his suit jacket. He pulled out some carefully folded copies of some documents and handed them to her. Tanja couldn't quite understand what it was about. It looked like a contract to buy property. The contract referred to the same address as their apartment address in Klaipėda but it was regarding a unit on the ground floor.

Tanja looked at George's name on the document as the buyer. "I'm confused, are you buying property?"

"Yes, he doesn't know it, but Tadas is about to be our neighbour."

Tanja looked down in disbelief. It was an act of kindness that surprised her; it was something she'd thought about and even discussed it with George, but in her new life as a mother to three demanding ones, it had been a fleeting thought and yet, he had carried it out.

"George – that's so sweet; I can't believe it; that was so kind. I can't wait to tell him."

"It will be great. If you like we could put the deed in his name, but we may want to put it in our names. I was thinking about what I said about letting him stay in our place if we went to London. Tadas shouldn't feel that he is only in a place temporarily in case we come back. He should have his own place and, if we decide to leave, we can rent our place."

"How would you even think of this?"

"I saw the sign and I thought what would Tanja do – and I did it. When I think like Tanja, I always do the right thing for people. Asta helped me out."

Tanja blushed and looked down. The wine was also going straight to her head; the comment made her feel slightly ashamed; she didn't deserve that compliment.

George watched her blush and then continued. "I wish I were more like you, Tanja. I'm sorry; I know I've been hard to be around since I came back; lots of things going through my head. The gestures aren't completely altruistic, I guess I was hoping to win you back a little."

The comment surprised her, "What do you mean by that?"

"I know I just showed up out of the blue. I know you have emotional baggage – and it's because of me; I'm sorry I put you in that position. Life is funny."

Tanja didn't quite know how to respond, she took another sip of wine and leaned forward, "Sorry George, what do you mean by emotional baggage?"

"With Mantas, I know it's been tough. You downplay it for me, but I live with two blabber mouths. Maria gave me the headlines and then I pumped Vlad for the details. I think I understand the extent of the relationship now. I'm sorry – men are possessive."

"And you're not upset? I mean about 'emotional baggage'."

At that point, the waiter returned. Tanja forgot what was on the menu, but George had recalled the dishes they'd ordered on their first date and so he asked if they could order those.

"Well, not really. When I was in that cell, I learned to accept things I couldn't control. I also know you pretty well; I know you wouldn't physically cheat on me; although the perfume the other morning caught me off-guard."

"It was just that I wanted to feel better about myself. George – look at me..." She took both his hands and looked him in the eyes, "I would never cheat on you. How did you even know about the perfume?"

"When you're locked in a cellar, your senses become pretty astute, you listen for every sound, sniff at every scent. I know how loyal you are, you've always been loyal. I think I even know why you're so loyal; when your father left, you had to take on part of his role; I think you promised yourself that you'd never be like that, but... I also know you're conflicted."

The starters were served and Tanja smiled at the waiter; she wanted him to go quickly so George could explain that comment.

"When I was in that cell, at one point, I wasn't just a prisoner in body, I had become trapped in my own mind. My thoughts would just repeat – I mostly thought about you and Maria, but sometimes I'd try to think about different things, but I just got caught in the same cycles. I couldn't break free; I just wanted to go back. I learned a lot about perspective in those two years – I know you're going through some turmoil, that you're stuck, but I want you to know that it's ok. If you want to have a relationship with Mantas, I'm ok with it. I'm not ok with a physical relationship, but I'm ok with an emotional relationship. I trust you."

Tanja looked into his blue eyes and she felt a surge of admiration toward her husband. That evening, he wasn't quite the ogre that he had seemed since his return. She put down her fork and asked him to give her his hand. She now had her own topics that she wanted to explore.

"George – you once said that we don't keep secrets. What happened in that cell?"

George sighed and pushed back from the table a little. He let go of her hand but she offered it again and he held it. "I'm not quite ready yet; it's not a secret, but I'm not quite ready to talk about it. It's a bit different when you've been the victim of an assault; it's hard to talk about it. It wasn't all bad; you're not allowed to talk about it – it will be between us only, I succumbed to Stockholm Syndrome, I bonded with one of the hostage-takers, I'm pretty sure that's why I am here now. I think some strings were pulled."

Tanja replayed the words in her mind. He was obviously in pain while discussing it and she wanted to blurt out that she knew what it was like to not want to talk about it. She felt such sympathy at that moment; he wanted to open up, but he said that the timing wasn't right. She knew that feeling as well.

George continued, "Anyway, my sweet, let's change the subject. Ok? Let's just finish on the previous thing then we'll talk only about happy stuff. So, I'm ok with you seeing him with the baby; as long as there's nothing physical. If you decide that won't work for you, then you need to come back and we need to talk about what the future is for us. If you decide you want to choose someone else, I won't stop you; but you shouldn't leave me because you think I don't love you enough. You are the love of my life. You are my soulmate; you complete me."

Tanja squeezed his hand. That night, her characterization of George had shifted from admiration, to sympathy and now, she felt something else, she wasn't quite sure how to describe it. It might have been that she was wearing the same dress or dining at the same restaurant or eating the same food, but somehow, that night, she felt the same way about George as she had when she last sat at that table - when she was 19 years old. It might have been the wine, but a tear came to her eye. "I agree to everything; I love you; I would never betray you."

She leaned forward and kissed him. He smiled at her and played with her fingers with his own fingers. Then, he looked at her and posed one final question.

"By the way, where is Mantas these days? He hasn't been round."

"Stockholm."

As the two made their way home after that candlelit dinner, Tanja held his hand. She looked down at her new coat and squeezed his hand even tighter. George asked how they should tell Tadas tonight, but Tanja told George that she preferred to wait till morning. She still wanted the night to be about just the two of them.

When they arrived at the apartment, Tadas was watching the television on a very low volume. Tanja took off her coat and shoes and tiptoed to him to enquire, "How did it go?"

Tadas smiled and stood up and kissed her on the cheek, "Lots of chaos, Vlad helped; it was hard to get the girls down, they wanted to play. Ata had a feeding just a few minutes ago; I changed him."

She grabbed Tadas and embraced him and held him for a minute. Tadas thought it was an unnecessary embrace; all he had done was watch some children for a few hours. Tanja broke the embrace and looked at him, "I love you, father."

Tadas now blushed, "Has she been into the wine?"

Tanja giggled and George affirmed that was indeed the case.

As Tadas made up his bed for the night on the sofa, Tanja collected a bottle of her expressed milk from the fridge and made her way into her bedroom, past her sleeping son. She placed the bottle on the nightstand and made her way to the bathroom. She looked at herself in her new dress. She knew what she was going to do now; it was her turn to give a present.

When she returned to the bedroom, George was already in pyjamas and laying in bed. She turned off all the lights. The room was illuminated by a single dim nightlight that stayed on at night so she could attend to Ata. She stood in her dress and slowly started moving as if dancing to music that wasn't there. He watched her; she watched him watching her. She slowly pulled down one of the straps from the dress, then continued to move in front of him, then she let the other one fall. She turned her back to him and pointed to the zipper on the back of the dress. He pulled himself closer to her and unzipped it. She let it fall to the floor, then gently used her foot to kick it to a corner of the room. She then slowly removed a stocking, then another one and threw them in the corner.

She then climbed on top of him on the bed with just her undergarments remaining. She leaned down and kissed him. She still knew what he liked; she started kissing his lips, then she worked her way down his face to his neck and began nibbling at it; he started to move with the stimulation of the gentle kisses on his neck. She then began undoing the buttons on that pyjama top and, once complete, she took her hand and rubbed and kissed his chest. He started caressing her hair and kissing her forehead. She pulled at his sleeve to indicate that he should remove the pyjama shirt. She kissed him on the lips and then sat on top of him, just looking at him. If she had just stopped and looked without saying anything to anyone in the world, she would have felt nervous, but she wasn't nervous with him, she could just sit there on top of him and look at him and she could just think.

He was rubbing her sides now and one of his hands made its way to her bra clad breast. She smiled at him. He took both his hands now and fumbled with the clasp at the back until it sprung free. He touched her breast and then he leaned forward to gently tease it with his tongue. Tanja redirected his attention to her other breast, the one that Ata didn't favour. It was engorged, and as he gently sucked on it, she could feel milk being released. With anyone else, she would have been embarrassed, but it aroused her and gave her relief, she beckoned him to keep sucking it.

Now, it was her turn. She removed herself from the sitting position on top of him and removed her panties. She then recommenced the kissing of his chest and slowly worked lower. He was already protruding from his pyjama bottom and she just gently kissed him there. She then worked her way back up to his tummy and gently touched the tip of it; just enough to make him groan in anticipation. She put her finger to his lips; he shouldn't moan with Ata at the foot of the bed and her stepfather in the sitting room.

She then took her hand and placed it firmly on him, gently stroking him and then she kissed her way back to the location and tugged at his pyjama bottom until she was able to pull it free and then she used her foot to fully remove those pyjama bottoms. She then began kissing him there then teased him with her tongue, then inserted him into her mouth. He was shaking now; shaking and trying not to moan. He kept putting his hands on her head to stroke her and then he'd remove them when the pleasure became overwhelming.

Then she stopped, she sat back on top of him again. She looked at him.

This wasn't about pleasure for her, it was about pleasing him. And the act of pleasing him was arousing her; she wanted him; she wanted him to want her – and he clearly did. She wanted to give herself to him. She raised herself slightly and slowly inserted him. She wanted him to feel her completely; she didn't use protection; she was breastfeeding anyway so didn't feel it necessary; besides, on that night, she didn't care. She didn't want anything between her and him.

Tanja just sat there for a minute and looked at him and periodically kissed him and said "I love you," A memory came to her while she sat there. She remembered the last time that she'd felt this type of arousal – she even remembered the date – it was Christmas Eve 1996 when her daughter was accidentally conceived. She gently began swaying and moving on top of him. She could feel him gently scratching her back. She moved faster; he started groaning again and, without stopping, she put her hand over his mouth.

He was sweating a little now, Tanja knew that he didn't want to finish – that he wanted to keep going, but he was close and she wanted to get him there. She wanted him to feel that pleasure. He whispered to her to slow down, but she moved faster and kissed him harder and put her hands around his hips and gyrated on top of him.

It was all over quickly, George almost screamed out, but she got her hand back quickly over his mouth. He shuddered instead and groaned. When he was complete, she just sat on top of him and moved gently, she wanted him to stay in that position and not extract himself.

He looked at her in the bath of the nightlight, "I'm sorry, sweetheart, it was a bit quick, it's been a long time, you're wonderful."

Tanja smiled, "Do you still want socks for Christmas?"

He smiled back; she gently pulled herself away and kissed him. She got up and returned to the bathroom, just to clean herself up and, when she returned, he lay there wearing his pyjama bottoms. She asked him to remove them, she wanted to be cuddled tonight without clothes between them.

She got into bed and cuddled up on his chest and drew circles with her fingers through his chest hair. She kept pulling herself closer to him; she wanted her body to touch as much of his flesh as possible. The couple fell asleep to the light of a nightlight in the master bedroom of Tanja's apartment in Klaipėda.

Around 4 am, Ata became antsy and Tanja got up and brought him to their bed to nurse him. He refused the bottle and demanded his favourite breast; Tanja acquiesced and smiled as she thought how men were so typical. After nursing, she returned him to the bassinette, but she couldn't sleep. There were too many thoughts going through her head, she just drew circles and designs in George's chest hair. It must have been close to 5 when he began to speak.

"What are you thinking about, my girl?"

She kept drawing the circles in his chest. "George – it's about Ata; it's about how he was born." She paused to continue drawing, "He wasn't an accident."

She paused again and George must have felt like he needed to be supportive, "That's ok, sweetheart, it doesn't matter, none of it matters, we have a son." He had clearly misunderstood what she was trying to say; she knew it had been a poor choice of words.

"No, I mean it was an accident for me. Mantas tampered with a condom; he put a pin in it."

She kept circling; he didn't say anything at first. She was glad that he didn't; she didn't want him to say anything, this was something that she had to say. She could feel a tear coming to her eye and then it slowly trickled down her face onto his chest and then another one trickled. She was having strange emotions – she was sad to recall it, but also relieved that she had spoken the words. It was the first time that she had spoken the words and it was therapeutic to have said them – and to have shared those words with the same man that had given her two children who were conceived not from subterfuge, but out of love that they once shared for each other.

George finally broke the silence, "It's ok, sweetheart, we got Ata out of it." He stroked her hair and waited a minute before he continued, "Tanja – it's not my place, I don't want to be perceived as demeaning him, we went through all that last night. I don't want to make you any more conflicted, it's just..." He went quiet for another few seconds as if he needed to find more diplomatic words but then he just said them, "it's just, I'm not a lawyer, but I think, if we were in the West, that might be considered... well, a form of rape."

Tanja kept circling, "Yes, I think you're right."

Tanja circled for a while and a few more tears came to her eyes until she nodded off again. She awoke again to hear Maria trying to get through the master bedroom door. Tadas was trying to defend the door and kept asking Maria to leave them alone and let them sleep. Maria seemed to abide by the command by wandering off somewhere, but then Tanja heard the doorknob turn. She had clearly tricked Tadas and now she had gained access. To prevent Tadas from trying to catch her, she leapt onto Tanja; she flew onto her as if she were a superhero. Tadas scurried to the door; Tanja smiled and said it was ok, it would be impossible to keep her out anyway.

Maria climbed to a space between her mother and father and got under the sheets and looked at her father. "Why you naked?"

"It was hot in here last night." Tanja smiled at the double entendre.

The response seemed to be sufficient for Maria who began talking about a dream that she'd had. At that moment, buoyed by the commotion, Edita wandered in and made her way to her father's side of the bed and climbed in to listen. She lay on her father's chest and just listened. The commotion was too much for the baby who also occupied that room. He began to cry and also demand attention.

Naked Tanja got up and closed the master bedroom door and retrieved her infant from the bassinette and went back to her place in the bed and began nursing her son.

Maria provided intricate detail about her dream. There was a princess of storks and she lived on a cloud. Tanja smiled; the girl had a crazy imagination. She suckled her son and caressed his hair and gently began making little circles in his hair with her fingers.

Maria was now explaining how the princess had a family of storks and there was a prince stork and three baby storks and they slept on a white cloud. Tanja couldn't figure out whether Maria was explaining a dream or whether she was making up a story or whether she'd had a dream and was embellishing it. She was pretty much describing the five of them in that bed.

Tanja looked down at her son and listened while Princess Maria gave increasing detail about the stork family. "Then, the princess stork would leave the cloud every day and she would bring children and luck to people who lived in the villages. The daddy stork was in charge of doing it for people who lived in cities…"

Tanja smiled; she was pretty sure she knew where that idea came from, it was one of Luce's favourites. Then, as she ran circles through Ata's hair, a thought came to her. Luce had told her that her predicament wasn't difficult at all; the woman was annoyed that Tanja had raised the subject with her. Now, Tanja understood it. In that bed were the four people she loved most in the world, she looked down at Ata who was taking turns between dosing and suckling; she looked at Maria who was still going on about the apparent dream, she looked at her daddy's girl, Edita, who was cuddled up with her father and she looked at George – the dead man who the universe had returned to her and whom she was considering denying. At that moment, she envisioned the five storks sitting on their cloud. She wasn't conflicted anymore, the storks had brought more than luck, they had brought truth.

Tanja continued to listen to the story and draw circles in Ata's hair. She had become a suspicious person, but she hadn't been before. She had become a self-centred person, which wasn't like her. She had become a schemer and that definitely wasn't her. She could be unkind, but she was a kind person. She now knew how Mantas felt after the accident - the dress, the restaurant from their first date, George's concession, her desire to please him, the confession of her assault, the story of the stork – they were all signals. She kept thinking to herself and repeating the same phrase in her head, 'I don't want to be the person I've become; I want to be the person that I was'. She kept repeating it in her head, but it was hard to focus on the words when Maria kept talking. Finally, Tanja found herself saying it out loud, she hadn't intended to, it was just hard with Maria always talking. "I don't want to be the person I've become; I want to be the person that I was."

Maria stopped, "What does that mean?"

"Nothing," replied Tanja.

Maria then recommenced, "Then the baby storks grew up and now they had to bring luck to people, but they didn't know how…"

Tanja eventually decided that it was time to get up. She was the first to leave the crowded bed. She handed Ata over to George, Maria shifted herself over to Tanja's side of the bed, so the whole family could shift. Maria kept describing the storks. Tanja donned her house coat and opened the bedroom door and entered the sitting room. Tadas sat on the sofa with Vlad, who must have just woken up.

"Good morning, gentlemen, I'll make a special breakfast for us, ok?" said Tanja.

"Thanks, sweet, but I had breakfast during the stork story; I'm going to head home," said Tadas.

Tanja blushed a little before replying; she wondered what else he'd heard from behind that door. "Actually, I need your help, can you help set the table?"

Tadas thought it an odd thing to ask; he'd never been asked to do that before, but he stood up and she pointed him to the dining table. "And use the good crystal juice glasses and the nice plates and cutlery from the cabinet. Ok? Oh, and I'll fish out a table cloth; we'll have a proper table cloth this morning as well."

Tanja disappeared for a minute and then reappeared with a table cloth and place settings and handed them to Tadas.

Tadas was confused, and perplexed, by the request. He'd spent the previous evening caring for her children, including a very rambunctious Maria. He wanted to go home and rest; now, he was being asked to set her table, but he didn't complain. This was his adopted family, if he were asked to set the table, he would do it, but he couldn't figure out why he was doing it; it was no one's birthday… unless maybe it was Luce's birthday; maybe she'd come to breakfast.

When he was finished, he called to Tanja and asked if he could go. Tanja asked him to stay; she wanted him to stay for breakfast, even if he didn't eat anything. Tadas was about to protest, but decided against it; he didn't have much to do today anyway and maybe it was a special occasion; it seemed to be a surprise.

While Tanja prepared pancakes, the remainder of the family finally emerged from the master bedroom. George carried Ata and offered him to Tadas who smiled while he cuddled the infant. Maria had stopped talking about the storks; she was much quieter now; she had had her moment and now she was likely hungry. As soon as Ata was handed to Tadas, Edita placed her hand in George's hand and he held it for her.

Tanja finally emerged with a stack of pancakes and invited all the assembled to join her at the table. Edita was the first to sit and look at the pancakes, then she looked at George and tried to say the English word 'bakfast'. George smiled, "Yes, sweetheart, 'breakfast', good girl, smart girl." Maria had been in the process of sitting herself and now she had new material for her story, "Oh, now I remember, in the dream, you were an English stork, but your name wasn't Edita, it was Diana. You were quite pretty in that dream, but your sister was prettier..."

While Maria provided the latest edition of the story, Tanja went about pouring juice and serving pancakes to the girls, while Tadas cuddled Ata in his chair as he sat beside George.

When the whole family was seated, the assembled began their attempt to put a dent in the pile of pancakes. As Maria's mouth was now full, Tanja decided that it was time to begin.

"Family – you are likely wondering about the table cloth and glasses – I have a special announcement."

George smiled at her; she was going to take ownership of his idea; it was validation of that idea – she obviously loved it. Tanja continued.

"The patriarch of this family is our beloved Tadas. Tadas does everything for us; he took care of us when we had no daddy, he watches over us. He is the king of all the storks."

Maria was about to interject, so Tanja kept talking, "We take you for granted, we know that. So, we bought you a small present. We hope you don't find it self-serving; it kind of has something to do with your living arrangements. Effective December 15, you will be our neighbour... We bought you an apartment on the ground floor."

Maria was the most excited; she jumped to her feet and ran over to Tadas and hugged him which caused Ata to stir and cry, George relieved the old man of the infant in his arms. Vlad also jumped up and hugged him and then George tried to shake his hand while balancing the fussy infant in his lap.

Tadas just sat in confusion and then looked perplexed, "I don't understand; I have a place to live; I like it there; you should save your money."

"It's an old dingy Soviet flat; you deserve more and we have already contracted to buy it, so it would have to stay empty."

"You could rent it; I'm sorry, Tanja, it was a nice gesture, but I can't accept a gift like that; I can't take something like that from my own children."

Tanja could have been dismayed by the response, but she knew how to play Tadas; she knew his motivations, she knew his perspective well. She was about to exploit that knowledge.

"Well," she looked down, "that puts us in a position, we were talking about moving back to London for a while and renting this apartment – it's much more valuable. We were hoping to ask you to keep an eye on the tenants and help them if they needed anything. If you won't move in, we'll have to rethink London. It's a shame, George was going to be a director there, Vlad had a great school there, we were hoping to send Maria to a pre-school there. Oh well, I guess fate is sending us a message."

Tadas looked down and was clearly thinking.

Vlad spoke up, "Are we really going back to England?"

"We were thinking of it; it was such a good school for you and we were hoping to find a princess preschool for Maria." Maria's face lit up; Tanja would have to explain that it was just an expression later, but, for now, she needed Maria onboard.

"Is there really a school for princesses?" asked Maria.

"Well, I'm not sure, but I guess we'll never find out." Maria looked toward her grandfather. He raised his head and looked at Tanja.

"I know what you're doing. You're tricking me into taking that apartment," then he smiled, "but I'm not going to hold my family back, I'll take the damn thing, but I'll pay you rent."

"That's fair, so after breakfast, I'll get the calculator out and we'll calculate each time you took care of the children, each time you helped me or Vlad – oh, and we need to add up all the stuff that you did for our mother, especially when she was ill. Then, we'll assign a monetary value to that work, then I'll research a fair market rental value for the apartment. We'll then take your credit and assess the number of months of rent that we owe to you. Until I do the calculations, I don't know what number that will come to, but I know it would exceed your life expectancy. So, I think we'll have to look at a cash settlement. While we are repaying you while you stay in the flat, we'll give you a one-time cash settlement, but don't try to hold us over a barrel during negotiations. We want you in that apartment so we are negotiating from a position of weakness."

Tadas sighed and then he smiled. "You sometimes remind me of your mother. She could be a very difficult woman."

It was Sunday afternoon when Tanja finally decided that she would call Mantas. She had decided not to call him on Saturday. She spent the day feeling happy. In the end, Tadas was pleased. He'd be close to them and have modern conveniences and close proximity to things. He deserved to spend his days surrounded by nice things and she felt happy about it. In fact, she felt very happy about it. It felt nice to do something kind for someone so deserving. She knew it wasn't her idea, but that didn't matter. It was the type of thing that she liked to do for people and used to do for people and it was a beginning – she would now start doing more of those types of things. In her mind, she positioned it as helping return to the person that she once was.

There was one other item that she had been pondering and may have been partly the reason that she had delayed calling Mantas. She needed to think it through. It was the type of logic that Mantas had inspired her to consider; it was the type of logic he would understand. She had carefully studied the contract that George had signed for Tadas' apartment. She read it several times; it was the second time that she'd seen that type of contract, Asta had had her sign a similar contract when she bought her own apartment, but she hadn't really studied it at that time; the negotiations had been such a whirlwind. There was one phrase on the most recent contract that she focused on and it was certainly on the previous one as well. "Both parties approach this contract in good faith and with clean hands."

It was the "clean hands" part that got her thinking. She went through the bookshelf and found a contract law textbook that George had used for a course he'd taken at Sheffield University. She was pleased when she found the reference in the index at the back of the book. She turned to the relevant page, "The clean hands doctrine establishes that both parties must have acted ethically and without bad faith." It went on to say that a party may be relieved from granting a remedy in a contract dispute if the other party had approached the contract with dirty hands. It was a phrase at the end of the description that she felt was most compelling, "He who comes into equity must come with clean hands."

It might have been an innocuous clause in a contract. A clause that had likely been in any similar contract for the last hundreds of years. However, Tanja had decided that contract doctrine applied to her own life. She extrapolated that legal concept even further as she considered two other terms that appeared in that contract - joint tenancy and sole ownership.

Based on that doctrine, Tanja passed a verdict. Maria and Edita were subject to joint tenancy. Their coming to this earth was approached by two parties who had contracted with clean hands. If she grew to hate her husband, or they divorced, she would always have a moral obligation to share them. The same did not apply to Ata; the clean hands doctrine had been breached; she was his sole owner.

Her verdict didn't really change anything. In fact, Ata might even see more of Mantas now that she didn't need to sneak around. However, her verdict meant a great deal to Tanja, and she felt relieved that she had made the determination. She was no longer obliged to Mantas because of Ata. She no longer had a moral obligation to him; she no longer owed him equity.

On that Sunday, she waited till George wandered into the kitchen. She wanted him to be there when she called Mantas. He was trusting her and she wanted to demonstrate complete transparency.

"Good afternoon, Mantas."

"Hi sweetheart," he whispered in reply.

"You can speak up," said Tanja.

"Are you alone?"

"No, but it's ok; you were right, I had a word with George, he's ok with us meeting up privately."

"Really?" he then whispered again, "I missed you."
"I missed you too, I was wondering if you wanted to see Ata?"
"Today?"
"I think that would be ok." She then dipped the mouthpiece and looked at George, "is that ok? can you watch the girls?", "yes, Mantas, George can watch the girls. The weather's ok; how about an hour? I can walk over."

Mantas frantically cleaned the flat. He'd been away for a fortnight and hadn't had the energy to clean up the day before. He was anxious to see her; the last meeting hadn't ended well and now she seemed so official on the phone. He was hoping he could make a better impression today.

His heart fluttered when he heard the knock at his door. When he opened it, Mantas looked at her; she had a big smile on her face; he hadn't seen that smile for a while; she looked radiant; somehow younger.

She pushed his son in his pram into the sitting room. Mantas went to kiss her on the lips, but she offered her cheek instead.

He removed his prize from the pram; he was more confident with Ata now. He couldn't believe how much he'd grown; he now opened his eyes more and seemed more aware of what was going on around him.

Mantas carried him to the sofa and sat next to Tanja and cuddled his infant.

"So, I missed you; sounds like you had it out with George; no more secret liaisons?" Mantas asked.

"That's right," replied Tanja.

"In some ways, I'll kind of miss them; they added mystery to our lives."

Tanja didn't reply. She just nodded her head, then she changed the subject.

"Mantas – before you left for Stockholm, I was planning to have a serious talk with you about the future; things have changed over the last fortnight, but I'm hoping we can still talk for a minute."

"Of course, my sweet."

"So, we've been spending the last few months talking about forgiveness. I want you to know that I now forgive you." Mantas spared a hand from his infant and reached out and squeezed her hand, but she retracted it, she wasn't finished yet.

"But I'm forgiving you only partly for you; I'm really forgiving you for me. I need to move forward with my life. I am very fond of the new Mantas and that's also a reason that I've decided to forgive you. I think the accident changed you."

"It did," Mantas replied.

"But, can I say something? At our last meeting, you said that you could prevent Ata from going to England. I know it was from the best of intentions, but it frustrated me, then I let it go, then it frustrated me again. Ata is my sole responsibility; I decide where he goes."

"I understand; I'm sorry Tanja, I just thought you were looking for a way out. I mean – it sounded like George was pushing you into something."

"I know, I know, I've learned a lot about George in the last few days as well; I misunderstood a few things about him. Mantas – I have to confess something to you. A few weeks ago, I was actually contemplating a life for you and me. I don't know if I was daydreaming or what, but that's what I was thinking about." Mantas eyes seemed to light up, so Tanja continued.

"And I'm sorry if I led you along, I didn't intend it. I've been on an emotional rollercoaster, there was George's disappearance, then the pregnancy, then the accident, then George returning from the dead. I was looking for something I thought was missing; you were the forbidden fruit and I also felt obligated to you because you were so kind to me and because you were Ata's biological father."

Mantas eyes now dropped; she had intentionally thrown in the word 'biological' as if he wasn't worthy of being a real father. It was clear to him he was about to hear the word 'but'.

"But," continued Tanja, "I now realize that I love my husband. I know that sounds odd, but I realize now that I chose him and now, I know why I chose him. I chose him not because I got pregnant or had an accident, I chose him because I loved him. I chose him to father my children, because I wanted to share them with him." She paused a minute to see if Mantas was digesting her words; he looked down at his son and was pondering, he clearly was. He looked sad.

"I'm sorry, Mantas, don't be sad. I've told you before that you'd be so many girls' dream man. But I want to tell you something else, I hope you find love like that one day. It's different than passionate love. I was passionate about you, but now, I realize it wasn't love or it wasn't the love that I have for my husband. I recently felt passion for him, but my love for him is something else. He understands the person that I was, he knew me then and it's the same person that I want to be again. While you were away, he did a kind gesture for someone whom I care about and, when I asked him why he did it, he told me it was because it was something that I would have done. He was right, in the past, I would have done it; I want to be that person again and I can only be that person with him. It's funny, you'll think it's corny, but something in the universe pushed him back to me and I almost pushed him away. I regret that now; I was pushing away the love of my life."

Mantas looked down at the infant in his arms who opened his eyes and stared back at him, "I understand, Tanja." Then, Ata started to cry. "Do you need to feed him?"

"No, that's a request for a nappy change. Do you want to try to change him? After that, we should really get going. We'll leave you to clean your hands."

It was Christmas Eve afternoon. Tanja was alone as she looked out her window to the Danė River. It looked so quiet on that final Christmas Eve of the millennium. She thought about that river; it was her river and she loved it. Whenever she felt down, she looked at it. Then she looked at the fire; she'd already lit it in honour of the day; it was so cozy in that apartment. She would miss it; she would soon be in England again. George would go first early in the new year; then Tanja, Vlad, Maria, Edita and Ata would follow in early February. It was a new life in another familiar town with another river.

She looked at her wedding photograph. A funny thought passed through her head; she had almost thrown it all away. Mantas had taken the news about England well. It was evidence that his transformation was real; he had become a different man. He asked if he could visit; Tanja said he could. They would also return for summer holidays and he'd be able to see Ata then. Tanja looked at the photo and thought that she hoped Mantas would find his soulmate as well.

She was surprised to hear the key in the lock. George had taken the whole family out to see Santa who was entertaining requests in the lobby of the Klaipėda Hotel; Maria was so excited about it. Tanja wondered why they were back so soon.

It wasn't the returning family; it was Luce.

"Oh hi, sweetheart," Luce said as she came through the door. "I just wanted to drop off some gifts for the children; I'll put them under the tree."

"We got something for you as well, Luce." Tanja made her way to the tree and extracted a little jewellery box from underneath it, "It was Maria's idea; open it at home."

Luce laughed, "If Maria chose it, the theme is either royalty or storks."

Tanja smiled, "Yes, you are right; I hope you like it... Luce – thanks for everything; not just for taking care of the kids all year, but for helping me. It was a rough year; I couldn't have made it through without you."

"I think you're a stronger woman than you give yourself credit for."

"I am now; I feel like I'm getting back to normal after that pregnancy and then the accident and the issues with Mantas. Thanks for setting me straight. I needed someone to tell me about the storks and clouds; there's a lot of wisdom in those villages." Luce smiled.

"So," continued Tanja, "what's up for tonight? Your family arrived yet?"

"Yes, I'll miss my daughter this year with her entertaining her in-laws, but my son's family arrived this morning – son, wife and 3-year-old. Ahh, Tanja, the wife just found out that she's losing her job – the day before Christmas Eve; they'll have to stay with me for a while. The timing's not great; with you leaving, I won't be able to subsidize them as much anymore. It'll be difficult for them."

Tanja now had a way to repay Auntie Luce and she jumped on it, "Actually, I don't see anything difficult about it. It's perfect timing. We haven't put the apartment up for rent yet. If they can hold a few weeks, we can let them have it."

"Tanja – they can't afford to stay here."

"Who said anything about afford?"

George, Tadas, Vlad, Ata and the girls all returned around 3 o'clock that afternoon. Maria was on her best behaviour. Santa had told her that he might consider her requests – but she would have to be extra good. So, she helped take her sister's coat off and was eager to help George to remove Ata's outdoor gear as well. Tanja smiled; it was another good day. She'd brokered the deal with Luce; in exchange for keeping the place in good condition, her son's family could live in the flat until summer. Then, Tanja's family would have a place to stay for their holiday. It was not only a good plan for Luce's family; it meant that Tanja's family would be able to stay in the beautiful apartment again in the summer.

Maria kept asking about when the presents could be opened and when Santa would come. George was coy; he insisted on English customs; Santa would deliver presents overnight and everything would be opened in the morning. It was a way of buying as much good behaviour as possible.

Dinner was a great feast of herring, roe, beets, carrots, mushrooms and afterward the family played games. As per local tradition, Maria, followed by Edita, had to throw their slippers at the door. As unmarried women, if the slipper pointed outward, they would get married and leave home over the following year. Maria's pointed inward; Edita didn't really understand the exercise, but her sister showed her how to stand with her back to the door and helped throw the slipper. It pointed outward. Tanja giggled, "Even if the law allowed it, no man is going to take daddy's girl." Tadas laughed; Maria gave Tanja a dirty look.

When the festivities were over, Tadas retired to his new ground floor apartment; he'd return in the morning. Maria and Edita were easy to put to sleep; Maria was keen to demonstrate excellent behaviour. Vlad took himself to bed and then Tanja put Ata into his crib. The master bedroom was now very crowded as George had recently installed a crib; Ata had outgrown the bassinette. She kissed Ata on his head as he stared up at the mobile that George had affixed to the crib. Tanja turned the timer on and the rabbit, frog, dog and cat began to circle and Ata smiled at it; he loved the rabbit, he would try to follow it with his eyes. Tanja kissed him again and said, "Happy Christmas, little prince." She then made her way back to the sitting room.

It was now just her and her husband by the fire. He sat on the sofa and watched it and listened to the crackling of the fire. She cuddled up with him in front of that fire and listened as well.

"Tanja – this is going to sound odd, but last Christmas Eve night; I tried to communicate with you. I mean I repeated some phrases in my mind and I was hoping you could hear them."

Tanja smiled, "Last Christmas Eve night, I stared at that photo on the mantle and told you I would see you in heaven one day."

George laughed. "Oh," said Tanja, she jumped off the sofa and retrieved something from under the tree. "You can open your present early."

George smirked, "I know exactly what is in that package and I need them and I'm glad that you got them for me because we are running out of places to put children." George unwrapped the package and looked at his new socks. Tanja giggled.

George looked at the socks and then at her. It was time to tell the story. He told Tanja about the buffoons that had captured him, then about the man that had beaten him, then about being transferred to the basement, then about the interrogator and about his haircut and his release. He told her about the lies that he'd told about who took him hostage and where he thought he was. He told her about being on the cusp of insanity and the books and the cigarettes and the shaving ritual and the trays. However, mostly he talked about Lamia. He told his wife how he had loved a teenage girl, who had saved him; saved his sanity; saved his life.

Tanja just listened and held his hand. Occasionally, a tear would come to his eye. She would lean over and kiss him. After the whole story was complete, he paused for a minute, "It's hard to explain; I mean I think she was like a guardian angel, sent by God. It's hard to understand."

Tanja looked into his eyes, "Actually, for me, it's not."

Acknowledgements

I gratefully acknowledge the contributions of Cindy Blankley in Copenhagen. Cindy provides technical consultation to several Scandinavian fashion labels. She is a voracious traveller, cultural observer, reader and literary critic. Cindy spent countless hours reviewing the storyline and assisted with significant revisions. Cindy has been a close friend and mentor for over 30 years and I'm truly blessed to have her in my life.

I am also thankful for the contributions of Cam Anderson. Cam is well known in the Vancouver arts community. He is a philanthropist and champion of FutureLegacies.ca. Cam critiqued this novel and provided suggestions for storyline revisions.

I'm also indebted to my friend, Soraya, for providing advice related to the Lebanese storyline.

Manufactured by Amazon.ca
Bolton, ON